John Arden

Three Plays

The Waters of Babylon
Live Like Pigs
The Happy Haven

Introduced by John Russell Taylor

 Penguin Books

Penguin Books Ltd, Harmondsworth, Middlesex,
England
Penguin Books Inc.,
3300 Clipper Mill Road, Baltimore 11, Md, U.S.A.
Penguin Books Pty Ltd, Ringwood, Victoria,
Australia

The Waters of Babylon first published in Penguin
Books 1964

Live Like Pigs first published in Penguin Books 1961

The Happy Haven first published in Penguin Books 1962

Copyright © John Arden, 1961, 1962, and 1964

Made and printed in Great Britain by
Cox and Wyman Ltd, London, Fakenham,
and Reading

Set in Monotype Bembo

Contents

To Gwalchmei Francis Arden

Who put his head out in October,
Kept it out until November,
Drew it in then.

       Please remember:
He was young enough to take his choice.
What he did not like he did not have to face.
We who are older
Must needs be bolder.

The pen must crawl:
The black ink fill the waiting space:
For tortoise and child alone
The shell is an honourable home.

                             J.A.

Introduction

The years since 1956 have been a time of violent and rapid change for British drama : there have been not one 'New Wave' but several, fashion succeeding fashion and wave succeeding wave with dizzying speed until all attempts to find some consistency in the New Drama movement have been defeated and we are left simply with a number – a very encouraging number – of individual writers who continue to write interesting plays and have in common only the fact that ten years ago we had not heard of any of them. One of the most strikingly independent of these writers, and, if one may venture to prophesy from work to date, one of those most likely still to be writing major plays in ten or twenty years' time, is John Arden.

The first thing to strike one about Arden, looking back over a career which already includes seven full-length plays and six shorter plays for stage, radio, or television, is the remarkable degree to which he has succeeded in ignoring fashion, or at least in forging his own fashion, choosing early his own line, and then sticking to it with a dogged, take-it-or-leave-it consistency. When the New Drama started with *Look Back in Anger* it was in a realistic mode and a socially conscious mood; Arden's answer was a radio play written partly in verse, partly in prose, on a semi-allegorical subject heavy with myth and esoteric lore. When, almost in spite of this, he was approached by the English Stage Company, which at that time seemed likely to become the London home of committed drama, the first play he offered them was a verse drama on a subject from Arthurian legend; the next was THE WATERS OF BABYLON, which, even more puzzlingly, turned out to be a play, written partly in verse, about prostitution and municipal corruption, and which, moreover, did not take up any of the attitudes that a

7

subject with such obvious social implications might then have led theatre-goers to expect.

Since then Arden has continued to shatter any preconceptions we might have about what to expect from him almost before they have formed in our minds, disregarding entirely the fashion for the theatre of the Absurd which swept British drama after the fashion for commitment, writing period drama at a time when everyone else was preoccupied with the contemporary scene, and gnomic comedy-dramas littered with ballads and rhymed dialogue set squarely in the present at a time when everyone else seemed, egged on by the example of Brecht, to be looking to the past. And all this without ever appearing to write as he does just from perversity or a determination to be different for the sake of being different. Arden is a genuine original, and far more important than the differences between his plays and those of his contemporaries is the internal consistency which makes them a logical, coherent progression, all first, foremost, and unmistakably the product of one exceptional mind.

To a certain extent Arden's originality may be explicable by the oddity of his background in the general context of the new drama. He was born in Barnsley in 1930, and is virtually the only dramatist of his generation to have been to both public school and university. He studied architecture at Cambridge and Edinburgh, and has practised as an architect, but also at school and university took a more detailed and scholarly interest in English literature and the history of drama than most, with the result that he is probably more clearly, intellectually aware of what he is doing in his plays than virtually any other dramatist writing in Britain today: if he writes a nativity play it is in the light of his studies of medieval mysteries and miracle plays; if he incorporates a ballad in a dramatic scene its function is governed to some extent by his thought about the ballad tradition and ballad imagery. Knowing what one is doing in this way is of course a mixed blessing: many of the learned verse-plays of the 1900s were too weighed down by knowledge and theory ever to get off the ground as living drama. But in Arden's case, given an intuitive flair for the theatre and stage effect, this particular danger is remote, and the advantages of his brand of constructive intelligence emerge without any of the concomitant disadvantages.

Arden seems to have been drawn to drama very early on; his schoolboy literary efforts included a tragedy about the death of Hitler written in the style of *Sweeney Agonistes* and a pseudo-Elizabethan verse drama on the Gunpowder Plot. While at Edinburgh he wrote a period comedy called *All Fall Down*, about the building of a mid-Victorian railway, which was in fact his first staged work, being put on by a group of fellow students. This he now regards as prentice work, and he dates the real beginning of his career as a dramatist from his radio play *The Life of Man*, which won a B.B.C. Northern Region prize for original drama and brought him to the attention of the impresario Oscar Lewenstein, who in turn brought him to the notice of the English Stage Company. *The Life of Man* is a strange work, telling of the illfated last voyage of a packet-boat with a mad captain and an odd Welsh seaman who seems to be a sort of avenging angel disguised as a scape-goat, but already it contains many characteristic features of Arden's mature style: the unpredictable alternation of racy, idiomatic prose and quite highly wrought formal verse, the extensive use of traditional song and ballad, and in the Welsh sailor Jones's evocation of his roaming shepherd life an interest in the bold, free, nomadic life of the 'sturdy beggar' which was later to bear spectacular fruit in LIVE LIKE PIGS.

Meanwhile, though, came the first play in this volume, *The Waters of Babylon*. It was accepted by the English Stage Company as the initial venture in a new series of experimental productions-without-décor staged on Sunday evenings for members of an associated club, the English Stage Society. The idea behind these productions was that in this way new talent among writers, and for that matter directors and actors, could be tried out with a minimum of risk and expense, and if the initial response seemed to justify it the productions might subsequently find a place in the ordinary repertory of the company. Such was certainly not the case with *The Waters of Babylon*: it never reached more than the one performance, and was generally greeted with extreme puzzlement if not outright hostility. And yet, looking at it again today, it is difficult to understand why. Once one has cleared the initial hurdle of the style, with its unexpected mixture of verse and prose, the story is quite easy to follow; the play is by no means obtrusively experimental. It simply describes a few disreputable days in the life of a Polish architect-cum-pimp, Sigismanfred Krankiewicz (known as 'Krank'), who attempts a little rigging of a municipal lottery in order to pay off another Pole who is blackmailing him into permitting a bomb plot to be hatched under his own roof. So far, so good: picturesque low-life, cheerful tarts, a gallery of more or less crooked local politicians brightly caricatured, and some vividly rounded central characters whom Arden has been fond enough of to incorporate in later plays as well: Krank in his television play *Wet Fish*, Charlie Butterthwaite, 'Napoleon of Local Government', as the central character of *The Workhouse Donkey* and on the fringes of a couple more. Why then did the play prove so difficult for its first audience?

The answer to that is the key to the greater or lesser difficulties which audiences have found with all Arden's work: you never know where he stands in the play. The subject of *The Waters of Babylon*, taking in as it does such topics as prostitution, the ethics of local government and the propriety of officially sponsored gambling (the play began in Arden's mind, he tells us, as a satire on the Premium Bond system), would lead audiences to expect that a point of view was going to be offered on some or all of these questions, that the author's general attitude on them would be clearly conveyed, and that indeed the prime purpose of the play would probably be to convey it. But not at all. The central character, for instance, Krank, is not only a pimp, but claims to be an heroic victim of Buchenwald when in fact he served there as a member of the German army. He should be a monster, but in the event it is not at all unfair to call him the play's hero: he is

certainly one of the most amiable and generally liked of the
people in the play, his relations with the string of prostitutes he
manages could hardly be friendlier, and all the time he succeeds in wriggling out of whatever too-easy classification and
judgement we might from any given piece of information be
tempted to force on him. This is characteristic of Arden's
treatment of all his characters and of the ideas they might be
supposed to stand for: no clear separation of the people in the
play into good and bad, heroic and villainous, is possible; they
are all, even the most boldly conventionalized like the upright
negro councillor Joseph Caligula, the fatuous M.P. Loap, and
the shifty chauvinist Henry Ginger, too complex to be com-
fortably pigeon-holed and so dismissed from mind.

Which, of course, was very disturbing to audiences used,
whenever a play dealt or appeared to deal with a 'social' subject of some sort, to a clear pattern of blacks and whites. It was
not so much that the blacks and whites did not come in the
expected places: controversial, thought-provoking plays
which set out to turn our ideas on a certain subject upside-
down were nothing new. But it was very worrying if the play
seemed on the contrary to present no unmistakeable blacks and
whites at all. Plays which limit themselves unequivocally to
private matters, to hermetic battles of will or the ravelling
and unravelling of intricate emotional entanglements, can
get away with leaving their moral principles undefined, but a
play which introduces pimps, corrupt politicians and even
Nazi war criminals without making it clear that the author is
against them is all too liable to be interpreted instead as being
for them.

What Arden was in fact up to emerges more clearly in *Live
Like Pigs*, the first of his plays to be given a full-scale public
production. Here again the subject appears to be social, and
here again there is a determined refusal to take sides on a
number of questions where almost any audience would con-
ventionally be inclined to suppose that side-taking was im-
perative. The centre of the play this time is a conflict between
two families in adjoining semi-detacheds on a new housing

estate. The families, one is tempted to say, represent two different, incompatible ways of life: the Jacksons are good, solid, respectable, impeccably conventional members of the lower middle class; while the Sawneys, who are moved somewhat against their will into an ordinary little house next door, are essentially nomadic vagrants, the last descendants of the Elizabethan sturdy beggars now barely existing on the fringes of a society which has no place for them.

But a difficulty immediately arises here: the two families are created primarily as individuals, each with his or her own faults and virtues, and as soon as one begins to suggest that they are in any way representative of anything other than themselves one runs up against all sorts of contradictions and complications; whatever they are they are certainly not average examples of it. In a more general sense, though, it remains true that the head-on collision between the Jacksons and the Sawneys does remain a conflict between two ways of life. It is just that the two levels upon which the play works – as a social drama embodying certain general points about society, and as a personal comedy-drama played out between two groups of highly idiosyncratic individuals – are quite separate, and neither is artificially modified to bring it into line with the other; especially does Arden refrain from limiting his characterization of individuals in any way to fit them into some general thesis.

Even when this is accepted – and audiences during the play's brief run at the Royal Court found it difficult enough to accept – the play's shocks to conventional expectation are not over. For on the level of a quasi-symbolic conflict between two ways of life we would still, normally, expect the author to take the part, in general, of one side rather than the other. The popular side to take would be that of the Sawneys, romantic figures from the past, noble savages we might say – though in the event there is precious little of nobility about them – who bring a tonic gust of fresh air into the shabby, constricted world of modern suburban conformity. On the other hand, a play written to exalt the Jacksons ('an undistinguished but not contemptible family' as Arden calls them in his introduction to the text) and their civilized, responsible way of life in an ordered welfare state, is not at all inconceivable. But we would normally expect one thing or the other. Either, our pre-conceptions would lead us to suppose, the dramatist must be for order, authority, and all the rest of it and against the forces of anarchy and disorder, or he must be against established complacency and for those who rebel against it. Arden's unique contribution is his ability to avoid both these pat formulations, and to write a play which gives both sides their due, without sentimentality and without a hint of patronage. We may ourselves choose a side to sympathize with, if we really have to, but the choice remains ours; the playwright too has no doubt his own views on the matter, but the last thing he wants to do is to force them on us.

The third play in this volume, THE HAPPY HAVEN, fol-lowed Arden's next major play the strange semi-historical drama about the nature of violence, *Serjeant Musgrave's Dance*. It takes up again the tragi-comic form of *Live Like Pigs*, and like *Live Like Pigs* it deals with a 'social' subject of the sort upon which one might expect any dramatist to take a strong line; which one would expect him to choose, indeed, largely because he had a strong line to take on it. It is about life in an old folks' home, and about the experiments performed by the doctor in charge, using the inmates as involuntary guinea-pigs, to produce a scientific rejuvenator. Now presumably all audiences can be assumed to be, if only in the vaguest, most sentimental fashion, sympathetic towards the old; moreover, whatever our ideas about experiment in medicine, we would probably most of us have some reservations about experiments conducted on unwilling or unsuspecting subjects. We would also probably incline to think that such matters were not the ideal subject for broadly grotesque comedy. And yet Arden here cheerfully offers us precisely that (a 'pantomime', he originally subtitled it), and in addition leans over backwards to show us the doctor's side of things as well as that of his patients, while depicting the old people themselves as anything but sugar-coated sentiment-traps: they are permitted to be as good or as bad, as pleasant or unpleasant, as people of any other age-groups; they are in fact less 'old folk', a special case, than just people who happen all to be over sixty.

All this made the play seem to its first audiences at the Royal Court at best mystifying (whatever was Arden up to?), and at worst a heartless joke in the worst possible taste. (The fact that, for mainly practical reasons, the play was acted almost entirely in masks did not aid easy comprehension either.) Looked at more coolly, however, it seems one of his richest and most satisfying plays: a lot of it is very funny, and some of it is very beautiful. The tough, unsentimental characterization of the old people seems to me to give the play humanity, to make it in any sense that matters a more sympathetic picture of the old than any rose-tinted fantasy, because it gives them, what the sentimentalists generally strip them of, real dignity and independence and forbids us to insult them with our easy pity. Technically it is probably Arden's boldest play yet: the mixture of highly formal verse and extravagantly informal prose has never been more stark and uncompromising, and its success bears out Arden's contention that 'If people are speaking formal verse with lines that rhyme, the audience does not have to worry whether it sounds natural. They are talking poetry. It's with the half-and-half thing that one is in trouble.'

But above all what one takes away from the play, beyond even its bounding theatrical vitality, is the splendour of its great moments of eloquence, like Mrs Phineus's speech in the second act:

> I'm an old old lady
> And I don't have long to live.
> I'm only strong enough to take
> Not to give. No time left to give.
> I want to drink, I want to eat,
> I want my shoes taken off my feet.
> I want to talk but not to walk
> Because if I walk, I have to know
> Where it is I want to go.

I want to sleep but not to dream
I want to play and win every game
To live with love but not to love
The world to move but me not to move
I want I want for ever and ever
The world to work, the world to be clever.
Leave me be, but don't leave me alone.
That's what I want. I'm a big round stone
Sitting in the middle of a thunderstorm . . .

Of that sort of writing, with that sort of hardwon strength and sinew, only John Arden has the secret in the modern English theatre; it already makes it presumptuous to call him promising, but makes one look forward to his future achievement with more certainty than one does that of any other dramatist working in English today.

JOHN RUSSELL TAYLOR

The Waters of Babylon

First produced at the Royal Court Theatre, London, on 20 October 1957 and directed by GRAHAM EVANS

List of Characters

KRANK (Sigismanfred Krankiewicz), *a Pole*
PAUL, *a Pole*
CONOR CASSIDY, *an Irishman*
CHARLES BUTTERTHWAITE, *an Englishman*
ALEXANDER LOAP, *an Englishman*
COUNCILLOR JOSEPH CALIGULA, *a West Indian*
HENRY GINGER, *an Englishman*
AN ENGLISH POLICEMAN
BATHSHEBA, *a West Indian*
TERESA, *an Irishwoman*
BARBARA BAULKFAST, *an Englishwoman, an architect*

SCENE: London, early in 1956.
NOTE: As the scenes of this play are, to some extent, unlocalized, the sets should in no way be realistic. Where it is necessary to indicate a particular locality, this must be done rather by suggestion than by outright illustration.

The sort of scenery I had in mind was the eighteenth or early nineteenth century sort, which involved the use of sliding flats or drop curtains which open and close while the actors are still on stage – a method still in use in provincial pantomimes.

Act One

KRANK *is discovered, yawning and stretching. He is a slight, fair man, aged anywhere between thirty and forty-five, with an undistinguished Central European face, steel spectacles, and receding hair. He is wearing a dirty jersey with a vee-neck, and trousers, and gym-shoes: no more. He has a coffee-pot, a cup, and a sandwich. There is a macintosh lying about.*

As the curtain opens, there is heard a crescendo then diminuendo of noise, as of an Underground train passing.

KRANK [*confidentially, to the audience: he has a light foreign accent*]: Half past seven of a morning. What kind of day is it? Cold, I think, yes, cold, rainy, foggy, perhaps by dinnertime it will snow. No? Perhaps not snow, it is after all spring. March, April, May, even in London. I do not think – even in North London, perhaps, not snow. Breakfast, what sort of breakfast, this coffee it is not very fresh, is it? After the nature of an archaeological deposit, more water more coffee into the pot every morning, but at the bottom it has been there six weeks, seven, it's like drinking bitumen. Why don't I wash my cups and plates more often than only once a week? 'Cause I am a man of filthy habits in my house, is why.

[*Train goes past again.*]

That's the electric train, it goes past. Metropolitan railway upon its embankment. To give the sun a headache before he even gets over the rooftops. In London, always the sun has a hangover, I think, every damned morning.

[*A banging overhead.*]

And that? Oh that's the Irishman upstairs. That's Mr Conor Cassidy, that's another foreign man lives in this London. *He* does not like getting up in the cold mornings, neither, Cassidy.

[*More banging.*]

Cassidy. Will you stop, please, your bangings and crashings over my head. Over the head of my bed. Over my breakfast. What is the matter with this salami? I think, somebody, they've dropped it on the floor. It would disgust a drain-layer. But not me. For me, breakfast is to be enjoyed.

[*He enjoys it.*]

[*Enter* BATHSHEBA, *a very pretty black girl, dressed for the street.*]

BATHSHEBA: Mr Krank.

KRANK: Get out.

BATHSHEBA: I'm feeling so tired, Mr Krank.

KRANK: Well so am I tired. I've told you before, between half past seven and eight o'clock of the morning I am neither elegant nor delightful.

BATHSHEBA: Not to look at, Mr Krank, no sir, indeed you're not.

KRANK: Nor to talk to, nor to make love nor nothing else. I have slept alone tonight, I am an Englishman this morning, Bathsheba, I have bad temper like a grindstone, and where is my *Daily Mirror*, you haven't even brought it?

BATHSHEBA: I left it upstairs, I guess.

KRANK: In Cassidy's room, no?

BATHSHEBA: I was never in the room of that boy.

KRANK: No?

BATHSHEBA: Never.

KRANK: I don't think I believe you. Even if you tell me the truth, so what? You were sleeping with someone, weren't you?

BATHSHEBA: Well, if that's not what you want me to do . . .

KRANK: But not with people I know, not people who live here in my house. You must not confound a proper commercial business with . . . with all sorts of other things, with my friends, with your friends, with all my other businesses. O.K.? Now where's my *Daily Mirror*? I want to read it before I go out.

BATHSHEBA: I don't want you to read it. I want to hear you sing.

KRANK: In the mornings I don't sing.

BATHSHEBA: Yes, you do.

KRANK: Get out.

BATHSHEBA [*producing some notes of money*]: There's the money.

KRANK: What money?

BATHSHEBA: My last night's money. What you sent me out to earn.

KRANK [*counting it*]: Is this all of it there is?

BATHSHEBA: I'll give you the rest when you sing me your song.

KRANK: What song?

BATHSHEBA: The song, you once called it your Dolorous Song.

KRANK: Oh. In the mornings I do not sing.

[*She waits.*]

O.K. The true story, this song, of the life of, of the life of me, of Krank. This was myself, you see, at an altogether different time of the world. I make the song so that I can sometimes remember.

BATHSHEBA: Remember?

KRANK: Remember what perhaps by now I ought to have forgotten. After all, more than ten years . . . I will sing.

[*Singing:*]

> As I went down by Belsen town
> I saw my mother there
> She said, go by, go by my son, go by,
> But leave with me here
> Your lovely yellow hair.
>
> As I went down by Auschwitz town
> My brother looked out of the wall
> He said, go by, go by my brother, go by,
> But leave with me here
> The lovely strong tooth from your skull.

As I went down by Buchenwald town
And there for my sweetheart I sought
But she whispered, go by, Oh my darling go by,
You leave with me here
The lovely red blood of your heart.

[*Noise of train passing.*]

BATHSHEBA: I don't understand all that song, what it's about. All the names of them foreign places you been? Man, you must have travelled wide.

[CASSIDY *enters. He is a young Irishman of cunning and insolent appearance. He is wearing London Transport uniform.*]

KRANK: Get out.

CASSIDY: I will not. Why, hello, Bathsheba, and you irrigating the morning wilderness of London with your tropical two eyes.

KRANK: Cassidy, you madden me with your noise. For your room this week, the rent is outstanding.

CASSIDY: And I'd come to pay it, so. Here y'are, fifteen silver shillings, count it yourself, all genuine and resonant like icicles. Ting, ting, jingle, jingle.

KRANK [*taking the money*]: You had a woman in with you last night. I'm not deaf. Is five shillings extra.

CASSIDY: There was nobody with me at all. There's all the second floors. Number six the Attic's after barring up and fastening his door. I couldn't be in at him without bursting the lock. What'll you do about that?

KRANK: Look, I let you pay reduced rent so you help me run these lodgings, I leave it to you what to do: O.K.? Five shillings extra for last night. I'm not deaf.

BATHSHEBA: Mr. Krank, there's all the money I owe you, Mr Krank, I always pay all the money I owe anybody, always.

KRANK [*pocketing this further money*]: H'm.

BATHSHEBA: Mr Krank, will you give me some breakfast?

KRANK: There's some coffee in that pot. And finish my sandwich. Tonight, Bathsheba, you can have a vacation. Tonight you sleep with me. There's too many very untrustworthy people around here. When you're not on the streets you come in with me. O.K., *Mister* Cassidy?

CASSIDY: Well then, won't that cancel out me extra five shillings? Let alone allegations of . . .

KRANK: You'd best go to work, you'll be late. I don't want to be there before you.

CASSIDY: Plenty of time, now. I've a piece of information for you, Mr Krank.

KRANK: Oh.

CASSIDY: At the Brompton Oratory, after Mass, last Sunday morning . . .

KRANK: I wasn't there, last Sunday.

CASSIDY: Sure I know you weren't, but this young fellow was. He seemed to be expecting you.

KRANK [*sharply*]: What young fellow?

CASSIDY: One of your own lot. Some sort of foreigner. He knew me. I don't know how: he says, 'Where's Mr Krank?', he says.

KRANK: Well?

CASSIDY: So I says to him, 'I don't know.' So he says, 'Tell him I'll see him soon,' he says. He gave me his name. After the Holy Apostle . . .

KRANK: I can guess it. Paul was his name.

CASSIDY [*disappointed*]: Why, sure it was, too. Then I've told you no news at all. I'll be off to me work. Oh, there's a fellow in the passage asking for you now. It's not the same one. Will I send him away?

KRANK: I don't want to see him. . . . Send him down here.

CASSIDY: I will. Oh, this boy at the Oratory, I didn't like his face at all. It was a face in a cold broken mirror, all kinds of bits that didn't fit, all full of bad luck. Not like Bathsheba, now: sure you could look at *her* face until . . .

KRANK: Out.

CASSIDY [*calls off and upwards*]: You can come down, Mister, he'll see you. Watch the steps in the dark, they're fitted with the most perilous declivities.

[*Enter* BUTTERTHWAITE. *A miserable elderly man, of*

shabby genteel appearance, cadaverous and with a West Riding accent. KRANK *is reading and* BATHSHEBA *eating, so he finds himself ignored.*]

CASSIDY: Here he is, and here I'm away. Begod, I love you, Bathsheba. [*Exit* CASSIDY.]

BUTTERTHWAITE: Er. Are you Mr Krank?

KRANK [*without looking up*]: Sometimes.

BUTTERTHWAITE: Good morning. Er. Good morning, Miss. My name's Butterthwaite. You wrote me a letter. [*He takes a letter out of his pocket.*]

KRANK: Indeed? I write a great many letters to a great many people. What did I write to you?

BUTTERTHWAITE: Er . . . well . . . I . . . er . . .

KRANK: Read me what I wrote to you.

BUTTERTHWAITE: Well, you just wrote like . . . er, 'Come next week and see me, and have some breakfast. Together we will talk business.' That's all. I was right puzzled I can tell you . . . I don't reckon you recollect it was in the bar at the 'Coach and Horses', you asked the barman to pass me this note, I mean, I wondered . . .

KRANK [*looking up at last*]: Oh yes, I recollect it. Bathsheba, will you go away please. I made a mistake about the break-fast. I never eat breakfast, so I haven't any to offer you: I am sorry. You come back here tonight, Bathsheba.

[*Exit* BATHSHEBA.]

Now look Mr er . . . Butterthwaite, I've been delayed this morning, I am very late for my business. So we waste no time, O.K.? First, I'd better explain why I asked you to call and see me. I have been informed that you are in some sort of authority upon the complications, the intrigues, the tricks, traps, and tramlines of your English bureaucracy.

BUTTERTHWAITE [*showing interest*]: Ah.

KRANK: Is it true?

BUTTERTHWAITE: Well now, if you'd asked me that about twelve years ago, I'd have answered you downright, Mr Krank. Aye it's true.

KRANK: But now it is not.

BUTTERTHWAITE: Oh no, I wouldn't say that. Not right final, like that. But since I was last in practice, there's been a lot like of changes, you know. I'm bound to be a bit rusty.

KRANK: In practice. What is your profession?

BUTTERTHWAITE: I was a Napoleon.

KRANK: I beg your pardon?

BUTTERTHWAITE [*livening up*]: A Napoleon of Local Government, I was. The term is not exactly mine, but it was coined in the provincial press. But it meant me, Mr Krank . . . me, Charles Butterthwaite. 'Vote for your Uncle Charlie and get pudding to all your dinners.' And they did. And they got it. Though I say it myself.

KRANK: You fascinate me.

BUTTERTHWAITE:
Aye. I'll tell you the tale.
As a young lad I began in Trades Union Offices.
Railways, smoke, black steel, canals, black stone.
That were my town, and where sets the power?
Mill owners: I saw that. Hundredweights of them.
Murky money. But not for me, not for our Charlie.
Conjure up the adverse power from out the crowded smoke:
Union Headquarters. Only a young lad: I begin: I go on:
From Union on to Council, Councillor to Alderman,
Alderman to Mayor, unfolded power of scarlet
broadening back and belly: but that weren't the secret:
it's not gold chain nor scarlet carries right power.
Committees. Chairman of this one, Secretary of that one,
Housing Development, Chamber of Trade,
Municipal Transport, Hospitals, Welfare Amenities.
Eat your Christmas Dinners in the Lunatic Asylum,
Colliery Canteens, in the poor old Borough Orphanage,
Weekly photo in the paper in a paper hat and all
Cheery Charlie Butterthwaite: there was puddings to them dinners.

KRANK: Indeed, indeed.

BUTTERTHWAITE: But not any more. I've forgot the taste of puddings.

The Waters of Babylon

KRANK: What happened to you?

BUTTERTHWAITE: I had my misfortunes, like. So do we all.

KRANK: Ah yes, indeed.

BUTTERTHWAITE: What have I been once and look at me now.

KRANK: Yes. I need someone to advise me, Mr Butterthwaite: over these difficulties I am running in, with – what you call – the Local Authorities. English process, and so on, it is still somehow strange . . .

BUTTERTHWAITE: Ah well, of course, you being as you might say, a foreigner it would no doubt. . . . You'd be a kind of Czechoslav, I take it.

KRANK: I would not. I am not a Czechoslav, nor yet am I Lithuanian, nor yet Byelo-Russian. I am a Pole. O.K.

BUTTERTHWAITE: Eh, no offence, you know.

KRANK: Will you work for me, Mr Butterthwaite?

BUTTERTHWAITE: Nay, I don't know. Where's the advantage?

KRANK: Advantage?

BUTTERTHWAITE: Well, what do I get out of it?

KRANK: A fair proportion, certainly, of whatever I can get out of it.

BUTTERTHWAITE: It's difficult, you know. I'm like a foreigner myself in this city, and I'm that long out of touch. Exactly what is it you want me to do?

KRANK: I'll explain, I'll explain. But look, now I must go to my business, I take a bus to the Baker Street Underground Station, if you come with me we can talk as we go. I'm sorry about the breakfast, come on.

[*The noise of a train is heard.*]

[KRANK *puts on macintosh and they walk together. Scene closes.*]

BUTTERTHWAITE: Well, that's all very well, you know, but I mean to say, I mean . . .

KRANK: Do I understand you, Mr Butterthwaite, that you're asking me for money? I have no money. How can I give you money? When you have assisted me as I require, then we shall both have money.

BUTTERTHWAITE: There is such a thing as a retainer, you know, like, a little on deposit . . .

KRANK [*crossly giving him a note*]: Oh, take ten shillings. Now I shall have to go without my lunch, very likely.

BUTTERTHWAITE: But exactly what is it you want me to do for you?

KRANK: My house, you've seen it. A well-conducted lodging-house. I have eighty people in it . . .

BUTTERTHWAITE [*flabbergasted*]: In that house – eighty people . . .

KRANK: Certainly. The most of them West Indians, East Indians, Cypriots, so forth, so on. Thirty shillings a week, one room one bed, I provide packing-cases if they wish to make any additional furniture: one lavatory: one gas-ring every landing: and a tap for cold water.

BUTTERTHWAITE: Well, I don't know: I say, I'm not surprised you're in bad favour with the Council.

KRANK: I *have* had to indulge in certain, ah, subterfuges. Eighty people, they say, is too many for the one building. Also I charge extra if a lodger wishes a guest for the night. I don't see, why is not that legitimate? But yet I have had this trouble . . . they *will* talk about a disorderly house. To be frank, they are persecuting me. And that, I come to England to avoid. O.K.?

BUTTERTHWAITE: But I don't reckon you need *me*, a good solicitor's what you want.

KRANK: No, no, no, no, no. A good solicitor would defend me, would he not, against the bureaucracies; but I, Krank, am not any longer in this a man of defence. I am to attack. In this I must be positive. So, I see you: I know you're more useful than a whole palatinate of solicitors. To begin: I intend to acquire a second house, to convert it to similar lodgings.

BUTTERTHWAITE: That's asking for trouble. The Sanitary Authority alone . . .

KRANK: . . . must be on my side. You will find me a way to arrange it. O.K.?

BUTTERTHWAITE: Eh, I don't know . . .

KRANK: Well, here we are at the Underground station. Good morning. I'm sorry about the breakfast. Oh, get into touch with me, come early of a morning to my house: or in the evenings, shall I say, always I can find *you* in the bar of the Coach and Horses? Good morning, Mr Butterthwaite.

BUTTERTHWAITE [*bewildered*]: Good morning, Mr Krank. [*Exit* BUTTERTHWAITE.]

[KRANK *comes forward as the scene opens. Discovered are a characteristic London Transport signboard, reading 'Baker Street' and another reading 'Gentlemen'.*]

KRANK [*walking round by one side of the stage*]: Baker Street Station. Here is that extremely convenient arrangement, a gentlemen's convenience with a door at either end of it. A most remarkable, and, I think, beautiful phenomenon. I am about to be reborn: in this twentieth-century peculiar ceremonial womb, glazed tiles and electric light beneath the golden pavement stones of London, hygienic underground renascence, for *me*, is daily routine. Where is the lavatory attendant? Wash and brush-up fourpence.

[*Enter* CASSIDY *with a mop and bucket, and a hold-all.*]

CASSIDY: Ah hello now, Mr Krank, you're a little late this morning. Here's a neat cubicle vacant for you, and here's your clothes all ready.

[KRANK *goes behind a screen and changes his clothes.*]

Would you be after reading your *Daily Mirror* now you took from me?

KRANK [*from behind screen*]: I have looked at it, yes.

CASSIDY [*industriously mopping the floor*]: And is there any news in it? I hadn't had time at all.

KRANK: News. Oh yes there is news.

CASSIDY: Some Royal Occasion perhaps? Or some praise-worthy betrothal announced combining Saxon Spectacle with warm Levantine money and money with true love –

and how nice if we could keep all the teenagers off the streets.

KRANK: This morning no Royalties nor no Betrothals.

CASSIDY: But some sort of threat no doubt to popular morality: some new and abominable traffic in the souls of men, or the hearts of women, or the bodies of youth; some beast in clerical or scholastic shape unmasked.

KRANK: Nothing so interesting, I'm afraid; one item only, it caught my attention. [*He comes out from behind the screen, dressed in a dark suit, made-up bow-tie, white shirt, carrying an umbrella. He has changed his spectacles for heavy horn-rims. He hands his original clothes in the hold-all to Cassidy.*] The Russians are coming to London.

CASSIDY: Glory God, the whole atheist lot of them? Trampling through my lavatories, with their feetfuls of frozen snow – I'm going to put in for a thirty-shilling raise and Bedamn it: I'll do it this day.

KRANK: Not quite the lot of them, only two of importance. I expect you'll have heard of them. The paper thinks they're funny, it calls them the Bulge and Crush, how amusing, read for yourself, I make haste to my office.

CASSIDY [*accepting the paper*]: Why sure, Mr Krank, sure, I'll see you in the evening. What a desirable bright day it is for subterraneous employment. [*Exit* CASSIDY.]

[KRANK *comes forward as the scene closes.*]

KRANK: Indeed. My employment, as you observe, is now immaculate, professional, appropriate to this body sparkling new from its matutinal rebirth, you see, I am a man of no one condition having no more no country, no place, time, action, no social soul. I am easy and able to choose whatever alien figure I shall cut, where and wherever I am, in London: not any place in London but all places of London, for all of it and none of it is mine (Central European paradox). Now Ladies and Gentlemen, my respectable existence, a skilful Polish architect in a good English office, reputable West End address, Liberal working hours nine-thirty to five-thirty, and my name is not quite just Krank.

The Waters of Babylon

[*The scene opens to discover a drawing-table with architect's instruments, etc., and a telephone.* BARBARA *enters, a square-faced young woman, age thirty-five, in a smock. She is not unattractive, but businesslike.*]

BARBARA: Sigismanfred.

KRANK: Good morning, Miss Baulkfast.

BARBARA: You are late again.

KRANK: Everywhere this morning I am late. I miss the train, I meet a sort of person I have no wish to talk to, he talks to me two hours and a half.

BARBARA: When I appointed you my senior assistant, I told you I expected you to set an example to the rest of the office.

KRANK: Forgive me, Miss Baulkfast. It *is* 'Miss Baulkfast' today, I think, not 'Barbara'?

BARBARA [*rather grimly*]: I think it had better not be Barbara again.

KRANK: Now why that, gracious lady?

BARBARA: Because I think it is better. We have a new client coming to see us this morning. He wants a house built.

KRANK: Let us build him one. It is what we are here for, no?

BARBARA: Have you completed the Contract Drawings for that school up at Hampstead?

KRANK: Not yet.

BARBARA: Why not?

KRANK: Not yet had time, Barbara ... Miss Baulkfast. Forgive me.

BARBARA [*angrily*]: Oh, for God's sake, Sigismanfred, I asked you to have them finished last night.

KRANK: Sigismanfred?

BARBARA: Mr Krankiewicz. It's a ridiculous name, anyway.

KRANK: It's a very interesting name, is mine. Sigismanfred. Did I tell you ever how I came to be called it?

BARBARA: Yes. These are the electrical layout drawings for the Willesden factory contract. Check them, please.

KRANK [*aware that she is taking no notice of him*]: My grandfather, his name was Axel Krankiewicz, he was born in

Warsaw, 1848. It was always his romantic sorrow, he had not been born twenty years earlier, so he would have been able himself to take part in the great and splendid events of that year throughout the nations of Europe. When my father was born, he named him Sigismanfred.

[*Enter* LOAP, *a man of about forty with elderly and petulant manners. He is immaculately dressed as for Westminster. Neither* KRANK, *who is talking, nor* BARBARA, *who is studying drawings, notices his entry.*]

Not after any national or liberal leaders of the age, for that would have had a taste perhaps of journalistic vulgarity, but after two most overweening heroes of poetry and history respectively. They possessed the soul of my grandfather. They were Manfred, the creation of your English Lord Byron, who defied the laws of God's greater creation: and Sigismundo Malatesta, the Italian Renaissance Tyrant, the wickedest man in the world.

LOAP: God bless my soul.

BARBARA [*startled*]: Oh. I beg your pardon, I didn't hear you come in . . .

KRANK [*unabashed*]: And *I* the eldest son of my father, received his identical name of Sigismanfred, to remind me doubtless of how different the fate of Poland, had my grandfather been born some twenty years earlier.

LOAP [*uneasily*]: How very extraordinary, er . . .

KRANK [*introducing himself with a short bow*]: Krankiewicz. Sigismanfred Krankiewicz. *I* am not the man to liberate my country. All my efforts are devoted to the liberation of myself.

BARBARA [*crossly*]: Mr Krankiewicz, *please*. I beg your pardon, sir . . . er . . . good morning . . . er . . . can we help you in any way?

LOAP: Miss Barbara Baulkfast's office?

BARBARA: Yes, I am Miss Baulkfast.

LOAP: My name is Loap. I had an appointment . . .

BARBARA: Of course, Mr Loap. Do take a seat. This is Mr Krankiewicz, my chief assistant. Mr Krankiewicz: Mr

Alexander Loap, our – prospective – client. He is a Member of Parliament for . . .

KRANK: Loap, Loap, Alexander Loap. You are Member for the Constituency in which I live, Mr Loap. The wrong side of the park. Most remarkable.

LOAP [*with professional enthusiasm*]: Well, well, *really*, a Constituent. I am indeed delighted, sir . . .

KRANK: I do not have a vote. I am not a British Subject. Don't worry.

LOAP: Oh.

BARBARA: Now, Mr Loap, business. You wish us to design you a small house, do you not?

LOAP: That is correct. A commodious, but by no means large, ah quite small, in fact, ah, house in the country . . . it will not exactly be for myself . . . it, ah . . .

[*Enter* TERESA, *a splendid Irish girl, with red hair worn very long. It is evident that a considerable amount of money is being spent on her adornment.*]

TERESA: Certainly not for himself. It's for me.

LOAP [*very out of countenance*]: Why, Teresa, my love, I did not expect you here today . . . ah. Miss Baulkfast, may I introduce . . .

BARBARA [*too flustered to know better*]: Mrs Loap, how do you do, your husband has just been . . .

TERESA: He's not my husband. But he's building me a house all the same. I don't trust him to tell you what I want and get it right, so here I am to control him. I heard him say the house will be small. It will not. I want a good size to it so I'm not always cannonading against the corner of the bath when I'm trying to get into the kitchen . . . [*She sees Krank.*] Oh God, who am I looking at? It, it isn't little Krank . . .

KRANK [*taking her up very smartly*]: Krankiewicz is my name, gracious lady. I don't think we have had the pleasure . . .

TERESA [*slyly*]: Oh is that it? Sure, maybe you're right. Mistaken identity after all. You're an architect, are you, mister?

KRANK: I am the assistant of Miss Baulkfast.

TERESA: Why, isn't that lovely, now, and I'm the harlot of Mr Loap.

BARBARA: I am afraid ...

LOAP [*sweating with embarrassment*]: Excuse me, must introduce, very glad to, ah, Miss Delaroy: Miss Baulkfast, our architect, Miss Delaroy, my ...

TERESA: All right – let's talk about the house. I'll tell you what I want. There's to be a good-size parlour or drawing-room or whatever you'd call it, and a dining-room separate. I don't eat in annexes any more at all. And the kitchen with everything in it, freeze, cook, wash, dry, everything, and the bathroom must have two showers, one over the bath and one in one of those transparent sentry boxes, and a spray nozzle affair additional between the taps of the bath. Oh God, and I want a bed like a Cathedral, with purple quilting going right up the wall behind our heads and two, three mirrors I can take a survey of meself in, top to toe front to back, whenever the notion takes me. And carpets as soft as custards in every room and corridor. Now you know what I want, Alexander, you arrange it with this good lady.

BARBARA: Well, Mr Loap, I have here a few sketches which might give you some idea of the sort of thing we can do for you ...

KRANK: Not those, that's the Willesden factory, I think.

BARBARA: Oh dear, I'm unaccountably confused. Thank you, Mr Krankiewicz.

[BARBARA *and* LOAP *study the drawings at the table.*]

KRANK: Your name, Teresa, it was not always, 'Delaroy'.

TERESA: Neither was your name always ... whatever you said it was.

KRANK [*seriously*]: Ah, there you are in error. Long before I was anything else my name was without doubt ... But yours used to be ...

TERESA: Flaherty was it, or maybe Delaney? When you first picked me up on Euston arrival platform and perfect gentleman you were, carrying me string bag, you asked me so compassionate, 'Would you be the young lady seeking domestic service in a decent Catholic family?' and I says to you, 'I would,' and little did I know of the ladder of shame and sorrow you'd set me tender feet on: Till today there's a house to be built for me for £5,000 . . . That day when I met you, I said me name was . . .

KRANK: Lonegan.

TERESA: It was not. That was me first lie in London. Me real name is Cassidy. I didn't dare to use it, I was afraid the 'domestic service' 'd get home to me mother or worse to me grandmother, or worse still, me brother Con.

KRANK: Con . . . Conor Cassidy?

TERESA: Of course.

KRANK [carefully]: He is, I suppose, still living in Athlone?

TERESA: Somebody said, no. I think he's come to London. Some sort of job with the Transport. Executive I shouldn't wonder. Oh he's always the boy for ambition is Con.

KRANK: Yes, I know what you mean.

TERESA: And why do you work in a place like this? Sure you made a lot more money the way you were before.

KRANK: Yes, but I was not . . . like here, I can find myself in touch, with, if you like, Members of Parliament. Architecture, building, it is a trade, I thought I'd learn it, then see what happened. Always useful no? But I have not abandoned other interests and businesses. *Now* I send assistants to meet the Irish Mail for me, when they have time. You know, I *do* take great credit for you, Teresa – you had never met me, where would have you been now?

TERESA: And to think that my first one, you found him for me, sold bad apples off a barrow at the corner of Praed Street . . .
[*The telephone rings.*]

BARBARA: Oh, damn the thing. – Hallo, Barbara Baulkfast's office. Miss Baulkfast speaking . . . [*coldly*] Oh. It's for you, Mr Krankiewicz.

KRANK: Thank you. Hello, here is Krankiewicz . . . Who? I've never heard of you . . . Oh, *Paul*, is it you, is it? Now look, I told you, I am not to be telephoned at the office . . .

No, no no ... Proszę mówić po Polsku. Ktoś moӡe podelechiawać. ... Khrushchev, Bulganin? Nie wygłupiaj się ... [*Abruptly*] Nie ma o czym mówić ... *No, I can*not* see you, Paul. If you are going to be waiting for me always on the Oratory steps, I shall never go to Mass again. Then you will be punished eternally. Good-bye. [*Rings off.*] Excuse me, I tell him not to telephone me here – he telephones.

LOAP: Khrushchev, Bulganin?

KRANK: I beg your pardon?

LOAP: I don't wish to seem inquisitive, sir, but I did overhear ...

KRANK: Oh no, nonsense, Mr Loap, two Polish words, quite different, no connexion whatever.

LOAP: Naturally I am not one to interfere with, independent thought, all have of course great sympathy, refugees, ah, iron-curtain of totalitarianism: but the Government is exceedingly anxious, and so indeed, is the Opposition that the forthcoming visit should in no way suffer from, ah ...

KRANK: Indiscreet demonstrations.

TERESA: Or boys throwing bombs?

LOAP: Be quiet, Teresa. This is a serious matter.

KRANK: Mr Loap, I do not throw bombs; neither do I demonstrate. It is not in my nature to do such things. Don't worry.

LOAP: I see. Thank you. Now, Miss Baulkfast, I have an appointment at the House in precisely half an hour, so I shall take my leave. As I say, I am impressed by the quality of your work, but *cost*, Madam, cost, is the key note. I shall have to give the matter much further thought.

TERESA: Indeed. So all is benificence and bounty as usual.

LOAP: Good morning, Miss Baulkfast. Do you accompany me, Teresa? I will see you to a taxi.

[*Exeunt* LOAP *and* TERESA.]

---

* Please speak in Polish. Someone may eavesdrop ... Khrushchev, Bulganin? Don't be silly ... There is nothing to talk about.

BARBARA [*in a strained voice*]: What has there been between you and that girl?

KRANK [*airily examining a drawing*]: Nothing, dear Miss Baulkfast, that need cause you to lose your sleep.

BARBARA [*indicating herself*]: What has there been between you and *this* girl?

KRANK [*as before*]: Nothing, dear Miss Baulkfast, that ...
[*Turning on her very suddenly.*]
Now listen to me: To look for true love in a naked bed
It is more dangerous, perhaps more vain,
Than burgling a house on fire,
Pearl diving under a whirling roof of sharks,
Hewing pit coal when the narrow air hangs dead along the galleries.
Where is your gain?
You do not have to do it for a living.
You do not have to fight it as a war:
You look for too much, and you look too far.
That way you find nothing but another person's pain.
And then you delude yourself, it's a fit pain for *you* to bear:
Though all you know about it is a muttering you would hear
Drift into your ears when you think you're asleep in bed.
Alone in bed, I mean: *I* never talk in my sleep.
It looks like I've lost a page from the Specification of the Hampstead school. Do you know where it might be?

BARBARA: You are a great deceiver of women, Sigismanfred. One day, I think, one of them will finish you.

KRANK [*airily*]: Oh, I don't imagine that is very likely.

BARBARA [*exploding*]: No, no? Do you ever imagine anything, do you have the smallest conceivable scruple of a notion of a grain of an idea ...
[*Enter* PAUL, *a haggard man in a dark duffle-coat.*]
What do *you* want?

PAUL [*like Krank, he has a light foreign accent*]: I beg your pardon if I intrude. I am from the Holocaust Heating and Engineering Company. Always trusting to meet your every requirement. I understand you wish to use our products in a factory at Willesden. I could discuss the contract with you, Madam, now, if you desired, or some other time . . .

BARBARA [*unsteadily*]: My assistant will discuss the contract with you. I – I think I have another appointment. Mr Krankiewicz, entertain the gentleman. [*Exit* BARBARA.]

KRANK: So. A heating-engineer are you now?

PAUL: I am. I am, in fact, my dear friend. Do you wish to talk about heating your factory?

KRANK: No. I wish to know why the devil you come here, I have given up going to church because you lie in wait for me behind the confessionals: I have given up answering the office phone because you terrify me over it continually. At least you do not know where I live. Or do you?

PAUL: Yes.

KRANK [*resigned*]: It is clear there is to be no escape, Paul, will you tell me, please, what it is you want?

PAUL: I want *you* to remember, you are a citizen of Poland.

KRANK [*wearily*]: Dear Paul, I am no longer a citizen of any-where.

PAUL [*dramatically*]: The Russians are coming to London.

KRANK: I read now and then the newspapers.

PAUL: What are we going to do about it?

KRANK: *Me*, I intend to do nothing about it.

PAUL: There are others who do not so intend.

KRANK: Let me point out to you – it has been officially requested by the leaders of the Polish Community in England that nobody does anything to disturb Queen Elizabeth's peace. I have no doubt some *gentle* kind of a demonstration, some carrying of banners and laying of wreaths, may likely take place. But strange, Paul, you are not a man I can envisage . . . you laying of wreaths . . . no.

PAUL: No. What I intend to do is not gentle, it is not passive, nor floral, nor processional, Sigismanfred, I am going to blow them up.

[*Telephone rings. Enter* BÀRBARA.]

BARBARA: That'll be for me. It's that bloody headmistress up at Hampstead. Hello. Barbara Baulkfast's office. Miss Baulkfast speaking. . . . Good morning Miss Fisher. . . . Yes . . . Yes . . . I quite understand. You want the colour scheme for the infants' classroom as it was before, the dove-grey and signal-red . . . Yes, Miss Fisher, they *have* started painting it blue. I'll order them to stop . . . Good morning. You heard that, Krankiewicz. Send out another Variation Order. After all, she's the client. [*She turns to leave.*]

KRANK [*to Paul, from whom he has not taken his eyes*]: You must be out of your mind.

BARBARA: Are you talking to me?

KRANK: No. I er . . . it's the Willesden factory, he wants to put in an oil-burning boiler instead of the gas. But . . .

BARBARA: Arrange it to your satisfaction. Only, remember, all these things have got to be paid for. [*Exit* BARBARA.]

PAUL: No, Sigismanfred, I am not out of my mind.

KRANK: God's mercy on to London, Paul, how do you possibly think you can . . .

PAUL: It will be perfectly easy. I have my job . . . I work for a firm making boilers, radiators, taps, screws, gas-pipes, electrical appliances, all of them things that each, with skill, can provide some necessary part of the – bomb, mine, infernal machine, or what you'd call it. Everything that is . . .

KRANK: Except your explosive.

PAUL: Ah, yes. The explosive will be furnished by Władysław. As you know he has means of access.

KRANK: I did not know.

PAUL: It's true, he has. All we want, Sigismanfred, is some-where safe to assemble our device.

KRANK: *And* somewhere safe to go and set it off.

PAUL [*humourlessly*]: That is being planned for.

KRANK: Why not assemble it in your radiator factory? If all the parts are manufactured there . . .

PAUL: Don't be a fool.

KRANK: Thank you.

PAUL: You owe me five hundred pounds.

KRANK: Oh, no I don't.

PAUL: In 1946 that money was lent to you by Josef, my second cousin from Poznań. Some disreputable deal, I don't care to remember ... But *I* have taken over the debt from Josef in settlement of a – a private dispute between us. Here is your acknowledgement of the loan. Your signature is incontestable. [*He produces a paper.*]

KRANK: So?

PAUL: I want it. Five hundred pounds.

KRANK: I haven't got five hundred pounds.

PAUL: Yes: it is, perhaps, so large a sum, you cannot immediately realize it; so, I will permit you to pay me in kind.

KRANK: What kind of kind?

PAUL: The use of your house at the end of next month for the purposes I have already implied.

KRANK: No.

PAUL: Yes.

KRANK: But you cannot carry out political conspiracies in my house. I will be ruined. Anyway, there's more than enough goes on there as it is.

PAUL: It is the only safe place. I know your elusive habits, Sigismanfred. Władysław has had you observed for quite a long time. You are not so clever as him, but I think you may be more clever than English Security. All *our* premises are liable to be watched. *We* are too well known to the M.I.5 as indefatigable patriots: but you are known only as ...

KRANK: Never mind what. You are over-rating me. *My* 'elusive habits' were designed to protect me from women, from creditors, from my tenants, from my own old convictions: not from the Special Branch.

PAUL: It does not matter. When we are ready, we shall expect a room, and privacy, and such assistance as we ask. In return, I forget the five hundred pounds, and also I forget to do my Honorary Englishman's duty of informing the police about all your different businesses in the northern part of London. You will hear from us soon.

[*Enter* BARBARA.]

In the Willesden factory, Mr Krankiewicz, a gas boiler would be by far the most suitable. I will prepare estimates accordingly. Good morning madam. Always trusting to meet your every requirement. [*Exit* PAUL.]

BARBARA: Gas boiler.

KRANK: Yes, on this particular contract, I think . . .

BARBARA: Very well, I'll leave it to you. Did he give you a price?

KRANK [*vaguely*]: Five hundred pound . . .

BARBARA: What?

KRANK: Er . . . no. He didn't give me a price. We shall hear from him later.

BARBARA: You never told me what you had to do with that girl.

KRANK: Just old, old acquaintance is all. Don't worry.

BARBARA: Just old acquaintance. Like me?

KRANK: Not very much like you. Don't worry. Half past twelve. Are you not lunching with a client today?

BARBARA: Good heavens, so I am. I must fly.

KRANK [*airily*]: O.K., dearest Barbara, you fly. Good-bye.

BARBARA: God destroy your bloody breath, Sigismanfred. [*Exit* BARBARA.]

KRANK: Not until somebody gives me five hundred pound. Keep these people away from my house. . . . Bombs, violence, conspiracy, all of it again, pale faces, sweaty fingers, jigging on my heart, hooded fanatic eyes like letterboxes watching me. I was alone, and confident, and uninvolved. Now look at me. Should I tell the Police? Police: No. I am Krank. I must stand uninvolved. Five hundred pound. At least I have over a month to get it.

[*He sings and dances a little step dance between the stanzas.*]

O when I was young
I played with a gun
And all the other children in a row
I shot them through the head
Till they lay down dead

And then I did not know
Where to go,
Where to go.

But the children they arose
And came creeping from the ground
And they fired silver bullets up my stair
They woke my true love,
Who was sleeping up above,
Till she ran from me
Tearing out her hair,
Out her hair.

They drove down the doors,
And set fire to my roof,
And they pulled away the pillars of the wall;
I stood in the street
With the rain upon my feet;
While my house so majestical
Did fall –
Oh did fall.

CURTAIN

Act Two

Noise of train passing. CASSIDY *discovered. He is not wearing his uniform, but a black suit.*

    [*Enter* BATHSHEBA.]

CASSIDY: Are you after meeting the boat train, Bathsheba?

BATHSHEBA: Man, half the week I've been meeting it. Waterloo, Victoria, Charing Cross.

CASSIDY: Anybody on it?

BATHSHEBA: Two today from Trinidad and there was one from Jamaica. I brought them along for to see Mr Krank. Will he keep them, maybe? No, I don't know. Not what I'd call real proud-jetting young women, not what I'd call flying fish or torpedoes. No sir, just kind of sad and quiet gentle sea-weed laid out dark on a hard cold beach. You've been along to meet a train too?

CASSIDY: The Irish Mail, no less. And there they stepped down from it, six beautiful doxies, Sea-weed? – No sea-weed but all roaring gorse, wild whitethorn, a chiming tempest of girls, turned that dirty Euston into a true windswept altitude, a crystal mountain-top for love. Or for Mr Krank's finances, which is more to the bloody purpose.

BATHSHEBA: Did you bring them here?

CASSIDY: I did not.

BATHSHEBA: Why not?

CASSIDY: Sure they'd a pair of chattering old magpies of nuns with 'em, 'March strictly past the wicked enticing man, girls, straitly away past him, and drop your eyes to the platform, God preserve us from the man, God help us and save us'. And who goes to Mass more commonly than Cassidy? What would you call me but the epitome of religion, what's Baker Street station but crumb of a warm loaf expansive to my leaven of perpetual devotion? Royalty and strength to His Holiness the Pope.

BATHSHEBA [*uncomprehendingly enthusiastic*]: Royalty, Royalty.

CASSIDY: And may the bones of Oliver Cromwell crumble in the ground. Crumble and rumble, rumble and crumble.

[*Enter* BUTTERTHWAITE *full of excitement. He carries a great bundle of newspapers.*]

BATHSHEBA: Glory hallelujah.

BUTTERTHWAITE [*sings*]: Hallelujah, Hallelujah, Hallelujah! Every Christmas up north we'd reckon to do 'Messiah'. Ah, there's a good thundering work through into the fling of that chorus, I'll tell you, and then, what about the Refiner's Fire, eh? Hear *that* one holler, as it comes running up shaft. [*Sings*] 'For He is Li-i-ike a Refi-i-i-ner's Fi-ire' . . . [*He holds up papers.*] But I've got it, I've got it. Your Uncle Charlie's got it, every detail fixed and prized for him. Where is he? Where is he? I'm bawling at his door.

CASSIDY: He's above in the house passing words with some women.

BUTTERTHWAITE: Words d'you call it, what I've got here it's more than words, I can tell you, it's Power, it's Potential, it's congenital Might and Force. And between you and me, Mr Cassidy, it's money. [*Sings*] 'The Trumpet shall sound and the Dead sha-all be wakened.'

[*Enter* KRANK *in his macintosh and a cloth cap.*]

A Merry Christmas, Mr Krank.

BATHSHEBA: Merry Christmas.

CASSIDY: Merry Christmas, many of them, barrel-loads of bloody beer.

KRANK [*annoyed*]: Merry Christmas, we only just had Christmas: what the hell you all talking about? Is more noise down here than when the Underground goes past . . .

[*The train passes and drowns his words.*]

When the Underground goes past. Three young ladies upstairs, what is it you think they think of it all? Howling and screaming like a cellarful of gelded cats, like I kept a brothel house down here, like you all wanted the police in here after us. Is that what you want? I tell you, these days, that is the *last* thing must be let to happen in this house. O.K.

CASSIDY: Oh, and how long is it you've been so respectful to the police?

KRANK: Never mind: do as I tell you. I hope, Mr Butterthwaite, you are come here to some practicable purpose.

BUTTERTHWAITE [*a little dashed*]: Aye, well I am: but, er . . . if you're not in right mood, like, I can . . .

KRANK: I am in the right mood for good sense: not for foolishness. What have you for me?

BUTTERTHWAITE: What have I for you? I've got everything for you. I've got such a scheme here – who said I'd no notion, who said I'd lost my touch; who said that Cheery Charlie Butterthwaite there was nowt left of him but press cuttings? I'll show 'em.

KRANK [*looking at the bundle of papers* BUTTERTHWAITE *gives him*]: I don't know what all this is. What is it? What will it do for me?

BUTTERTHWAITE: What you want it to do. It'll put you and the Borough Council together like that. [*He holds up crossed fingers.*] Two mouths, ten fingers, four little feet, in a big brass bed, that's you and them: Mister and Missus, and devil take the lodger. 'Course, you'll have to play it careful. Bold, aye, but careful. Stand to reason, you know.

KRANK: Indeed? You fascinate me. But at this present unfortunate moment I am no longer concerned with the coition of myself and the Borough Council. What I would like to know: will your scheme, Mr Butterthwaite, bring to my imminent pocket five hundred pounds?

BUTTERTHWAITE: Five hundred pounds? It'll bring you thousands.

KRANK: So? But how long, how long?

BUTTERTHWAITE: Ah, it'll take time: but I reckon we could guarantee you five hundred in no more than a month or two. Of course, that warn't exactly, you know, what you'd set me on to find out. But still . . . Now then, for details. What I'd reckon'd be best . . .

KRANK [*studying papers*]: One moment, wait. Cassidy, Bathsheba; if you please – out.

BUTTERTHWAITE: I thought, maybe, Miss Bathsheba, she maybe, might be of help to us.

KRANK: Indeed? O.K., Bathsheba. Stay.

CASSIDY: If she stays, I stay. What the hell should Bathsheba do, that you keep secret from me? Carry on, Buttery boy, let's hear the story.

BUTTERTHWAITE: A matter of interest, what do you want the five hundred for? Because if . . .

KRANK: Never you mind.

BUTTERTHWAITE: Oh very well, very well. So long as I get my percentage.

BATHSHEBA: And for me, Mr Krank? Me too, for a percentage?

[KRANK *takes her on his knee and fondles her as he reads.*]
[*A train passes.*]

CASSIDY: Percentages on the house me boys, tonight, hey?

KRANK: As well as I can make it out, your extraordinary handwriting, Butterthwaite: what is here, it is some ' sort of arrangement for swindling the electors of this Borough out of their savings?

BUTTERTHWAITE: Swindling – Mr Krank, the scheme is in the nature of a Municipal Lottery, as you'll see.

KRANK: To start with it's illegal, I'm afraid.

BUTTERTHWAITE: Eh, it's not illegal. If the Borough Council sets it up for us . . .

KRANK: The Borough Council. But how . . . ?

BUTTERTHWAITE: It's nowt but a modification of what's always been successful, years ago, up north, scores of Corporations, I tell you I'm *experienced*. The Borough Council first sets up . . .

KRANK: But how to hell we can get the Borough Council to set such things up for us?

BUTTERTHWAITE: But that's where our Joe comes in. Now as I was saying . . .

The Waters of Babylon

CASSIDY [*bemused*]: Oh God, I'm dancing on the twirly water, who's this fellow Joe, anyway?

KRANK: Quiet.

BUTTERTHWAITE: The Borough Council first sets up a Municipal Savings Bank. Connected, very like, with Co-operative Society. Now then, your Bank might not do too well, so what happens? You offer a Premium, every month, every quarter, when you want, and you draw for it, and the winning ticket gets – whatever you want to give. Folk put their money in. Who draws it out? We do.

KRANK: By what means?

BUTTERTHWAITE: That rather depends on how well we get on with Joe.

CASSIDY: I'd rather you told me, Mister, who the bloody hell is Joe?

BUTTERTHWAITE: Oh aye, Joe. I thought I'd made that clear.

KRANK: No. You had not. Please to make it clear. Who is Joe?

BUTTERTHWAITE: Joe is the new Napoleon of this Borough. Leastroads, he will be, by time I'm through with shaping him. As soon as you'd done talking to me the other week, I said to myself, 'What this Borough needs is a new Napoleon, and what Mr Krank needs is to be like Grey Eminence, behind him.' I'd have taken on the job myself, but you know, I'm an old man – I don't reckon I've got right stamina any more. So I took a look at your Council, took a good look at all of them, and out of them all I selected Joe.

BATHSHEBA: Joe – Joe for Joseph – why, man, it's Joseph Caligula you got on your mind.

BUTTERTHWAITE: That's right – aye, she's right, Joe Caligula, the very lad I mean.

BATHSHEBA: But that one, he comes from Barbados, just like me, Mr Krank, all away from Barbados, and look at him now . . . so marvellous and main, he sits and he rules the Council of the town.

KRANK: You know him, Bathsheba?

BATHSHEBA: It's all of we spades we know him, Mr Krank. He's a real famed boy, Joe Caligula. Oh yes, he's the black bully ruler, he's the stamping boy to prove no faster blood in London than Joe's jump of life.

[*Noise of train passing.*]

KRANK: Joe Caligula. Councillor Joseph Caligula. Yes, I think I have heard of him. I think I had better meet with him. O.K.

BUTTERTHWAITE: O.K. It's two o'clock, it's Sunday: I'll tell you where he'll be. Speakers' Corner, Hyde Park, he goes every Sunday, he stands on his platform, he makes speeches all afternoon. He does work hard at his trade, you know. Perhaps you'll like to go and listen?

KRANK: Excellent thought. Let's all go and listen.

[*They come downstage as the scene closes.*]

How wonderful a symbol of your English democracy: The Corner of the Park. So sylvan, so arcadian, so pregnant a lesson to the errant Totalitarian. So joyous an expanse of sweet Independent Liberty informed by true reason and the dictates of Conscience. Let us all go there and listen.

[*There are discovered three speakers' stands, as follows:*
JOE CALIGULA's *with a placard reading,* 'Joe Caligula. Only friend of Coloured Londoners. Destroy Discrimination'; HENRY GINGER's, *reading,* 'England and the Foreign Peril. We are betrayed'; LOAP's, *reading,* 'Our Foreign Policy is a Balanced Road to Peace.'

[CALIGULA *is a spectacular black man, very big and bold, well dressed in a camel-haired greatcoat and grey homburg.* HENRY GINGER *is a seedy little man, with long grey hair and a reedy cockney voice. When the scene opens they are all three talking at once. Throughout the scene their speeches, unless otherwise indicated, are addressed directly to the theatre audience.*]

CALIGULA: I stand for the Right of the Coloured People in this Country. We are loyal subjects of the British

Government, but we must have full liberty, we must have freedom, we must have freedom.

HENRY GINGER: There are untold thousands of criminal foreigners in this country. They are being let in by the British Government, a monstrous threat to our liberty, a threat to our freedom, to all our freedoms.

LOAP: The considered Foreign Policy at the present time, of this Country, Expand the Good influence of the British Government.

CASSIDY: Well, and here we are. Now which of these three is the glorious Napoleon?

BATHSHEBA: Do I have to tell you? Oh, see him with your eyes, man.

KRANK [*indicating Loap*]: One thing you didn't tell me: *he* was going to be here. How exceeding inconvenient. I must not be observed. [*He turns his collar up and pulls his cap down.*]

CASSIDY: I don't see the Irish Republican Army today . . .

KRANK: Quiet.

HENRY GINGER: I know very well that I'm not listened to, but I shall fearlessly continue to deliver the truth . . .

CASSIDY: That's his usual place, there, where that little fellow is.

CALIGULA [*in a sonorous Old Testament voice*]: Five years, six years, I have lived in this London. What do I find in the streets and high houses of this city, what do I find for my people beneath these aching pavements and up under these glittering roofs . . . for my people, whose skins are of the dark coal forest and whose spirits are the fire and wonder that hides inside that trodden coal, O my dark people; I find we still are told, Go down, Go down, here is enough warm light already, you are come among us uncalled-for, as smoke and shadows to drench out our fire in alien ugliness and our own guilt for it. But I say no man can hold us down, shall send us down again, shall choke the sweeping hinges of our wide wide progress and our open pride of life: for we are breaking up and out into our own time of the world, and we never shall go down.

BATHSHEBA: Glory, glory yeah man.

KRANK: Are you quite sure he is the most suitable for our purpose?

BUTTERTHWAITE: Nay, what good's a Napoleon, without he's got strength.

CASSIDY: Oh Lord, to me he's just a roaring nigger. Let's go and listen to one of the others, for God's sake. [*He goes over to Loap.*]

LOAP: We feel, and, I say, the Prime Minister feels, that, to this circumstance, that is to say, the forthcoming visit of the Russian Leaders – as a necessary if indeed a not entirely inappropriate manifestation, or, yes, a trend towards possible peace, ah, mutual co-operation, co-habitation ... co-, to coin a phrase, co-existence with the mighty Soviet Union. This momentous visit, must not, I have made it my personal, my personal charge, to see that it must not be marred or spoiled, that all should concerning it ...

CASSIDY: Oh what the hell do you think you're telling us? You tell *me* a thing, Captain.

LOAP [*to Cassidy*]: What is that, sir?

CASSIDY: My brother Seamus comes across the water to live in London, he's a peaceable decent man like yourself, and what happens to him? They make him join the British Army.

LOAP: I fear, I ...

CASSIDY: Two bloody years, Captain, oppressing Minorities in the English Colonies, and putting the bayonet into pregnant women ... that's what they're after making him do. Now he has a friend, see, his name's Paddy Riley, *he* comes to London. 'Begod,' says he, 'I want to be a fireman in the Brigade.' 'What's your nationality?' they ask him. 'Holy Ireland,' says he. 'Begod boy,' they tell him, 'there's no place for you in the Fire Brigades of London, you're no more than a bloody foreigner,' they tell him. Now is that justice, Captain, I put it to you square, should you call that justice?

LOAP: I, ah, I don't – I was endeavouring to discuss – Mr

49

Khrushchev and Marshal Bulganin, sir, is my subject. I must ask you to let me keep to it.

CASSIDY: O, Mary in Heaven, there's no justice at all.

[*He goes towards Henry Ginger.*]

CALIGULA: You think I am a bitter man, I am cruel, full of revenge, I want racial wars and bloodshed – no, it is not true. All I want, all I demand, is the knowledge in this country that my people are your people, the Queen of England's people, that we have some claim to live in London without being feared, suspected, laughed at, sniffed at, we don't stink, you know, and we do change our underwear as often as most of you; sniffed at, sneered at, patronized, entertained with that wrong friendliness that says, 'I know you are inferior, but I am such a jolly fellow, such a gay dog, that I can forget it – unlike some of my unneighbourly neighbours. So have a drink, old fellow. Let's hope we're not observed.' Perhaps above all we claim our rights to live without being prayed upon by the avarice of pimps and landlords, black or white, disguised as human beings, into whose malevolent houses are trepanned so many cold bewildered travel-tired dark strangers before they've even been in London half an hour.

KRANK: Oh dear.

CASSIDY: Sure, that one's the noisiest black man I ever heard in me life! I can't catch one word this little creature's discoursing. Speak up, speak up will you, and let's have some notion of your argument.

KRANK: For the sake of heaven, Butterthwaite, what sort of convenient Napoleon is this?

BUTTERTHWAITE: Now don't you try and cross the Trent when you've not yet got as far north as Luton. Everything's . . .

[*To* CALIGULA, *who comes down from his stand.*]

BUTTERTHWAITE: Good afternoon, Councillor Caligula, I trust as how you're in health?

CALIGULA [*when not orating, he has a grave courteous manner*]: Why, Mr Butterthwaite, I am indeed most happy to see you.

I am your debtor, sir, for the recent invaluable assistance you have rendered both to me and my work. I have put your project before the Borough Council and it has found favour. There is much work to be done, sir, in the ward I represent, and in many others. Evil houses to be pulled down, vicious tenants to be evicted, plague spots to be burnt out. Your Savings Bank Scheme, properly used, will give us great help, Sir.

BUTTERTHWAITE: Aye, well, the Lottery should act as a bit of an inducement . . .

CALIGULA: Yes, indeed. Particularly among my improvident countrymen.

BUTTERTHWAITE: I wonder, Councillor, if I might introduce to you a gentleman who . . . [He turns to look for KRANK but finds him shaking his head and taking evasive action.]

[Meanwhile BATHSHEBA thrusts herself in front of Caligula. He is not to realize that she is associated with Krank or Butterthwaite.]

BATHSHEBA: Councillor Caligula, it's Bathsheba. I'm from Barbados, just same as you, you know my folks back there . . . or maybe, maybe you know 'em, you bet you know 'em. My pappy he was a man like a black old battle remembered in a song. Only one eye left to him, only one ear, all cut about to the shape of a scallop shell, 'Half-past-two-half-past-three' they used to call him 'cause them times of every day he was wild wild drunk, he would go and he'd fight against the sailormen for gold rings and dollars, way down along on Silver Beach . . . You know him Mister?

CALIGULA: No, child, I never knew your pappy – but I know you and I know the way you choose to live in this town.

BATHSHEBA: I keep a gentle warm bed, Councillor, wide and gentle. I could rock you to sleep easy as a swooning ship in a loud storm. I could be the arrow-compass for all your ranging dreams, Councillor. Oh yes.

CALIGULA: What could you do in London you couldn't in Barbados? Only here, there's more money and more wicked men after it. Child, you may be wide and gentle, you may have pretty tits and hips, child, but all you are with them is just a waggling fool.

BATHSHEBA: Oh.

BUTTERTHWAITE [*recapturing Krank*]: Councillor Caligula, this is Mister Alfred Cash, the Polish gentleman I was telling you about, Councillor. Mr Cash is as it might be the moving spirit behind our Savings Bank ... it were his own original idea entirely, let's be proper modest about it. He's the one worked every bit of it out.

KRANK [*frantically aside*]: What did you say is my name?

BUTTERTHWAITE: I reckon he's got a right name for it, eh, Alfred Cash, Cash means money. ... Good Cash brings you the Good Cash, eh? [*He laughs uproariously and nudges.*]

BATHSHEBA: Councillor, I'm going.

CALIGULA [*to Krank*]: I am very honoured, sir. You must be a person of great financial acumen.

BATHSHEBA: Good-bye Councillor, I'm gone. [*Exit* BATH-SHEBA.]

[*Enter* PAUL *unremarked by the others.*]

HENRY GINGER: But, I stand here and fearlessly say it, it is the monstrous army of foreign agents calling themselves Political Refugees, who for years have been insinuated, O with cunning, into the midst of our Society ...

CASSIDY: Where's your evidence?

HENRY GINGER: ... And we have welcomed them. Refugees? Where do they come from? Czechoslovakia, Yugoslavia, Lithuania, Hungary, Rumania, and, perhaps above all, Poland.

PAUL: What is that you say?

KRANK [*recognizing Paul*]: Oh my God, I get out of this quick, Excuse me, Councillor, but ...

CALIGULA: Are you going, sir? I too will have to take my leave, I have a meeting ...

HENRY GINGER [*to Paul*]: I have documentary proof that half the Poles in this country were nothing more than active collaborators with the Nazi Gestapo ...

[*Exit* CALIGULA *with his stand and placard.*]

PAUL [*furiously*]: That is a lie. I will not speak of myself, but there, over there, I see one of my compatriots, he will support me. Sigismanfred Krankiewicz. Sigismanfred, come here.

LOAP: I repeat, in extending the hand of friendship ... [*He breaks off, noticing Krank.*]

[GINGER *writes in a notebook.*]

KRANK [*who has almost managed to sneak away*]: Paul, is it, Paul, there seems to be some mistake ...

PAUL [*magnificently*]: This man has been in Buchenwald. I know it for certain. Now will you dare to tell *him* what you have been saying to me ...

HENRY GINGER [*doubtfully*]: He may have been in Buchenwald, oh yes, that's very likely.

PAUL: And I myself was two years in Siberia, prisoner of the Soviets, and after that for two years I fought in most bloody campaigns, in Italy I fought ... Who captured Monte Cassino?

LOAP: I repeat in extending the hand of friendship to our Russian friends ...

HENRY GINGER: And that is another thing. I have heard unimpeachable information that there is a clear plot, a Polish plot, to sabotage the visit next month of Comrades Khrushchev and Bulganin ...

PAUL: You have heard nothing but unimpeachable dogs-vomit, you foul old man; I will not stand here and listen ...

HENRY GINGER [*very fast and nervous*]: What I'd ask you is this, why didn't the Poles go back after the war? I'll tell you why not ... they were afraid, because they knew that the People's Government in Warsaw knew that they'd worked for the Nazis. And now they're all working against a just peace settlement with the Russian people and the Progressive Soviet Statesmen. They're all criminals and traitors, that's what they are.

PAUL: Lies, lies, lies, pull him down, the dirty slanderer ...

HENRY GINGER [*shouting into Paul's face*]: Yah, warmonger,

where's your Iron Cross, where's your Swastika, you Fascist?

[PAUL *pulls Henry Ginger off his stand and jumps up himself.*]

PAUL: Now hear my words, Englishmen. I am a Pole. I am proud of my nation. I did not ask to be an exile in this country, I did not ask to have my own country betrayed into the belly of the atheist tyrants . . .

CASSIDY: Ha, ha, hurrah.

PAUL: Nor did I ask to walk the streets of London and look on in silence while the vile murdering butchers who have killed my family and enslaved my friends walk and talk and smile among your graveyards and your picture galleries, and smear the gloves of your delicate Queen crimson with the reek of their hand-grasp.

LOAP [*to Paul*]: Sir, if you please, I must beg you to moderate . . .

CASSIDY: Send him down, David.

PAUL [*to Loap*]: Roll back into your mudwallow, you slobbering crocodile.

LOAP [*to a Policeman who has already wandered across the back of the stage once or twice during the scene*]: Officer, Officer, for heavens' sake restore order . . .

[CASSIDY *pulls Loap off his stand and damages his placard.* HENRY GINGER *scuffles with* PAUL.]

HENRY GINGER: Nazi, Fascist, Reactionary, Warmonger, Anti-British, that's what he is, why don't you arrest him, Officer – he's Anti-British, I tell you . . .

KRANK: Cassidy, come here, will you come back here . . .

CASSIDY: Ha, ha ha hurrah, where's the police, where's the bloody peelers . . .

POLICEMAN [*strongly clearing the stage*]: Come on, come on now, break it up. You there, you there, come on, move along, out of it the lot of you. Oh, it's you, is it, Henry Ginger, you behave, old man, or you'll find yourself inside again for Inciting a Breach. Come on, come along now, break it up, can't you?

[*Exeunt all save* LOAP *and* POLICEMAN. HENRY GINGER *carries away with him his stand and placard.*]

LOAP: Thank you very much, Officer. Much obliged to you.

POLICEMAN: That's all right, sir. . . .

[*Enter* TERESA.]

. . . Here, you, young lady, we've got too many of your lot round here already; get moving.

TERESA: Well, I declare.

LOAP [*embarrassed*]: It's all right, Officer, I, ah, I know this lady.

POLICEMAN: Eh? Indeed? Well, if you say so, Mr Loap. Good afternoon, sir. [*Exit* POLICEMAN.]

TERESA: And the same of it to you, Superintendent. You after enjoying now an agreeable half-hour with your politics, Alexander?

LOAP [*following her*]: How many times . . .

TERESA [*looking at what is left of his placard, etc.*]: They don't seem to have left much of your little platform for you.

LOAP: Teresa, how many times have I to tell you . . .

TERESA: This Balancing, now, it must be a difficult art. I used to live once with a boy from the circus, he made out he was an Equilibrist, but not after dark begod he wasn't. I only let him have me for a fortnight – the lunatic grunting crab. It was like sharing your pillow with a steam-shovel.

LOAP: Teresa. *Will* you listen to me.

TERESA: Oh, what's the matter now?

LOAP: Time and time again I have told you I will not have you hovering around me in public places. It was quite bad enough in that architect's office, but in . . .

TERESA: And what about the Architect's office, anyway? If you're to build me a house at all, I'm going to have some sort of opinions, I imagine, and not let your generous money be thrown away on a pie-dish of a cabin that wouldn't be appreciated by a pigman. Besides, I became reacquainted with a very old friend in that office, and that's one pleasure you'd never begrudge a girl surely.

LOAP [*reflecting*]: A very old friend. So you did. I knew he was familiar. Bulganin, Khrushchev.

TERESA: What?

LOAP: Khrushchev: Bulganin. Of course . . . Good heavens. Your old friend, Teresa, how well do you know him?

TERESA: Oh, well enough.

LOAP: Do you know where he lives?

TERESA: I know where he used to live.

[*Enter* BARBARA *in some agitation. Unobserved she stops to listen.*]

LOAP: Where?

TERESA: Never you mind. Anyway, I think he's moved.

LOAP: Now understand me, Teresa. If you are to get this new house as I promised, you are going to have to earn it.

TERESA: *Earn* it. And what do you think I'm after doing every other night for the past six months . . .

LOAP: Be quiet. You find out where this fellow, Krankiewicz, where he lives now. I want you to go to his house, and I want you to watch what he's up to.

TERESA: What he's up to . . . What should he be up to?

LOAP: Never you mind.

TERESA: Then what the hell am I supposed to . . . Oh, and, how extraordinary, here's the Architect-lady herself.

LOAP: Oh, good afternoon, Miss Baulkfast.

BARBARA: Good afternoon, Mr Loap.

LOAP: Are you . . . ah . . . taking a walk, Miss Baulkfast?

BARBARA: Yes, I – I am taking a walk. The park, it is, it is so delightful in the sharp weather, is it not? Miss Delaroy, I think?

TERESA: I am captivated with the renewed opportunity, Ma'am. And how are your affairs?

BARBARA: Very well, thank you. [*She takes Loap aside.*] I wonder, Mr Loap, you didn't happen to see my assistant anywhere round here recently, did you? My Polish assistant, you know. I thought I saw him among the crowd, and now he seems to have vanished. I wanted to tell him . . . er . . . something rather important, connected with the office actually.

LOAP: No, I haven't seen him, no. I am sorry.

[TERESA, *now up on Loap's platform, starts to sing.* LOAP *and*
BARBARA *attempt to carry on their conversation.*]

TERESA:

'Oh I built my love a castle
Of the marble stone so strong
And fastened up the doors on her
So she could do no wrong
I stood to guard her bedroom
With me pockets full of gold
But the wind blew down
    the corridor
And I caught my death of cold.'

BARBARA: I hoped you
like the sketch designs
for the house I sent
you last week.

LOAP: Yes, indeed, they
were most interest-
ing. I'll be calling on
you some day very
soon to go into it
more fully; but I can
tell you now, Miss
Baulkfast . . .

LOAP [*cont.*]: Teresa, I would be obliged if you would go and
do what I asked you to do.

TERESA: I'll finish me song first.

  'Oh if you love a lady
  And you know she loves you good
  You can lie her down in thorns and briars
  Or in a wild green wood
  But if she sees the thicket
  Has a fence or wall around
  She'll climb by night and take her flight
  And leave you on the ground.'

Isn't that the truth, now, Miss Baulkfast? Oh, God, Alexander, and now for Mr Krank.

[*Exit* TERESA.]

BARBARA: Mr Krank?

LOAP: Miss Baulkfast. About the house . . .

BARBARA: Krank? Krankiewicz. Krank. You have seen him,
haven't you?

LOAP: Now, now, Miss Baulkfast. . . .

BARBARA: And that girl knows where he is. Or she will know
where he is. And she is going to him. That's enough for
me.

LOAP: Miss Baulkfast, don't go. I mean, I meant to ask you

before, but ... Miss Baulkfast, will you have dinner with me tonight?

BARBARA [*losing patience*]: Oh, you stupid god-damned ... can't you see ... no sense of time or place or of ... God, what would you know of decorum, anyway. No, of course I won't have dinner with you, you pompous political idiot. [*Exit* BARBARA *after* TERESA.]

LOAP: Well. What an unbusinesslike young woman. Do you imagine that she treats all her clients like that? Yet she was highly recommended to me. And by a Cabinet Minister too. I don't understand it. [*Exit* LOAP *with his stand and placard. The Scene closes.*]

[*Enter* HENRY GINGER.]

HENRY GINGER: Sigismanfred Krankiewicz. I've wrote him in my book – if there's anything to find out, I'll find it out. Buchenwald, he says, does he? We shall see, we shall see. I wish I knew what the other one was called. Very violent character: tst, tst. But I'll catch him. I'll catch the both of 'em, I know 'em. Foreigners, doing down the interests of the English working man. But they've got to be smart to outreach Henry Ginger:

> Henry Ginger quick and hot:
> Against Conspiracy and Plot,
> Though the fool policeman sleeps
> Henry Ginger wakes and creeps.
> He tracks down Subversive Threat,
> And he'll rescue England yet.

Krankiewicz was he called? I've wrote him in my book. [*Exit* HENRY GINGER.]

[*Noise of train passing. Enter* KRANK *in old jersey and trousers.*]

KRANK: Butterthwaite. Butterthwaite, where are you? Where the devil are you?

[*The scene opens to discover* BUTTERTHWAITE *sitting reading a newspaper on a flight of steps which run up from the rear of the stage as from an area up to the street which is suggested by a platform across the back at a height of about five feet from the stage floor.*]

BUTTERTHWAITE: I'm out here in your basement area, Mr Krank. Getting a grip on some fresh air.

KRANK: Oh. What is it you think you are doing out here? I don't like you out here. You might be seen from the street.

BUTTERTHWAITE: You just listen to this. 'Councillor Joe Caligula's scheme for a borough Savings Bank and Public Lottery in which no one can lose is proving a great success. The popular Coloured Councillor told Pressmen today. The promise of bumper annual prizes has encouraged many North Londoners to invest in the new Bank. Asked when the draw for the first Premium would take place . . .'

KRANK: The popular Coloured Councillor said, 'Not for a long time,' I hope.

BUTTERTHWAITE: Something of that, Aye.

KRANK: Look here, how much money already we got out of this scheme?

BUTTERTHWAITE: Well, I . . .

KRANK: How much?

BUTTERTHWAITE: Nigh on a hundred.

KRANK: I want five hundred.

BUTTERTHWAITE: But not in one day. I said a month or two. You said all right. You want to butter your cake and lie on it, you do. We've got to take it gradual. I can't embezzle every penny as it comes in, just like shovelling up shavings and sawdust. We've got to have a floating reserve. Supposing somebody wanted to lift their investment out again suddenly? And, besides, there's always these daft old women, they put sixpence in, they take sixpence out . . . they're shuffling it back and forth all day like through a treadle hole. You'd think they were playing pontoon.

KRANK: This floating reserve, then, how much is in it?

BUTTERTHWAITE: About a thousand by now.

KRANK: I wish I could get at it, I wish I could get it in fast.

BUTTERTHWAITE: But I thought we said at least one month, or two . . .

KRANK: Yes, yes. We did. I am too nervous, is the truth.

BUTTERTHWAITE: Any road, we must be sure there's enough in for someone to draw a prize. We've got to let that aspect go above-board, or folk'll begin to talk.

KRANK: I hope when the prize is drawn, is still plenty for us below-board. O.K.?

BUTTERTHWAITE: Oh, aye, don't you worry.

KRANK: Besides, your Joe Caligula. I tell you what I think, Butterthwaite, I think that man he is honest.

BUTTERTHWAITE: Oh, never, never, never, never. He's a politician.

KRANK: Even politicians . . .

BUTTERTHWAITE: Look, I've been in the game all my life. I'll admit that there's been times when I've made, like, a miscalculation, but . . .

[*Enter* CASSIDY, *in uniform, above.*]

CASSIDY: Ho, ho, hello, hello, below there. Is it yourself then, Mr Krank? I've news for you – we'll have to start playing it bloody safe, man. There's somebody watching the lavatory at Baker Street station.

KRANK [*indicating Butterthwaite*]: Shut up. Not here.

BUTTERTHWAITE [*tactfully*]: If you want to talk private, perhaps I'd best be off.

KRANK: Where are you going?

BUTTERTHWAITE: Town Hall. There'll be nobody in the Savings Bank Office. I'll have a little session at cooking the books, eh?

KRANK: All right. But I tell you what I think, Butterthwaite. I think it is you leave me in the dark too much about what you do. You give me that ridiculous false name to Caligula. I look a fool. That I do not like.

BUTTERTHWAITE: Why it's a grand name, Cash, cash means money. Good Cash brings . . .

KRANK: I know. But I told you I wanted to be put into favour with the Borough Council. If you give a false name, how *can* Caligula know to support my cases? My lodging-house is . . .

BUTTERTHWAITE: Let me handle it my own road: I tell you I'm experienced. Look, have you suffered any sort of a nuisance from the Local Authority since I started in on my work?

KRANK: Well no, I must admit . . .

BUTTERTHWAITE: All right then. Leave it to me . . . leave it to your Uncle Charlie. I've got all my contacts laid out ready. I'm fixing the lot of them – I know what I'm up to.

KRANK: Does Joe Caligula know what you're up to?

BUTTERTHWAITE: Not yet, he don't.

KRANK: But listen . . .

BUTTERTHWAITE: Good-bye, I'll see you. I'll see you, Mr Cassidy. [*Exit* BUTTERTHWAITE, *above.*]

CASSIDY [*to Butterthwaite*]: Oh sure, sure.

KRANK: Now – *who* is watching the lavatory? Police?

CASSIDY: I don't think so.

KRANK: Wladyslaw?

CASSIDY: Who?

KRANK: A big thick man, black moustache. Polish, like me.

CASSIDY: Oh no, it's not him. It's that little fellow was preaching away against the foreigners in Hyde Park. Henry Ginger, I think was his name, now.

KRANK: Oh? Oh. I wonder what it can be *he* is after? Has he seen *me* there, my uses of that place?

CASSIDY: I couldn't tell. I wouldn't be surprised at all.

KRANK: This I do not like. [*Suddenly angry.*] There's other things I do not like, neither, Conor Cassidy. If it was not for you making abusive behaviour and your so amusing little riotings in Hyde Park, that man would not now be watching me into your lavatory. It is a great part of your fault, I tell you.

CASSIDY: Hey, wait a minute, now . . .

KRANK: And other things I do not like. If you were less interested in pinching the buttocks of the girls who come to this house, and were more interested in collecting the money that they owe me, there should be the less reason for me to

61

revile you. Now get upstairs and gather in some rent from my tenants. There is a lot of it due, O.K.?

CASSIDY: Oh sure, sure. But you watch the tones you're talking to me with, Mr Krank, I'm not a man to ...

[*Enter from the wings* BATHSHEBA.]

BATHSHEBA [*singing to a blues tune*]: He laid me down, he laid me down, he laid me down, Oh Lord. He laid me down so low.

CASSIDY: He's in a battering bad mood tonight, take care of your manners, now. And you take care of yours, Mister Conor Cassidy's no bloody Hebrew slave in Egypt, you know, despite his occupation. [*Exit* CASSIDY *into the wings.*]

[*Noise of train passing.*]

KRANK: Where have you been?

BATHSHEBA: Where you told me to go. Where you asked me to go. Where you begged me to go, Mr Krank. Where I couldn't have held myself from going, if you was to stake me down to your kitchen floor, with nails of burning fire. And what have I got for it? What have I got from Councillor Joe Caligula, that proud lovely roarer of this town? I got as much joy as is water in a kettle after five hours a-boiling: and that's all I gone and got. From any living man I never met less. I'm real downright shamed. Am I old, Mr Krank, are my round haunches withered, my belly shrunken-in, my bosom dropped to nothing? Is my face and lips a ploughed field full of dirty thistles? What am I like, Mister, that I get no joy at all? 'Cause I don't seem to have given none, the first time in my life.

[*Noise of a motor vehicle arriving, door slams, knocking.*]

KRANK: What's that?

BATHSHEBA: Up at the back door, I think.

KRANK [*calls*]: Cassidy, Conor Cassidy, see what is happening.

CASSIDY [*from off and above*]: I think it's some fellows at the door are looking for lodgings.

KRANK [*calls*]: Well see to them yourself. I'm busy down here. Considering it, Bathsheba, you need not go to Caligula again. You never told him, did you, that you came from me?

BATHSHEBA: No indeed. You said not yet to tell him.

KRANK: O.K. That damned fool Butterthwaite, he seems to be managing all my plans for me. I don't know why or where, or whatever he is doing. So perhaps it is better you should not go any more at present.

What are you like Bathsheba?

Thistles in a sour field?

That I do not see.

Nor do I see these witherings and wrinklings and shrinkings you talk of

I am no man for no woman, truly, Bathsheba:

I am a sort of a hole punched into the wall of the world

Letting in the strong wind to knock down the chimney-pots.

I am a sort of pocket in the serene sky

Rattling and bouncing the royal passage of airliners.

What reason can there be for *me* to so continually couple with these girls,

Black girls, white girls, yellow girls, all lamp posts in the fog . . .

[*Stamping and banging above.*]

More noise, more. What goes on up there? Cassidy?

[*Enter* TERESA *above.*]

TERESA: Delaroy is the name, Mr Krank, I'll thank you to remember.

KRANK: Teresa. You should not have found your way here. I never told you I was living in this house.

TERESA: I've not come on a sociable visit. I've been sent. I've been sent to spy on you, Krank. What do you think of that for a tale?

KRANK: Sent? By whom? Scotland Yard?

TERESA: Not at all. Alexander Loap, M.P. He thinks you want to murder the Russians.

KRANK: He makes a mistake, then, is all. I am at peace. So tell him, Teresa.

TERESA: I don't know that I'll tell him anything. It's none of his damned business. This house of yours, you know, it's a great improvement on your last. But begod, it's not any tidier, is it? Who's the lady?

BATHSHEBA: Bathsheba's my name.

TERESA: And mine's Teresa. Hello there. [*To Krank.*] You were kissing her when I arrived? Don't let me interrupt you.

BATHSHEBA: You hear what she says, man?

[*Enter* BARBARA *above and unnoticed.*]

TERESA: Put your arms around his neck, now, lovely, sit on his knee . . . he's small and he's bristly and he's short-sighted, and the sweaty little hands on him tremble like telephone wires: but with it all, if there's seven hundred people in a street and he out in the middle of them quite away from the sight of your eyes, you'd know he was there, you'd know he was there, always you'd know he was there.

BATHSHEBA: Not always the happiest thing you could know, is it, Mr Krank? But I don't scare as easy as I can lie down, ah no.

KRANK [*kissing her*]: No? No? So, so, so.

[*He sees Barbara.*]

Tonight it seems to be for me to be watched upon by everyone. Please come in, Miss Baulkfast. This is indeed a great honour. The humble little slum of poor Sigismanfred. Introductions: Miss – Delaroy, you know, do you not? And this is . . .

BARBARA: Miss Delaroy, I certainly know. I must admit, Sigismanfred, you astonish me. I felt sure I would find you in somebody's arms, but I thought . . .

TERESA: You thought at least they would be white and Irish?

BATHSHEBA: But they're not, they're not, lady. They're dark as a dolphin in the sea. I guess they're warmer than a dolphin, yes indeed.

KRANK [*getting up*]: Yes indeed. Barbara you are making me exceedingly angry.

BARBARA: Then we'd better get together again, hadn't we – see, we have just one thing left to us in common.

BATHSHEBA: You and me, lady, we seem to have something

in common as well, but I tell you I don't want to get together with you, not one mouthful.

TERESA: We've got all the three of us that something in common: but as none of us appear to have been having it simultaneous, I don't see any reason for hate and distaste. [*She takes a whisky bottle from her handbag.*] Here's a much better thought. We will all have a portion of this? Will we reconcile together our broken lives of Krank, or whatever you'd call them?

BARBARA: Certainly not. You're an outrageous trollop.

[BATHSHEBA *and* TERESA *laugh.*]

Sigismanfred Krankiewicz; you need no longer attend my office for architecture or for any other purpose. The money that is due to you will be sent on through the post.

[*The banging, etc., above is suddenly repeated and prolonged.*]

CASSIDY [*offstage*]: Mr Krank, Mr Krank, Mr Krank, for God's sake . . .

[*Enter* CASSIDY *in a panic.*]

For God's sake, come up above, man, and stop their bloody nonsense.

KRANK: What bloody nonsense?

TERESA [*aside*]: Holy Joseph and Jacob. The transport executive.

CASSIDY: How the dancing devil should I know what it's about? These fellows they come trampling in with all their clanking junk, and all over the passage and the bottom two flights of stairs . . . Authorization, they say they've got, to deliver it to Mr Krank's – Have they got Authorization? What the hell next? Have I got a Hydrogen bomb in me hip pocket?

KRANK: Hydrogen bomb? No, it can't be. These men, who do they tell you they are?

CASSIDY: I don't know who they are. They've come in a van called the Holocaust Heating or something. Are you truly having rows and rows of radiators put into this house?

KRANK: Holocaust – radiators – No. At least, maybe I am, I

don't know. But not yet, not yet, in God's name, they can't be wanting to come in *yet* . . .

[*Enter* PAUL *above.*]

PAUL: Excuse me.

KRANK: No, so soon.

PAUL: So soon. I hope it is not too great inconvenience for you, Mr Krank. Good evening, Madam, I think . . .

BARBARA: I think we have met, at the office? I didn't know you were doing private work for Mr Krankiewicz.

PAUL: A little contract only, Madam, one good friend to another.

BARBARA: Of course. Good night, Sigismanfred, I am sorry I have to go : but there is an invitation to dinner which I have just remembered. Good night, Mr . . . er . . . Holocaust.

PAUL: Good night, Madam. Always trusting to meet your every requirement.

BARBARA: Good night, Miss Delaroy. Do enjoy your whisky, and whatever bed you find access to tonight. [*Exit* BARBARA *above.*]

CASSIDY [*looking at Teresa, puzzled*]: Delaroy . . .

KRANK: Paul, come here.

[PAUL *starts to descend. The two girls are reclining voluptuously and passing around the whisky bottle.* CASSIDY *drinks.*]

KRANK: I owe you five hundred pounds.

PAUL: So I believe.

KRANK: Today, I have not got it.

PAUL: Not?

[HENRY GINGER *walks quietly across the stage above.*]

KRANK: But I am getting it, do you see, Paul, I am getting it.

PAUL: And so?

BATHSHEBA [*sings*]: He laid me down, he laid me down, he laid me down, oh Lord . . .

KRANK: I do not understand your hurry. I did not expect your, your radiators to be installed till next month. Why, the Foreign Tourists are not to be here till at least the month after that.

BATHSHEBA [*sings*]: He laid me down so low.

KRANK: I cannot deal with this sinister ironmongery in my house. Will you ask, please, your gentlemen to take it away.

[HENRY GINGER *passes quietly across above.*]

PAUL [*grieved*]: So, we are not to be welcomed here. I am disappointed. I had thought, Sigismanfred, that your true Polish spirit . . . Nevertheless, this house of yours it is so very convenient a place for us, I do not want to have to change now. Any other arrangements must be expensive and very difficult.

KRANK: But for five hundred pounds?

PAUL: You are not able to pay it.

KRANK: But soon, very soon. I *can* give you *one* hundred . . .

PAUL: Insufficient, my friend.

[HENRY GINGER *passes quietly across above.*]

But as you are my friend, I will not embarrass you more than I can help. Give me my five hundred by the end of this week and we will leave your house alone. Meanwhile I am moving into that vacant room at the back.

KRANK: It is not vacant. There are three Pakistani bus-conductors to come into it tomorrow.

PAUL: They must find somewhere else. I'm sorry. [*Exit* PAUL *into the wings.*]

BATHSHEBA: That's not a kind man, Mr Krank. He's neither kind nor joyful.

CASSIDY [*who has been looking at Teresa puzzled*]: Excuse me, miss, your face now, it seems some piece of it familiar – I wonder would you ever have travelled to Athlone?

TERESA [*dryly*]: I wonder.

CASSIDY [*still puzzled*]: I wonder, would you have ever worn your hair something of a different colour?

TERESA [*stung*]: *Indeed*, I would never so.

[*Noise of train passing.* CASSIDY *recognizes his sister.*]

CASSIDY [*beginning quietly, then bursting forth, scandalized*]: No, no more you would, no more you would at all. But sure, when you were younger, sure, you were a young girl as rapid as a housemartin, but you had the grace and decency of religion to wear it all roped-up under some proper hat, you did, or some scarf or some shawl – you never paraded the walks of the Shannon the likes of this, with a great long battle-flag of incontinence flattering into the eyes of every randy man.

TERESA: What are you talking to me about, Con Cassidy?

CASSIDY: It's not to you I should be talking, Teresa Cassidy, no, it's here's the fellow's done it, here's the beastly fellow's brought you to such grief and shame ... [*He has turned on Krank*] in the very flowering of your maiden's beauty.

TERESA: Gracious save us all.

CASSIDY [*thrusting his face at Krank*]: Whatever bed, was the word, whatever bed she finds access to tonight. Now listen to me, Mr Fornicating Foreigner ...

KRANK [*cuts him short*]: I will talk to you in one minute, will you give me *one minute*? – be quiet for just *one minute*? Thank you.

CASSIDY [*considerably cowed*]: The beastly fellow, the beastly filthy fellow ... [*He turns away muttering and helps himself to whisky.*]

BATHSHEBA: That's not a kind man, Mr Krank.

BUTTERTHWAITE [*calling offstage*]: Mr Krank, Mr Krank.

BATHSHEBA: I think he's doing you wrong, Mr Krank.

KRANK: Mind your own ...

CASSIDY [*lurching downstairs and growling at the audience*]: Wrong, is it, she says wrong, who's done my sister wrong, look at her, will you look at her, lusting away like a bloody female sea-lion, and she one time the most virginal white darling in all the world.

BUTTERTHWAITE [*entering*]: Mr Krank ...

KRANK [*very fiercely*]: Well Mr Butterthwaite, what bad news have you brought me?

BUTTERTHWAITE: I've just been to the Town Hall. Do you know what Joe Caligula's been and gone and done?

KRANK: He's not been and found out, has he?

BUTTERTHWAITE: No, it's not that, but it's very near as awkward. He's arranged the draw for first prize in the Lottery; Mr Krank, it's day after tomorrow.

KRANK: God above us. But now I shall never get that five hundred pound in. It will take us months and months.

BUTTERTHWAITE [*very miserable*]: God knows it will and all. I'm right sorry, Mr Krank. It looks like I've made a miscalculation.

BATHSHEBA: That's not a kind man, Mr Krank. He's neither kind nor joyful.

KRANK: Wait, wait, but one moment, is there maybe an answer? How much is he offering as the Premium Prize?

BUTTERTHWAITE: Four-fifty.

KRANK: It is enough. It is more than enough, Mr Butterthwaite, we must hold the winning ticket.

BUTTERTHWAITE: How can we do that?

BATHSHEBA [*sings*]: He laid me down, he laid me down ...

KRANK: Teresa, here is five shillings.

TERESA [*taking it*]: Mary in Heaven.

KRANK: Tomorrow you go to the Town Hall, and you buy with it one Municipal Savings Bank Certificate. O.K.?

TERESA: Anything at all to give you gaiety.

KRANK [*to Butterthwaite*]: Is there anyone in the Savings Bank Office now?

BUTTERTHWAITE: No.

KRANK: Then let us go there and see what we can plan. And this time there has got to be no miscalculation.

[*Exeunt* KRANK *and* BUTTERTHWAITE *up steps and above.*]

CASSIDY: Give that money to me.

TERESA: No, I will not.

CASSIDY: Then buy your bloody certificates, and – oh the shame and the grief of it – how well I remember the day your sainted grandmother, rest her soul in peace, St Patrick, St Bridget, St Mary Gipsy, pray for her soul, gave you your first rosary – 'Teresa,' said she, and the tears of love were like snow on the cheeks of her ...

TERESA: Indeed and indeed? And what would she think of you, High King Conor Transport Executive Cassidy, and you nothing more than a little foreigner's personal pimp.

CASSIDY: Do you tell me that? Me own sister tell me that.

[*Enter* CALIGULA *from the wings.*]

What are *you* doing here. How did you get in?

CALIGULA: I came here, sir, to see a compatriot of mine who lodges in this house. I entered quite normally through the front door.

CASSIDY: Well, your friend's not down here. But sure and I know you. The roaring nigger, that's who you are. Joseph Caligula.

CALIGULA: You are not mistaken.

CASSIDY:

> Councillor Joseph Caligula,
> He pulls down the houses
> Where we cheat the bloody niggers.
> He runs the local Savings Bank
> And cooks the bloody figures.

CALIGULA: Thank you.

CASSIDY: Thank you, Mister Councillor, thank you very very much. Teresa, you've taken the whisky, you bitch.

CALIGULA [*to* BATHSHEBA]: Hello, child.

BATHSHEBA: Hello, Councillor. You come a-looking for me?

CALIGULA: No. I came looking for this house. I had heard it is an evil house for our people.

BATHSHEBA: You think so, Councillor?

CALIGULA: I *know* so, child. And you ought to know it too. I had heard of the man who runs this house. I have never seen him, but they say his name is Krank. A bad name for a bad man.

BATHSHEBA: Oh not so bad. No no no, Councillor, not so bad as that.

CASSIDY: Sure it's a bad name. And it's not the only one he carries, neither. You'd find it highly interesting, wouldn't you now, if you heard his other, Councillor? Perhaps you know it already, they call him . . .

[TERESA *hits Cassidy over the head with the bottle. He falls unconscious.*]

TERESA: When he has the drink taken he behaves irresponsible. Before you came in, Mister, he was just after slandering his own grandmother. I have the drink taken too. So, I'm behaving irresponsible.

[*Sings air: 'The Wearing of the Green.'*]

> My love is like a thornbush
> On the middle of the moor.
> The winds have blown it black and bare
> Except for one white flower.

[BATHSHEBA *and* CALIGULA *are facing one another from opposite sides of the stage.* CASSIDY *lies between them.*]

BATHSHEBA: Councillor, you've been running away from me.

CALIGULA: No.

BATHSHEBA: Yes.

[*They begin to circle slowly round Cassidy, each keeping as far from each other as the size of the stage permits. They keep their eyes fixed on each other.*]

TERESA [*singing*]:

> The only road to reach it
> Runs mad with rocks of stone
> And underneath the branches lies
> A heap of soldiers' bones.

A very irresponsible song, bloody hell, it's an irresponsible song. Good night to the both of you. [*Exit* TERESA *up the steps and above.*]

BATHSHEBA: Or maybe, Councillor, I've been running away from you.

CALIGULA: What do you mean?

BATHSHEBA: You don't run in a straight line, I don't run in a straight line, but round and round: who follows who?

> Say I was the moon, you was the sun,
> Each one as near and as far from each one,
> Draw a circle, walk it round,
> Draw a circle on the ground.

CALIGULA [*determined not to let her bewitch him*]:

> You don't play that game with me.

BATHSHEBA:

> No? Say I was a rat and you was a black cat,
> You'd tear me down and break my back.

CALIGULA:

> No.

BATHSHEBA:

> Say I was a mackerel and you was a whale,
> You'd swallow me under, head and tail.

CALIGULA:

> No.

BATHSHEBA:

> Say I was the thorn-bush and you was the south wind,
> You'd strip off my leaves and my flowers and my rind.

CALIGULA:

> No.

BATHSHEBA:

> No? Draw a circle, walk it round.

CALIGULA [*beginning to be caught*]:

> Draw a circle on the ground.
> Say I was the lantern and you was the dark.

BATHSHEBA:

> You could thrust at me though, wherever I'd lurk.

CALIGULA:

> Say you was the reaper and I was the corn.

BATHSHEBA:

> I'd feed on your heart and your husk I would burn.

CALIGULA:

> Draw a circle on the ground.

BATHSHEBA:

> Draw a circle, walk it round,
> Say I was the red meat.

CALIGULA:

> And I was the fork.

BATHSHEBA:

> Draw a circle, walk it round:
> Say you was the lantern –

CALIGULA:

    And you was the dark.

    Draw a circle on the ground.

BATHSHEBA:

    Say you was the railing and I was the park:

CALIGULA:

    I am the lantern

BATHSHEBA:

    I'm all the dark.

    [*She breaks from the circle and runs up the steps and out, above.*
    He follows.]

Upstairs, upstairs, Councillor. I've got a room in this evil
house. Wide, wide and gentle. Easy, gentle and dark.

    [*She runs out and he runs after her.*]

CASSIDY [*groaning and sitting up*]: Somebody's hit me on the
head. I can't remember who. I was going to tell a man
something: I can't remember what. I *do* remember whisky.
Somebody's taken that. Oh God, what a world – it's nothing
but misery – fornication, shame, and misery: and never **a**
drop of whisky in between.

CURTAIN

Act Three

[*Enter* HENRY GINGER *with his notebook.*]

HENRY GINGER: Oh, very violent, very dangerous, I know, but I mean to have my words with him. Here he comes. I don't like his looks:

> But what care I for such malice,
> If Truth he brought to Birth:
> I am H. Ginger, fearless I stand forth.

[*Enter* PAUL.]

Hello. I'd like a word with you.

PAUL: You. How dare you present yourself before my face? How dare you?

HENRY GINGER: Fearless I stand forth.

[PAUL *offers to hit him.*]

That don't do you no good, you know. You don't want to hit, you want to listen. It's true, isn't it, you've got a plot to kill the Soviet Leader?

PAUL: Of course it is not true.

HENRY GINGER: You've got a plot.

PAUL: Oh no. You prove I've got a plot: go on, prove it to me.

HENRY GINGER: I didn't say I could prove it. Didn't say I knew your details. But I do know your confederate.

PAUL: Confederate?

HENRY GINGER: Mr Sigismanfred. Mr Buchenwald. Mr Krank.

PAUL: Well . . . he is a *friend* of mine, certainly.

HENRY GINGER [*pointing offstage*]: Is *he* a friend of yours?

PAUL: No. I would not say so.

HENRY GINGER: Then let's get out of his way. I've got a lot to talk to you about.

[*Exeunt.*]

[*Enter* CASSIDY *in uniform, suffering from a hangover.*]

CASSIDY [*vaguely invoking the audience*]: Who'll buy me a drink, now? That's all I need, boys, just one glass of the whisky, sit me down easy, and let me sort meself out. Bloody hell to it, I don't know, I'm all shocked and shook up. Would you believe me when I tell you, I've wandered every room upstairs and down, in the house of that, that copulating Croesus, that – oh never mind – the dark house of Krank, anyway. I've wandered every room, and not one drop, in one bottle, or one glass, or anything at all. And me head, oh me head, the back of me head, boys. What about the back of me sister? Ah, she's done more travelling on that part of her body than on either of two legs, and that's shameful certain. Two legs. Two keys, I've got two keys, you know, to every room in Krank's house. That's what he doesn't know. He thinks I've only got one. So, when he takes from me just one of those ones, I go straight to the room concerned: I want to know his purpose. Now what purpose do you suppose he has in making a bloody great bomb? Central-heating is it? I'll Central-heat his continental arse for him. I know about bombs, I do: I used to work for the Republican Army. Not as exciting as the London Transport, but maybe more educational. Here's Charlie Butterthwaite. If only he'd buy me some whisky, boys, it'll clear out me brain for me, and I'll know what way to go. Then you'll understand what I'm talking about.

[*Enter* BUTTERTHWAITE *carrying a pair of large brass cymbals.*]

Buy me a drink of whisky, will you? There's not been such discomfort to an Irishman since Wolfe Tone lost his shoe-horn in the bog.

BUTTERTHWAITE: I don't reckon you'd better have any more. You've got to do an important job for us at this meeting tonight.

CASSIDY: Sure I'll do the job. I'll do any job you want.

BUTTERTHWAITE: Look, if you make just one little mistake,

75

the whole show's mucked up. You've not forgot the signal, have you? [*He makes as though to clash the cymbals.*]

CASSIDY [*clapping his hands to ears in agony*]: Oh, God, don't do that, don't do it now. I can remember it.

[*Enter* TERESA.]

TERESA: Ah, Mr Butterthwaite, so I've found you at last. Here's the Savings Certificate. I bought it yesterday. Krank told me to give it to you. It's number Three Two Four.

BUTTERTHWAITE: No, no Miss, you want to keep that, you'll need it. All I want's the counterfoil.

TERESA: I haven't any counterfoil.

BUTTERTHWAITE: I hope you haven't. It's supposed to be left with the clerk at the Town Hall.

TERESA: Oh I see. So it was, too. How are you going to get it?

BUTTERTHWAITE: I'll get it, love, I'll get it. Quickness of the hand deceives the eye, eh? Come tonight, we'll need to be even quicker.

CASSIDY: Ah, the brave boys.

TERESA [*indicating Cassidy*]: And what part's he going to play in this prestidigitation? You're not trusting him for anything reliable, I hope?

CASSIDY: What part is it, what part? What part are you after playing these last five years, but sorrow and trouble upon the grey heads of them that has loved you ...?

TERESA [*angrily*]: Oh take him away, will you, take him away? The minute he sees me he thinks he's on the stage of the Abbey Theatre, or something. For Godsakes, take him away ...

[*Enter* KRANK *in his smarter suit, with a flower in his buttonhole and a fancy waistcoat.*]

CASSIDY: Ah, the brave boys. What they need, now, is a new opportunity. All for the lack of a little central heating.

BUTTERTHWAITE: What are you talking about?

CASSIDY: The Irish Republican Army.

KRANK [*aside to Butterthwaite – gives him some money*]: Get rid of him, Butterthwaite. Buy him a drink, why don't you?

CASSIDY: Oh, the tall gallant fighters – all them grand machine-guns they stole, and what the hell did they do? They left them in a warehouse at the back of the King's Cross for the bloody peelers to discover.

BUTTERTHWAITE [*gives some of the money to Cassidy*]: Look, Mr Cassidy, you go round the corner, and buy yourself a bottle. I'll come and join you in a minute.

CASSIDY: Will you so, truly?

BUTTERTHWAITE: Aye, I will too. Go, you go on.

CASSIDY: Another thing they did, they sent a poisonous mince-pie to the Chief himself of the Ulster Constabulary: and then they sent a message after to tell his wife not to eat it. Oh, the gallant fighters, so cruelly betrayed. [*Exit* CASSIDY.]

KRANK: Is everything arranged for tonight?

BUTTERTHWAITE: Aye, aye, I reckon so.

KRANK: Well, let us just consider again what we have to do. You and me and Caligula are on the platform. O.K.?

BUTTERTHWAITE: O.K. There may be others, you know.

KRANK: What others?

BUTTERTHWAITE: Oh, some of the councillors and that, very like. Most of them won't be there. They're not altogether so fond of our Joe, now he's working up as a Napoleon. They reckon there's a right place for right folk, but not as long as they're black, eh?

KRANK: I see. Now then: tedious speeches first are to be made. We come then to the great event. The drawing of the ticket. They're all in a drum, O.K.? The drum is whirled and whirled around. It stops whirling. And then the winner is drawn out by . . .

BUTTERTHWAITE: By Miss Bathsheba.

KRANK: *Bathsheba*. But that is not what was decided . . .

BUTTERTHWAITE: I forgot to tell you. Joe Caligula, he's fell for that girl at last. This is all his idea, this is. Very nice, too, eh, very sentimental.

KRANK: Does she know: does she know what to do?

TERESA: Sure I've told her what to do. As soon as the signal's given, every light in the building goes off. When they go up again, there she is with the ticket and, hey presto, she's drawn it out of the drum. Number Three Two Four.

KRANK: But when is she going to get hold of the ticket?

BUTTERTHWAITE: I'll put it into her fingers when the lights are gone out. It couldn't be easier.

KRANK: This is getting very complicated.

TERESA: There's one thing, though. Suppose somebody recognizes you, Krank? You appearing in public for the first time ...

KRANK: But not as Krank. As Cash. No one in this part of London has ever seen me in this suit, or these spectacles, or washed, or shaved, or brushed. Except Loap. ... Oh God. Loap.

TERESA: He'll not be around.

KRANK: Not?

TERESA: Sure, he's roaring and rutting after that whore of an architect of yours. He'll not be finding his politics in any *Public* Halls for a day or two, I dare say ... Do you know – there's one of my lady-friends tells me of a Cabinet Minister, no less, is looking for a new lady. Very good situation, first-floor flat in Pont Street, generous allowances, only required Thursday nights and Saturdays, rest of the week's your own, and he's not at all jealous. If Loap can give me an introduction to him, I'll promise not to tell the Sunday papers about Loap.

KRANK: Yes. Now, there's only one thing not fixed. What is to be the signal?

BUTTERTHWAITE: My cymbals.

KRANK: What?

BUTTERTHWAITE: Aye, it's what I said the other night, we must carry off this meeting with a bit of high style. Loud and Cheery, you know. Half the audience are going to be West Indians, and the other half'll be chronic Telly-gawpers looking for one of them give-away games. You've got to make it dramatic. Besides, the noise has to carry to Cassidy at the switchboard. That's underneath the stage.

TERESA: Con Cassidy, you've got Con Cassidy. . . .

BUTTERTHWAITE: There's nobody else . . .

KRANK: You have tested it. It will carry?

BUTTERTHWAITE: Aye, it'll carry. [*He clashes cymbals.*]

KRANK: Let me try, too. [*He takes the cymbals and clashes them.*] Good. Very good, I think. Yes. Use them by all means. [*He clashes them again.*]

   [*Enter* PAUL *followed by* HENRY GINGER, *who keeps obscurely in the background.*]

PAUL: Sigismanfred.

   [BUTTERTHWAITE *exits with* TERESA.]

KRANK [*jauntily*]: Aha, Paul, aha. I have something to tell you. Tomorrow at this time, either five hundred pound, or else a little iron bed in Pentonville Gaol.

PAUL [*drawing a revolver purposefully*]: Sigismanfred. I am your bed-maker. I would like you to go easily to sleep. [*He aims the gun at Krank.*]

KRANK [*backing away*]: Oh, Paul. No, please, please point it some other way.

PAUL [*grim*]: No other way. You have been my friend.

KRANK: Oh, Paul. Had you not better tell me the reason?

PAUL: Reason, I cannot believe it that you do not know. [*To Henry Ginger.*] Come on, come here. He wants to know the reason.

KRANK: So. Henry Ginger, is it not? Sir, I hope you found your hours well spent in the Baker Street conveniences?

HENRY GINGER: Oh yes, very well spent, yes, I make no doubt of that.

PAUL [*to Krank, sobbing*]: You said to me, you said to me, that you were two years in the Buchenwald Concentration Camp. Did you not say it?

KRANK: Certainly I said it. It was the truth.

PAUL: But he says . . .

KRANK: Well, what does he say?

PAUL [*with a tremendous effort*]: He says to me, that you were in Buchenwald yes, but Sigismanfred, you were no prisoner.

KRANK: Henry Ginger, words of truth, how should Henry Ginger know? He was not there?

HENRY GINGER: No, I wasn't, no. But what about them as was, what about Constantin; what about Ranewski; or Joachim Klarakiewicz, what about Braunstein, you know him, a little Jew with three warts under his jowl; what about Jean-Pierre Dumaurice, I think he was a Frenchman?

KRANK: So? What about them?

HENRY GINGER: All of them was once in Buchenwald. Now then, you see, all of them are living in London. They've told me some curious things, Mr Krank. When you was in Buchenwald? You used to be . . .

PAUL: . . . You used to be . . .

KRANK: I used to be a German soldier in Buchenwald. I helped to garrison the camp. And my principal occupation was to clean the officers' boots: but nevertheless, I was a German soldier, a volunteer, I used to wear the grey uniform, all right now, Paul, you have heard Henry Ginger's truth, all right, you shoot me.

PAUL [*terribly upset*]: Why, I do not want to shoot you. What is the good to shoot you? All I want – I want to shoot myself. You have been my friend. I *must* understand this. [*He lowers the gun.*]

KRANK:

You know, there's nothing difficult psychological, obscure
It's a most easy story, not very long. I will tell you.
1939, my part of Poland is invaded by the Russians,
So I find it convenient to join the Russian Army.
I clean the officers' boots. Amusing. Then, 1941.
My part of the Russian Army is destroyed by the Germans.
So I find it convenient – so, once again, I find . . .
I clean the officers' boots. Amusing? I did not ask
To be posted to Buchenwald. That was the time of the world
That I know to myself I have no year, town, or family,
The house of Krank is to be always an empty house.
Eighty people in it, lodgers? For me it is empty.
In Buchenwald was I prisoner, was I convenient soldier . . .

So many thousands of people all lost in that cold field.
Who knows what I was?

PAUL:

We know what you were.

KRANK:

But I don't know what *you* are.
Or you, Henry Ginger, or all of the rest of you,
With your pistols and your orations,
And your bombs in my private house,
And your fury, and your national pride and honour.
This is the lunacy,

[*Exit* HENRY GINGER *furtively.*]

This was the cause, the carrying through
Of all the insensate war
This is the rage and purposed madness of your lives,
That *I*, Krank, do not know. I *will* not know it,
Because, if I know it, from that tight day forward,
I am a man of time, place, society, and accident:
Which is what I must not be. Do you understand me?

PAUL:

No.

KRANK [*violently*]:

The world is running mad in every direction.
It is quicksilver, shattered, here, here, here, here,
All over the floor. Go on, hurtle after it,
Chase it, dear Paul. But I choose to follow
Only such fragments as I can easily catch,
I catch them, I keep them such time as I choose,
Then roll them away down and follow another.
Is that philosophy? It is a reason, anyway,
Why I am content to hold such a disgusting lodging-house,
And why I'd be content to get you and your bombs out of it.

PAUL: I do not know what to think of you. I was going to
shoot you, but how can I shoot a man who does not understand why I am shooting him? My bombs, did you say?
Where is Henry Ginger?

KRANK: Where indeed?

PAUL: Gone, gone. I have been led into a trap, yes, surely, why, now he must know – I'm going after him.

KRANK: Wait – Paul.

PAUL: After him, Henry Ginger. Led into a trap. [*Exit* PAUL *in a frenzy.*]

KRANK [*wiping his brow*]: That is a man I never feel safe with. He's mad, you see, terribly mad. I am now on my way to meet another madman, not quite so unsafe but not so far from it. I don't think he has a gun. [*He walks up and down the stage.*] Councillor, Councillor Caligula. Are you here? This is me Alfred Cash. I am waiting to see you.

CALIGULA [*off*]: Coming, Mr Cash. I won't be a moment.

KRANK: Good, he sounds jocund. I wonder is Bathsheba with him. Yes, so she is. How remarkably fortunate.

[*Enter* CALIGULA *with* BATHSHEBA.]

CALIGULA: Well, Mr Cash, I think everything is ready. I am most honoured that you are to be on the platform with us, on this pioneer occasion.

KRANK: It's a pleasure, sir.

CALIGULA: For me, indeed sir, a true pleasure. I would like you to meet the young lady who has consented to make the draw for us tonight. Bathsheba, this is Mr Alfred Cash: Mr Cash, meet Miss Bathsheba.

KRANK: I am delighted.

CALIGULA: She has been a victim, you know, of the devils and sharks of this part of the town. Against whom I fight, Mr Cash. Yes, sir, against whom Joe Caligula does not hold himself meek. Krank is the name, she lived in his house, but not any more. That man I have marked, Mr Cash . . . Mr Butterthwaite, I presume, will be with us tonight?

KRANK: Yes, I am sure that he will.

CALIGULA: I don't think any of the councillors are going to attend. I am conscious, nowadays, of a coldness towards our scheme, which I had not expected. But not among the people, no. There, there is enthusiasm. However, Mr Loap has promised to come along, later.

KRANK [*startled*]: Mr Loap.

CALIGULA: Our Member of Parliament. Now he has shown consistent interest in the scheme I believe even the Cabinet they have expressed interest. You may find yourself a famous man, Mr Cash.

KRANK: Yes; I rather think that I may.

CALIGULA: I must hurry from you now. I have last-minute arrangements to make. I'll see you on the platform shortly. You coming, Bathsheba?

BATHSHEBA: I'll just be in the way if you're busy. I'll stay with Mr Cash, till the meeting.

CALIGULA: If Mr Cash does not mind ...

KRANK: It will be a pleasure.

CALIGULA: Well, sir, till the meeting.

KRANK: Till the meeting.

   [*Exit* CALIGULA.]

What the devil do you laugh about? Everything, everything is ruined.

BATHSHEBA: Ruined, why ruined?

KRANK: The Member of Parliament. He knows me, Bathsheba.

BATHSHEBA [*disconcerted*]: Oh, lady, that's bad. But he's not coming right away. You've still got time for the draw, man.

KRANK [*suddenly*]: Let's hope so, by God. How intimate have you become with Mr Caligula?

   [BATHSHEBA *grins*.]

I see. Where did it happen?

BATHSHEBA: Your house, Mr Krank.

KRANK: So, so? What was he doing there?

BATHSHEBA: Prowling around. Oh lady, can that councillor prowl?

KRANK: Can he indeed. How much does he know?

BATHSHEBA [*voluptuously*]: Everything I could show him, plenty more besides.

KRANK [*sharply*]: I did *not* mean that.

BATHSHEBA: Are you really going to beat the signal with *these*?

KRANK: Yes. They belong to Butterthwaite. When he was a young lad. In the Trades Union Offices, I believe.

BATHSHEBA [*laughs and clashes the cymbals*]: There goes the signal. Draw out the ticket. Does it win? [*Clash.*] Lords, Gentlemen, it does. Give the money to Mr Krank. [*Clash.*] Oh Mr Krank, you certain are grand and elegant tonight.

KRANK: Why should I not? Perhaps my last opportunity.

BATHSHEBA: Sing me a song, Mr Krank.

KRANK: A dolorous song?

BATHSHEBA: Not that one tonight. You sing me a loving song, instead.

KRANK: For you and Joe Caligula?

BATHSHEBA [*sings*]:

> As I lay sleeping
> There came to my bed
> My love with no clothes on
> But a crown on his head,
> But a crown on his head.

> Oh he was as black
> As the night without stars
> His eyes were like steamboats
> Racing from afar.

> He came to my bed
> And he lay in my bed
> And he loved me all night
> From my feet to my head,
> My feet to my head.

CALIGULA [*off*]: Ha, Mr Cash. [*Enter* CALIGULA *agitated.*]

CALIGULA: Mr Cash, Mr Cash, have you seen Mr Butterthwaite?

KRANK: Has he not arrived?

CALIGULA: No, he has not. I have been waiting for him, what can have happened? We shall have to start without him, Mr Cash.

KRANK: Without him. But we can't do tha ...

[*Enter* POLICEMAN.]

POLICEMAN: Good evening, gentlemen.

CALIGULA: What can we do for you, Officer.

POLICEMAN: Councillor Caligula, I believe?

CALIGULA: Yes.

POLICEMAN: I'm Police Constable Robinson, sir. I am reporting as detailed to be present on your platform at the Drawing of the Premium.

KRANK: What for?

POLICEMAN: Just a matter of form, sir. In an observatory capacity, as you might say.

KRANK: Really.

CALIGULA: You haven't seen Mr Butterthwaite, have you?

POLICEMAN: No, I'm afraid not, sir. As a matter of fact, sir, between you and me, I'm not at all sorry I've been picked for this duty tonight. Me and Mrs Robinson, sir, as you might say, we have a bit of an interest ourselves. Only a couple of five-bob certificates, you know. But there's always a chance, isn't there? Of course if I was to win, being on the platform at the time, do you know what they'd call it, down at the police station, don't you? They'd call it Evidence of Criminal Collusion – laugh. Oh there's a lot of funny jokers in the force.

KRANK: Very diverting. Ha, ha.

[*The tabs open to a flourish of music. The full stage is discovered laid out for a public meeting – the audience being represented by the theatre audience. In the centre is a table draped to the floor with Union Jacks. On it are the usual carafe and glass, etc., and a kind of miniature milk churn, on trunnions, which is the drum for mixing the tickets. There are chairs behind the table. Hanging from the flies is a large poster reading 'Look after the pennies and the pounds will come running', 'Sixpence today saved is a pudding for dinner tomorrow'. There is a telephone on a small table.*]

[*Enter* CALIGULA, BATHSHEBA, *and* KRANK, *and take*

their places behind the table. The POLICEMAN *follows and remains standing upstage.* BATHSHEBA *lays the cymbals carefully on the table.*]

CALIGULA [*knocking for silence*]: Ladies and Gentlemen of this Borough: or shall I say my good friends – you all know me. I'm Joe Caligula. I'm the man the newspapers call the 'Chocolate Dynamo of North London' and the 'Black Banker with the Premium Punch' and various other things. And you all know what I'm here for. I'm here to give you that Premium Punch. I'm here for the drawing of the first ticket for the first prize in the first scheme of this nature ever to be put before the English public. With me on the platform was to have been Mr Alexander Loap, your Member of Parliament. I understand he has been delayed – an important committee at the House of Commons, I believe ... But he will be along, he assured me, in plenty of time for the draw. Also I had hoped to be supported by another gentleman – indeed I had intended he should have taken the chair – for without him, I can freely tell you, this scheme would never have begun to carry any sort of shape at all. I refer, friends, to Mr Charles Butterthwaite, like myself not a native of London, but ...

[BUTTERTHWAITE *crawls forward out from under the table. He is wearing a mayoral gown of scarlet and a gold chain and clutching a half-empty whisky bottle and a black cocked hat. Although he is very drunk the clarity of his speech is unimpaired.*]

BUTTERTHWAITE: ... But the erstwhile Napoleon of the north. Cheery Charlie Butterthwaite. Councillor you've begun without me. Why? [*He addresses the audience.*] Hello one and all. Here I am, then, in the flesh, large as life, me lads and lasses. Your old Uncle Charlie. Hark to your Uncle Charlie and get pudding to all your dinners. I'm sorry, I seem to have got a bit too much pudding to mine already. Alfred, your fault, you should never have sent me ...

KRANK: Ladies and Gentlemen ...

BUTTERTHWAITE: Well then, let's get this meeting moving. Just at present it's like one of them snooty fancy parties where the time stays seven-o'clock – cocktails-and-bits-of-biscuits till half past eleven at night, and nobody so much as splashes their boots. Councillor, the folk want livening, we all want livening, this is an occasion . . .

KRANK: Ladies and Gentlemen . . .

BUTTERTHWAITE [scornfully]: Nay, that's not how to do it. You're giving them nowt but dishwater, when they're bawling for mulligatawny. 'Ladies and Gentlemen.' Look at me. Here's the very gown that I was Mayor of our town up north in; nine times I was voted for Mayor, three times three is nine, and when I retired they give me a testimonial like, this gown, aye this gown and this chain, real gold, you know, none of your brass for tarnishing . . . and the old cocked hat as well. Here's how it should go on, fore and aft, aye like this eh, I look a proper Charlie, don't I? But put it on like this . . . [He alters it to a sideways position.] Then what do you get? Napoleon Bonaparte, that's what you get . . . [He suddenly becomes very melancholy.] Napoleon Bonaparte, erstwhile, erstwhile. . . .

Three times three
Did my conquests run
Against the moon, against the sun,
Three times three, Humber shall drain,
Ere Charlie Butterthwaite rise again.
Talk to 'em, Alfred. Have a go. Tell 'em the tale.
[He subsides forlornly.]

KRANK [very willingly]: Ladies and Gentlemen: after so exuberant an introduction, my few words, my very few words, are bound to appear a little lacking in excitement. Like Councillor Caligula I am not by birth English. Poland is my country: since 1939 I have the misfortune to be a political exile. But in so far as the place of my exile has been your wonderful, your beautiful city, London, by so much, so far, I cannot call it truly a misfortune. It is to me a great honour . . .

BUTTERTHWAITE [*with his hand on his bosom, moodily*]: Austria, Prussia, and Russia.

KRANK: ... a great honour ...

BUTTERTHWAITE: Austria, Prussia, and Russia. I conquered the first two, lads and lassies, no doubt about that. But Russia, ah Russia, there was a miscalculation.

KRANK: It is to me a great honour, a great delight, to be able to play this very humble role ...

BUTTERTHWAITE [*rudely*]: O shut your cake-hole, Alfred. This meeting wants livening up. Let's hear from the true Working People, let's see if they can't make a bit more noise. [*He addresses the audience, dividing them into groups.*] Now then, all you lot to the left of my hand, you're Austria. You lot to the right, you're Prussia. And you lot up top, are you listening? You're Russia. Now what I want you to do is to tell me who you are, and tell me all at once, when I give you the one-two-three. It's a grand way to get a gathering going this. They say old Wilf Pickles used it to warm up his legless pensioners before his broadcasts. All right now, on the one-two-three: Austria, Prussia, and Russia. Shout them names out, and shout 'em loud.

[*He picks up the cymbals and prepares to clash them.*]

One, two ...

KRANK [*violently checking him*]: No. Not now.

BUTTERTHWAITE [*recollecting himself and laying the cymbals on the table*]: Oh aye. Aye. We'll do without them. Now then ... one, two, three ... Eh, there could have been a lot more noise there. Again let's have it. One, two, three ... And again then. One, two, three ... Oh you disappoint me, you know, there's no two roads.

KRANK: Don't you think, Mr Butterthwaite, we should be getting on to the draw?

BUTTERTHWAITE: Eh lad, there's plenty of time.

KRANK [*fiercely*]: No, there is not.

[*The telephone rings. The policeman answers it.*]

BATHSHEBA [*aside to Butterthwaite*]: The counterfoil, Mr Butterthwaite, my counterfoil?

BUTTERTHWAITE: Eh, oh don't worry. [*He confidently puts his hand to his breast pocket. His expression changes and he begins a frantic search through all his pockets.*]

CALIGULA: Friends, I think it would be as well for me to explain the method of the draw. In this drum are all the counterfoils of all your certificates. [*He shows the drum full of tickets. The* POLICEMAN *has finished telephoning and whispers in Caligula's ear.*]

BATHSHEBA [*aside to Butterthwaite*]: Man, have you got it, have you got my ticket?

BUTTERTHWAITE: Eh, God, I don't know.

CALIGULA: Friends, I have just had good news. That telephone call was from our Member, Mr Loap. He regrets very much he has been delayed, but he is on his way here at this moment, and should be with us almost immediately. Of course, we will defer the draw until he comes.

KRANK: No.

CALIGULA [*surprised*]: Mr Cash?

KRANK [*wildly*]: I said, no . . . [*In his precipitancy he leans right across the table and with his elbow knocks the cymbals off the edge.*]

BATHSHEBA: Mind the cymbals . . .

[BATHSHEBA, KRANK, *and* BUTTERTHWAITE *all leap to catch the cymbals which fall one upon the other on to the floor with a considerable clanging. The drum of tickets is also overturned. All the lights go out.*]

BUTTERTHWAITE [*in the darkness*]: I tell you I've lost it, I've lost it I tell you . . .

CALIGULA: Keep your seats, friends, please keep your seats. It seems to be a power failure. The lights will very likely . . . [*The lights come on again.*] Ah.

[KRANK *and* BATHSHEBA *are discovered on their knees by the pile of tickets.* BUTTERTHWAITE *is sitting on the floor as though turned to stone.*]

BUTTERTHWAITE: Austria, Prussia, Russia.

CALIGULA: Oh dear, the tickets. Perhaps we had better . . .

The Waters of Babylon

POLICEMAN: Just one moment, if you please, sir. I think it would be better that nobody should handle the tickets at all, before the young lady takes her pick.

CALIGULA: But we must put them back into the drum.

POLICEMAN [*good-humouredly*]: I think it would perhaps look better, if you didn't, sir.

BUTTERTHWAITE: Waterloo.

POLICEMAN: Why don't we blindfold the young lady and let her have a stab at the heap on the floor?

CALIGULA: An excellent idea. It quite solves the difficulty. Thank you, Officer. Bathsheba. . . .

KRANK: Use my handkerchief, gracious lady. [*He ties it on for her. Aside to Butterthwaite.*] Did you give her the ticket? [*Aside to Bathsheba.*] Did he give you the ticket?

CALIGULA: Ready, Bathsheba? [*He leads her forward.*] Here is the pile. You just bend down and pick a ticket. Nobody can say they aren't shuffled now.

BATHSHEBA [*bends down resignedly and picks*]: I've got one. Here it is.

CALIGULA [*takes the ticket and unfolds it*]: Friends, I am about to read out the winning number of the first prize in our first pioneer premium draw. This ticket is number three hundred and . . .

TERESA [*shouting from offstage*]: Mine.

CALIGULA [*the rest of the number has been inaudible*]: And here is the lucky lady of tonight.

[*Enter* TERESA *from the wings.*] And her prize, my friends, for one five-shilling Savings Bank Certificate is four hundred and fifty pounds.

POLICEMAN [*with considerable diffidence*]: Excuse me a minute, sirs.

CALIGULA: Yes, Officer?

POLICEMAN: I didn't quite catch the number of the ticket, as read out – the lady was so quick.

CALIGULA [*slightly surprised*]: Number three hundred and seventy three was the number I read out.

POLICEMAN [*embarrassed*]: Oh, but that's my wife's ticket,

sir. Three-seven-three. There must be some mistake. Here look I've got the certificate. [*He produces it.*]

CALIGULA: It can't be a printer's error, surely. May we see your certificate, Madam?

TERESA [*realizing something has gone wrong*]: I think there is a mistake. It's number three-two-four. I must have misheard you. I'm sorry, I was so excited, you see. [*She hastens to leave the platform.*]

CALIGULA: Pardon me, Madam, but have we not met before? [*Enter* CASSIDY *from the cellar.*]

CASSIDY: Aha, well, so you've had the draw, have you ... and who's won the prize – Teresa, so it's you. I'd never have believed it. Has he given you the cheque yet? Give her the four-fifty, Mister Councillor, and sign it neat and good for her. Cassidy's her name. And *here's* the splendid fellow, Mr Alfred Cash himself, the moving spirit, milords, behind this fervour of financing. And I put it to you all, who is he? Mister Councillor, I put it to yourself, who is he? I was for telling you two days since, but there was reasons well known to you already. It's *Krank*.

BATHSHEBA: BUTTERTHWAITE:
No, no, no.   Waterloo, Waterloo, Waterloo.

TERESA [*furiously*]: Don't you be paying any attention to this drunken knacker. Sure he's me own brother, but for all the good of that I'd pour sewage on him in the street. Get inside with you, you dirty nasty fragment of a catechist's carnal meditation, you ...

CALIGULA [*knocking for silence*]: Wait a moment. Let us have quiet, please, quiet, please. [*To Krank.*] Sir, this man had called your name, Krank. I know of one Krank: a subtle and wicked enemy to the peace of life of many of my people. I also know that this man is both drunken and malicious, yet, as he lives in Krank's house, I cannot entirely ignore his accusation. What have you to answer, sir?

KRANK [*very winningly*]: It is true my name is Krank. And because I had heard of your hatred to this Krank, I told you it was Cash, so you should not hold against me the faults of my brother.

CALIGULA: Your brother.

KRANK: My brother Krank. Very disreputable. I know you will think there seems to be a lot of new brothers and sisters so suddenly appearing, but . . .

CALIGULA [*sombrely*]: I do think it, yes. And I do not believe you. Although I am a politician, I will admit I am not a very quick thinker. But my mind is slowly moving to another, and I fear catastrophic, conclusion. This Savings Bank, this Lottery . . .

KRANK [*savagely*]: This Lottery has been won by Mrs Robinson, the Constable's wife. I can assure everyone there is no trickery about *that*.

CASSIDY: What, my four-fifty pounds, you've let it be stolen by a bloody peeler? What the hell have you all been playing at, up here?

POLICEMAN: That's a very good question. Now I'd like to know a thing or two about . . .

KRANK [*decisively*]: O.K. O.K. Gentlemen, Ladies. I am Krank. Yes, I have no brother. I run a disorderly house and I exploit my under-privileged fellow men. Mr Caligula, you do right to be horrified. *But*, Mr Caligula, your horror would do you the more credit if it was not that you yourself have been, in more than a manner of speaking, a satisfied patron of my premises. Bathsheba, is it or is it not the fact that Councillor Caligula spent a night with you in my house, in bed?

BATHSHEBA: Oh, you shouldn't have said that. That's a bad cruel thing of you to say.

KRANK: Is it or is it not the fact?

CALIGULA: Yes sir, it is the fact. Let me make this clear to you, Mr Krank, to all the people in this hall. I'm not a preacher, I'm only a councillor, I have a body and a heart of love and they will drive, and I'm a warm man then, I'm a man of rash peril, like a pounding motor-bus in your thick streets of London, or a strong heavy bowl among the ninepins. And who's to tell the ride of love where it is to blame? Here's me, here's my woman, we make children together. What else on this world are we for? But to squat down in your black hell, your basement kitchen, counting and counting of moneys . . . You've cheated last night from the guests within your doors, where that is to blame anyone can tell. And I'm anyone. For the matter of the Savings Bank . . .

[*Enter from the wings* LOAP *and* BARBARA.]

LOAP: Constable, will you please see that nobody leaves the hall.

POLICEMAN: Why, Mr Loap, sir . . .

LOAP: Let nobody leave the hall, Constable.

POLICEMAN: Well, yes, sir – there's some funny things going on around here.

LOAP: I can well believe it. Pray be seated, my dear Miss Baulkfast. Councillor Caligula, Ladies, and Gentlemen, Electors of this Constituency, Fellow Citizens, as you know, my chief concern as your duly elected representative in Parliament has been my indefatigable support to a declared policy of renewed intercourse with the Mighty Soviet Union – to be achieved by the momentous means of meeting at the Summit. It is therefore with the gravest concern that I have discovered neither more nor less than a plot to murder the celebrated Leaders of the Mighty Soviet Union, during their forthcoming visit – yes, murder them, Fellow Citizens. In London. With a bomb.

CASSIDY: With a bomb.

LOAP: With a bomb. Miss Baulkfast, my dear, you told me that you had information incriminating at least two persons.

BARBARA: Yes.

LOAP: Do you see either of them here?

BARBARA: One of them.

LOAP: Who?

BARBARA [*harshly pointing to Krank*]: That man. He is Sigismanfred Krankiewicz. He is in league with another man, whose name I do not know. Under pretence of having

93

a Central Heating system installed, he is fabricating the bomb in his own house.

BUTTERTHWAITE: St Helena.

KRANK [*quietly*]: Gracious lady. You have what kind of proof for all this?

LOAP: Well, Officer, you heard the lady; arrest him.

POLICEMAN: He has a point, you know, sir, proof. I'm afraid till things are sorted out a bit more, I can't very well . . .

LOAP: His house is being raided, at this very moment, Officer. I can assure you that in less than five minutes you will receive orders to carry out the arrest.

POLICEMAN: I don't know, sir, it's a question of exceeding my duty . . .

[*The telephone rings.*]

LOAP: You'd better answer that, Officer. I think it will be for you.

[*The* POLICEMAN *answers the telephone.* LOAP *again addresses the audience.*]

Fellow Citizens, this man, he has tried to destroy our chances of peace in the world. At his house is a bomb. The police will by now have found it.

HENRY GINGER [*appearing at the back of the stage*]: Oh no they won't.

LOAP: I beg your pardon?

HENRY GINGER: They'll find no bomb. Me, Henry Ginger, I've just been to that house. There's no bomb there no more. Somebody's whipped it away.

KRANK [*bewildered, but thinking fast*]: Whipped it away? But how to whip away what was never there?

HENRY GINGER [*bitterly*]: It was there once, all right, all right. You've had a bomb there, all right. Concealing of Evidence, that's what you've been doing.

KRANK [*sincerely*]: I'm certain I have not.

CASSIDY: And I'm certain too. Oh, he's a truthful boy is Krank. Now what would he or any other Christian at all be wanting with a bomb? Up the I.R.A.: ha, ha . . .

POLICEMAN [*his telephone conversation finished*]: Seems like you're right, for once, Henry Ginger, old man. [*To Loap*] That was the Superintendent, sir. He says there is nothing in the nature of bombs to be found anywhere on the premises in question. Now, Henry, I'd like to know what you think you're doing here.

HENRY GINGER: I've come to watch our Mr Krankiewicz. I'm watching him.

> Though the fool policeman sleeps,
> Henry Ginger wakes and creeps.

[PAUL *bursts in at the back of the stage with his gun out.*]

PAUL [*distracted*]: But not for too long, no, Henry Ginger, you, you, you, you, you, you . . . what have you done with my bomb?

HENRY GINGER [*terrified*]: Nothing with your bomb. What are you talking about? Officer, he's a Fascist, he's mad. He's a mad Fascist, Officer, he's going to shoot me, help.

PAUL: Yes, Henry Ginger, I'm going to shoot you . . .

[HENRY GINGER *dodges in panic behind Krank.* PAUL *shoots and hits Krank.*]

PAUL: Oh no, but not you, not *you*, Sigismanfred – you are my friend – I did not mean . . .

HENRY GINGER: He's dangerous, he's Anti-British . . . you ought to have run him in long before this, you know. [*Exit into the wings.*]

POLICEMAN [*approaching Paul dubiously*]: I am arresting you on the charge of Attempted Murder, in possession of fire-arms; it is my duty to caution you . . .

PAUL: And *I* caution you, do not come any nearer. There are yet bullets, five of them in this gun. Sigismanfred, I have killed you, I have killed you.

KRANK: What did I say, that you are a lunatic, Paul: this quicksilver I told you, too difficult for you to catch. I'm not going to die, I don't think. Go on: quicksilver: run.

PAUL [*helplessly*]: I thought to have helped, for the people of Poland, for freedom from violence, I had thought. . . . For what value to kill Henry Ginger, even; a little poisonous screech-owl, is all . . . Nobody follow me. I swear I will

shoot. Good-bye, Sigismanfred. I did not mean to do it.
[*Exit* PAUL *into the wings.*]

POLICEMAN: Here, you come back here ... Stop him, stop
him ... [*Exit* POLICEMAN *after Paul. Shouts and police
whistles die away offstage.*]

KRANK:

I said I was not going to die;

Truth? I am afraid, I think it was a lie.

So, only a few minutes to live,

I must see can I not give

Some clearer conclusion to this play

To order your lives the neatest way,

For when after the voters have gone home.

Mr Loap and lady, there is no bomb.

Let the Bolshevik tyrants arrive:

Conviviality shall thrive

And the ceaseless peace no doubt ensue.

Councillor, that quick girl with you tried with me to cheat
   you, true.

Forgive her. She had a clever master:

But I'm almost sure you now can trust her.

The bomb, Cassidy, I think you stole it.

I hope your brave boys can control it,

For is it not the nature of such ammunition

To perpetuate partition?

Of your sister imagine no more evil.

She is now reaching Ministerial level.

So use respect. Good-bye, Charlie.

A pity the cymbals have had to clang so early.

Your Hundred Days were short I fear.

Ladies, come here ...

Bathsheba, Teresa, Barbara – Miss Baulkfast:

I'm going to declare my identity at last.

Place and time, and purposes,

Are now to be chosen for me.

I cannot any longer do without knowing them ...

So many thousands of people

In a so large a cold field.
How did they get into it?
And what do they expect to find?
  [KRANK *dies*.]

BARBARA:

Deceit upon his tongue. Quicksilver in his mind.

TERESA:

No money in his pocket. Shouting in his house.

BATHSHEBA:

Songs in his throat, lightning and thunder in his bed.

BUTTERTHWAITE:

Notwithstanding, Krank is dead.
I'm going to sing you a song:
  [*He sings* (Air 'The Ash Grove').]

        We're all down in t'cellar-hoyle
        Wi't'muck-slaghts on t'windows.
        We've used all us coyle up
        And we've nowt left but cinders.
        When t'bum-bailey comes,
        He'll never find us
        'Cause we're all down in t'cellar-hoyle
        Wi't'muck-slaghts on t'windows.

Now let's divide up like and sing it as a round
Then after that all the fold can go home. . . .
  [*The song is sung as a four-part round as follows:*
    Part one: BUTTERTHWAITE
    Part two: CASSIDY and TERESA
    Part three: BATHSHEBA and CALIGULA
    Part four: BARBARA and LOAP.
  BUTTERTHWAITE *clashes the cymbals three times.*]

THE CURTAIN FALLS

D

Live Like Pigs

Seventeen Scenes

First presented by the English Stage Society at the Royal Court Theatre, London, on 30 September 1958, with the following cast:

An OFFICIAL of the Local Housing Department	Alfred Lynch
BIG RACHEL	Anna Manahan
ROSIE	Margaretta D'Arcy
SALLY, her daughter	Daphne Foreman
COL, Rachel's son	Alan Dobey
SAILOR SAWNEY	Wilfred Lawson
MRS JACKSON	Peggy Anne Clifford
DOREEN, her daughter	Jacqueline Hussey
MR JACKSON	Nigel Davenport
BLACKMOUTH	Robert Shaw
THE OLD CROAKER	Madge Brindley
DAFFODIL, her daughter	Frances Cuka
A DOCTOR	Anne Blake
A POLICE SERGEANT	Stratford Johns

Directed by GEORGE DEVINE and ANTHONY PAGE

Décor by ALAN TAGG
Ballads set and sung by A. L. LLOYD

TIME: The Present
SCENE: A post-war Council Estate in a north-country industrial town

Introductory Note

When I wrote this play I intended it to be not so much a social document as a study of differing ways of life brought sharply into conflict and both losing their own particular virtues under the stress of intolerance and misunderstanding. In other words, I was more concerned with the 'poetic' than the 'journalistic' structure of the play. The reception of the production at the Royal Court seemed to indicate that I had miscalculated. On the one hand, I was accused by the Left of attacking the Welfare State: on the other, the play was *hailed* as a defence of anarchy and amorality. So perhaps I had better declare myself. I approve outright neither of the Sawneys nor of the Jacksons. Both groups uphold standards of conduct that are incompatible, but which are both valid in their correct context.

The Sawneys are an anachronism. They are the direct descendants of the 'sturdy beggars' of the sixteenth century, and the apparent chaos of their lives becomes an ordered pattern when seen in terms of a wild empty countryside and a nomadic existence. Put out of their fields by enclosing landlords, they found such an existence possible for four hundred years. Today, quite simply, there are too many buildings in Britain, and there is just no room for nomads. The family in this play fails to understand this, and becomes educated in what is known as the 'hard way', but which might also be called the 'inefficient way'.

The Jacksons are an undistinguished but not contemptible family, whose comparative cosiness is not strong enough to withstand the violent irruption into their affairs that the Sawneys bring. Their natural instincts of decency and kindliness have never been subjected to a very severe test. When they are, they collapse. I do not regard them as being necessarily typical in this. They are the people I have chosen for the play, because they illustrate my theme in a fairly extreme form.

To any producer interested in presenting *Live Like Pigs* may I offer one or two suggestions?

(i) The play is in large part meant to be funny.

Introductory Note

(ii) The Old Croaker-Blackmouth-Daffodil group have much the same effect upon Sailor's household as the Sawneys in general do upon the Jacksons.

(iii) The singing of the ballads should be in some way integrated into the action or else cut out. At the Court they were unsuccessful because the singer was put on the stage between the scenes and quickly taken off again so that no one was really clear whether he was in the play or out of it.

The setting is the interior and exterior of a typical council house. I do not think it necessary to build a whole house on the stage. This was done at the Court, and had the effect of slowing down the action considerably. Distinction between upstairs and downstairs can be made quite easily by arranging the upstairs rooms behind or beside the downstairs ones with only a foot or so difference in level. I have written all the stage directions in terms of a real house; but these can be modified by a producer without strain. The exterior scenes do not really need a complete front wall to be provided for the house (or houses, for the door and one window of the Jackson building are required). The sort of council house I had in mind is the dull sort – not one of the agreeable designs given prizes by County Planning Committees.

The Housing Estate has only too obviously been laid out by an unimaginative Borough Surveyor. It is wearisome to look at and contains no real feeling of a living town. Col's criticism of it to Doreen in Scene Three is entirely justified.

The rooms in the house are as follows:

Downstairs: Living-room
             Hall, with staircase, front door, and door into kitchen
Upstairs: Large bedroom
             Small bedroom
             Landing, with door into bathroom.

The kitchen and bathroom are not seen on the stage.

The Characters

SAILOR: He is a strong broad-shouldered old tyrant of seventy. He walks with a limp. His white hair hangs to below his shoulders and he has a long drooping moustache. He is the most barbarous yet least savage of the group.

RACHEL: A tall handsome termagant aged about forty, and carrying it easily. She has very long hair worn loose and an alarming tigerish laugh. Arrogant and harsh-voiced.

ROSIE: In her early twenties, short and stocky, and apparently sullen. Obviously put in the shadow most of the time by Rachel. She has, however, a basic sense of satire and true depth of passion. She is also very weary.

COL: Is a loutish youth of eighteen or nineteen, with a rather more urbanized approach to life than the others: though he stops very far short of being a genuine Teddy-boy. His clothes do have certain hints in that direction, but no more. He is much given to uncouth noises to supplement his speech, and has swift and violent mannerisms.

SALLY: Is a wicked little ten-year-old girl with Woolworth spectacles, and a great capacity for loud excitement. She idolizes Col.

BLACKMOUTH: He is described as half-gipsy, and looks it. He is twenty-eight years old, lean, and sexy. He is both insolent and obsequious, and can put on a kind of false joviality that does not take many people in. (It does take Col in, for a while.) When crossed, he gives clear indications of underlying mental unbalance.

THE OLD CROAKER: Has a voice from which her name clearly derives. She is a batty old hag, alternately skittish and comatose. Her voluminous rags make her look like an outlandish bird. When scared, she can be very self-effacing. So can her daughter.

DAFFODIL: Aged about seventeen, she has an old, old face like that of a malicious fairy. Her sideways smile is caused by a white scar that runs up from chin to cheekbone. She has some of her mother's mannerisms, as well as a sly juvenile lechery which is all her own.

The Characters

MR JACKSON: Is a man of forty-five who is in process of being pro-
moted from the working-class proper into the lower-middle. There
is nothing much to be said against him. He knows he has a dull life
and feels very hurt that when he looks for a little mild excitement he
should receive so much more than he bargained for.

MRS JACKSON: Has grown older quicker than her husband and has
not had a figure for several years, but does not mind. She loves her
gossip, and in general much resembles her neighbours.

DOREEN: She is a shop-assistant, eighteen years old, very nice, simple,
pleasantly dressed. She is not particularly well versed in the contemporary 'Teenage Culture' of her friends, but likes to think she is.

THE OFFICIAL: A typical junior-grade Local Government employee,
middle-aged and well meaning. He wears an old Burberry which
looks as though he slept in it and a bowler hat on the back of his
head. His outer pockets are stuffed with documents and his inner
ones with pens and pencils.

THE DOCTOR: Is a lady doctor and not a very pleasant one. She is
impatient with the members of her panel and by no means inclined
to put herself out for their convenience. Her diagnoses are accurate.
She is fifty years old.

THE POLICE SERGEANT: He is motorized and therefore wears a
peaked cap and not a helmet. If his methods are irregular and his
manner overriding, this is principally when dealing with those he
despises. He is honest enough: and no more of a bully than he would
claim to be necessary to preserve the peace.

The Songs

The stanzas of song at the beginning of each (or nearly each) scene are
intended to be sung as an introductory statement either just before the
set is discovered or while the lights are coming up. This song needs no
instrumental accompaniment, and the same tune, basically, could be
used for each scene. It should be a typical melancholy street-ballad,
dragging and harsh, and sung with the peculiar monotony associated
with the old fashioned street-singers. The same singer need not sing
each stanza if it is considered that a better effect would be produced by
varying the voices.

The first stanza of all should cut very violently into the hushed
hum-and-shuffle that normally comes between the lowering of the
house-lights and the rise of the curtain.

The songs sung by the actors in the course of the play should be to
airs of the usual folk-song variety, and unaccompanied.

Scene One

SONG

O England was a free country
So free beyond a doubt
That if you had no food to eat
You were free to go without.

But if you want your freedom kept
You need to fight and strive
Or else they'll come and catch you, Jack,
And bind you up alive.

So rob their houses, tumble their girls,
Break their windows and all,
And scrawl your dirty words across
The whitewashed prison wall.

Interior. Evening.
The OFFICIAL *is discovered half-way up the stairs, discoursing on the house.* ROSIE *sits in the living-room with her baby in a shawl and* RACHEL *stands in the hall. Both women have brought in several untidy bundles.*

OFFICIAL: And up the stairs we're into the bedrooms. There's the two bedrooms, one big, one small; and there's your bathroom off the landing. You didn't have a bathroom down on the caravan site, did you? Mrs Sawney! I say Mrs Sawney; aren't you coming up to look at your bathroom? [*He comes back down into the hall.*] Oh come on, missus, I've not got all day. Blimey, you'd think I was showing you round a condemned cell or summat.

ROSIE: Did you say it was a bathroom?

OFFICIAL: God help us. Of course, love, I said it was a bath-room.

[SALLY *has entered through the open front door.*]

SALLY: Bathroom? Is there water? Is there taps of water, mister?

RACHEL [*slapping her*]: You shut your noise, Sally.

ROSIE [*angry*]: Don't you go knocking her, she's not yourn, she's not yourn to go knocking her like that.

[SALLY *howls.*]

ROSIE: Shut your noise when you're told.

[ROSIE *slaps her.* SALLY *shuts up and then begins stealthily climbing the stairs.*]

OFFICIAL: Now look here, missus, do you want to see up-stairs or don't you?

RACHEL: Why? We've no choice, have we? You've put us to live here. Why can't we take our own bloody time looking at the place? So what if we *don't* like it? We've got no bloody choice.

OFFICIAL [*exasperated*]: Eh God, I'm a reasonable man ...

[*The baby cries and* ROSIE *rocks it and croons.*]

OFFICIAL: But where did you get all this fat nonsense from, hey? 'No choice', 'put you to live here' – *who* put you to live here?

RACHEL: You put us. Coppers put us – all the lot of narks.

OFFICIAL: Now wait, wait. I'm not the police, I mean look at me, Mrs Sawney, did you ever see a policeman my shape of figure? All that's happened is: Your old place down by the caravans has had to be condemned, well I mean: rightly – I mean a broken tramcar with no wheels no windows, I wouldn't put pigs – all the rain coming in on you and all, why ...

RACHEL: Our place, mister.

OFFICIAL: But *this* is your place. *This is* your place. You've to pay rent, of course, it's not much, though. You'll easy afford it; if not, you can go on the Assistance, you see ... Why it's a *good* house. It's only five years old at most: I mean look at it . . .

[*There is the sound of running water from the bathroom into which* SALLY *has slipped. The* OFFICIAL *turns angrily and hurries up the stairs.*]

OFFICIAL: What's that? Sounds like running water. . . . Where's that kid gone – God help us, in the bathroom. Hey lovey, hey, little girly, hey hey, what do you think you're playing at with them taps, water all over the bloody floor.

[*He goes into the bathroom and* SALLY *comes running out, down the stairs, and off through the front door. The* OFFICIAL *turns the taps off and comes slowly down himself.*]

OFFICIAL: I don't know. I don't know. A lovely house, I'd call it. I've not got a house like this, you know. *I* have to live in furnished lodgings, and like it.

[*There is a pause.*]

RACHEL: It's time Col was here with Sailor and the barrow. Why don't he come?

ROSIE [*nervously to Official*]: Can we: can we – is that . . . ?

OFFICIAL: What is it, missus?

ROSIE: Upstairs, you chased the kid off, she was only running water. Who's to tell us when we *can* run water?

OFFICIAL: What are you talking about? Nobody's to tell you. It's your bathroom. You can use it when you like.

ROSIE: Then what for do you chase the kid off? She was only running water.

OFFICIAL: She'd left the plug in the basin, it was all over the floor.

ROSIE: She's not your kid to chase. She was just having her play, that's all.

RACHEL: They ought to be here with the barrow. Wait all the bloody evening.

OFFICIAL [*embarrassed*]: Well, I'll have to be off to the Town Hall. I've given you the keys, I've done my job, and precious thanks I've got for it. [*He moves to the door.*] Just a while, and you'll get settled all right, Mrs Sawney. You know, you'll like living here. Honest, you will.

[SALLY *runs in again.*]

SALLY [*very excited*]: He's coming, he's coming, Col's coming, Col's coming, Col, Col, Col's coming.

[*She dances up and down.* SAILOR *and* COL *come in through the front door pushing a home-made barrow consisting of a packing case mounted on pram wheels. It is loaded with a great pile of household junk, topped by a chamber pot and an old-fashioned horn gramophone. They also both carry bundles. We hear their voices before they appear, grumbling angrily.*]

SAILOR: Two men to pull the barrow, one man pulls the barrow, one man walks beside it, that's *his* way.

COL: Ah, hold your old gob, will you, I'm leading as much of the weight as you –

SAILOR: One man to pull it, one man to walk beside – it's the strong lad, he walks beside; the old man, he has to pull; that's *his* way. [*He sees the Official.*] Who's this?

COL [*to the women*]: All the road up from the back bottom of the hill, he's carrying-on. Why don't I smash his face for him? [*He sees the Official.*] Who's this?

OFFICIAL: Mr Sawney? I'm from the Corporation, I've just been opening the house up for your good ladies and like showing them around. I think everything's in right order for you – if there's anything you want to know about –

SAWNEY: Want to know, is it? Do *you* know where we've been living, mister, until today, d'ye know *that*?

OFFICIAL: Yes, I know. Down the far side of the railway yard, on what they call the caravan site. No drains, no fresh water, no nothing.

SAILOR [*satirically*]: Ye wouldn't keep pigs in it, hey?

RACHEL: That's what he said to *us*.

SAILOR: Oh hoho, he's the grand man to talk. And look at the grand palace he gives us. [*He goes up the stairs.*] Look at it. Lovely. Lovely ... Mister!

OFFICIAL: Er, yes?

SAILOR [*calling sharply from the big bedroom*]: Whose is this house?

OFFICIAL: Well, er –

SAILOR: Whose is it?

OFFICIAL: Well, you might say it's yours, now, Mr Sawney.

RACHEL: That's what he said to *us*.

SAILOR: Then that being so, Mister, then that being so – I'll give ye one half minute to get off of this ground.

COL [*violently*]: Go on, you heard him, go on. Jump your bloody feet to t'other side o' that door.

OFFICIAL: Now just a moment, you can't do this sort of thing here –

COL: Are you going?

OFFICIAL: This is very silly of you, you know, this is very silly indeed . . .

[*He hurries out of the house as* COL *advances threateningly.*]

RACHEL [*shouting after him*]: Calling us pigs, would you! How'd you like a real screaming sow to raven your paunch for you, hey?

COL: I'll show him pigs.

SAILOR: Has he gone?

COL: Aye, he's gone. Ought to have put the boot through him. I'll show him pigs.

SAILOR: Bring the dunnage into the house, Col. Here we are and here we've got to live. But we're keeping *them* out from us, every bloody one of them. [*He stands astride and terrible.*] They call me Sailor Sawney and no man slaps his natter at *me*. Rachel, Rosie, help Col carry the dunnage.

[COL *and the women bring in more possessions from outside, including a very battered pram into which* ROSIE *puts her baby and leaves it in the living-room.*]

SALLY: Col told him, Col told him right proper. You told him proper, didn't you, Col?

COL: Get out the road, Kid. Run away to Sailor.

[SALLY *creeps timidly upstairs and peeps at Sailor in the bedroom.*]

SAILOR: Come away in, Sally, come away in, to Sailor.

SALLY: It's water in there. Taps of water. He chased me cos I run it. He did.

Live Like Pigs

SAILOR: Never you mind for him, little daisy, little sparrow.
　　You run it when you're minded. Our house, our taps of water.
　　[*He sings:*]

> Oh when I was a strong young man
> I wandered on the sea
> And many were the ladies
> That called unto me:
> With golden hair and scaly tails
> And eyes of bright green
> So many were the mermaid girls
> That swam all in the stream.

Scene Two

SONG

> To every woman is a man
> Or two or three or four:
> And she has not got a man
> Must fight a terrible war.
>
> Like mermaids in the ocean wild
> With babes upon their breast
> Will cross the bow of a roaring ship
> And sink it both keel and mast.

Exterior. Morning.

ROSIE *is sitting on the doorstep rocking the baby in the pram by pushing it backward and forward with one hand while she sorts a basket of clothes-pegs with the other.* RACHEL *comes out to the doorway, with a cigarette in her mouth.*

RACHEL: Where's Col gone?

ROSIE: He's gone out.

RACHEL: I know. I said where?

ROSIE: He went down the town. He says 'if my mam asks where I've gone, I've gone for a job' he says.

RACHEL: What like of a job?

ROSIE: He says, 'there's new building work along beyond of Woolworths –'

RACHEL: Aye I've seen it – they say offices for the Corporation. Are they taking men, are they?

ROSIE: Col says any labourers you want to ask. It's four bob an hour.

RACHEL: He didn't tell me he wor going.

ROSIE: He said for me to tell you, if you wanted to know.

RACHEL: Who are you to tell me – he's *my* lad!

ROSIE: You warn't around, so he said it to me. He said four bob an hour.

RACHEL: Well it's time there's *someone* brought it in. We've got rent to pay for this bloody dump. It's time Sailor went for some work. That bad leg of his been better six month, seven. He could work.

ROSIE: Well, you tell him then.

RACHEL: You tell him, he's your dad.

ROSIE [*stung*]: He'll work when he's ready. There's no one can touch that old Sailor once he's got his strength in. My mam, when she wor living, he'd be out on a job, wind a crane, dig drains, heaving barrels, what you like, all day he'd be at it; then into the boozer till closing – likely fight a pair o' men into canal dock, knock a copper over after – then home like a traction engine and revel her three times down to Rio without he'd even take off his boots. That's what my mam said.

RACHEL: Ach, your bloody mam.

ROSIE: And before that, when he wor a right sailor. He comes home from his voyage one time, and he says to her, 'Every water's got its wavetops, every house got its roof, but there's only one sailor's got *you*,' he says, 'and there's only one bloody sailor keeps you.' That was his last voyage of all, that. He come into Hull from Archangel on the ice and he lived with my mam till she died. What do *you* know about him?

RACHEL: I know he's been young and now that he's old. But I'm not old and I'm still with him. So that tells you. That bloody tells you. Telling me, you dirty bitch. What about the feller give you these two kids of yourn – call *him* a wavetop on the burning water, hey? You living with *their* daddy till you die? Burning likely you're living with him, hey?

[ROSIE *takes no notice and plays with the baby.*]

I said: Burning likely you're living with him. I said: Where he is, you'd *love* to roll and slumber. I said: Where he is, *you'd* carry your belly to the cookhouse door, wouldn't you, where *he* is, hey? Why don't you follow him –

[*While she carries on,* MRS JACKSON *comes out of her house and begins to sweep the steps. This is only an excuse for her to be out, however.*]

– You don't *know* where he is, you never *did* know. In one night, he serves you pretty Sally; in another night, serves you the other here. Off with the sunshine and where does he go? Or was it the rain?

ROSIE [*sullen*]: Rainy days. All you know of rainy days is stand under the arches at closing-time, isn't it? – 'Come in out of the wet, dearie, nice bit o' fun wi' Rachel, only ten bob, dearie, call it sheltering while the rain comes down and never tell a word to the Missus.'

RACHEL: And what about it so?

ROSIE: I've nothing about it. 'Cept there's some as offers for *five* bob. Young redheads and all.

[RACHEL *laughs with a bitter hiss and turns angrily away.* MRS JACKSON *comes across to them.*]

MRS JACKSON [*very friendly*]: Excuse me: it's Mrs Sawney, isn't it? The rent collector give me your name, he said you were coming to live here, so I thought, well, I'd just pop round the door and have a word – like, it's your first day here, and why not be neighbourly, I thought, and give 'em a call? Eh, isn't it a lovely day?

RACHEL: Who are you?

MRS JACKSON: I live next door, you see, so I thought why not be neighbourly; like, it's such a lovely day. Jackson's the name. My husband, my husband he works for Co-op you know; like he's their agent, drives around the villages all day in his van to the local branches; just in the grocery he used to be, but he got made Agent last year. By, he wor pleased, I can tell you. He's got his van, you see: he's like his own master now.... What do you think to the Housing Scheme?

RACHEL [*dourly*]: Housing Scheme, is it?

MRS JACKSON: Well of course, I mean, we think it's lovely. We've been here nigh on two year. I'll tell you where we used to live – you know when you went past the Town Hall, down by the Catholic Church – all them little mucky streets – eh it wor terrible. But they moved us out, moved us all out and pulled the lot down. That's where they're building new Corporation Offices, you know, now. Isn't it lovely here, though? Wide streets, bits of garden, and all. Of course, it's a long way from the shops and there's only the one public. But my husband, he reckons that's a good thing. He says –

RACHEL: Oh go to hell, you and your fizzing husband.

MRS JACKSON [*stopped gasping in midstream*]: I beg your pardon! . . .

[SALLY *runs out of the Sawney House and stares at Mrs Jackson.*]

RACHEL: I says go to hell. You're not wanted here. Keep to your own garden, you like it so much.

SALLY: Mam, mam, she's as fat as a pig, ent she?

SAILOR [*from indoors*]: Rachel! Rachel!

RACHEL [*shouts back*]: Oh so you're out of your bed at last! What d'you want then?

SAILOR [*appearing at an upper window*]: Chase that bloody cow out o' here, and get me a sup o' tea. Well, move to it!

[*He shuts window.*]

RACHEL [*to Mrs Jackson*]: Go on, get out of it.

MRS JACKSON: Well! Well . . . Of all the –

[RACHEL *goes into the house.*]

ROSIE [*wearily*]: Why don't you folk leave us alone? We didn't come here cos we wanted; but now we *are* here you ought to leave us be. [*To the baby.*] It's time you had your dinner, Geordie. In we go, in we go, in we go to dinner.

[ROSIE *goes in too.*]

SALLY: Pig, pig, pig pig, fat fat pig.

MRS JACKSON: Why, you little – [*She offers a blow to*

Sally, but SAILOR *indoors shouts again:* 'Rachel!', *and* MRS JACKSON *nervously lets her arm drop.*] I'll tell my husband of this. I never heard the like.

[*She goes into her house.*]

Scene Three

SONG
Wages at four bob an hour
What labourer will decline?
Yet you can earn you much more than that –
And I don't mean overtime.

Exterior. Evening.
COL *enters, from work, with an army haversack across his shoulder. He approaches the Sawneys' door; but instead of going in, he stands outside and shouts.*

COL: Hoy oy, where are you! Who's at home tonight?

SALLY [*appearing at a window*]: Sailor and Big Rachel gone to the boozer.

COL: Gone to the boozer.

SALLY: Me mam's gone selling clothes-pegs. Then she's to the boozer too. Left me to watch our Geordie. He's asleep.

[*The baby howls indoors.*]

Oh he's woke up again. I give him a clothes-peg to suck but he don't keep quiet. He don't, Col, he don't. You going to the boozer, Col?

COL: Maybe later. I only got one and six. They didn't have no more nor that in their pockets this morning: so where'd they get it from, hey?

SALLY: Big Rachel found, like, a wallet. In the road she found it. Three quid in it, see. Me mam had a half-a-dollar too. That mister he dropped it in the bathroom yesterday when I wor running the taps. He dropped it, see. Then me mam made me give it to her. Then there's her clothes-pegs and all.

[COL *throws his haversack down and takes out a number of carpenter's tools.*]

What you got there, Col?

COL: Off of the building site, these. How much for 'em, Sally, eh? Two quid? Sell 'em to Charlie, up the Sheffield Road. He'd give me two quid; two quid ten maybe?

SALLY [*laughing*]: Ey, Charlie, Snotty Charlie!

COL [*joining in with her*]:

Filled his pockets with oats and barley
Some for cakes and some for loaves.

SALLY: And some for sticking up his long red nose!

[*They both laugh.* SALLY *climbs out of the window, carrying the gramophone and three records.*]

SALLY: Col! Col! will you play us gramophone?

COL [*ungraciously*]: Gramophone . . . On there, then. I can't abide inside, you'd be a tortoise or summat, you've to live in this dump. . . . There wor four records. I say you've only brought three.

SALLY: It broke.

COL: Oh it did, eh? It's about time somebody broke *you*, you little . . . Here's the music for Col, boy. Listen at this one:

[*He puts on a record: 'Cigareets and Whisky'. He and* SALLY *listen with great absorption, joining in the words of the song at intervals and beating time wildly.* DOREEN *enters from the street and goes up to her front door. She opens her bag for her latchkey and cannot find it. After a moment's indecisive fumbling she rings the bell. There is no answer.*]

DOREEN: Oh dear.

COL [*enthusiastically picking up the refrain as the record ends*]: 'Drive you insane!' 'Drive you insane!' There's the boy he wrote that, knew the truth.

DOREEN [*looking at him dubiously*]: I say –

COL [*glances at her, and then turns to the gramophone*]: We'll put it on again, kid. God, he's a good song, this: *he* knows a man's life, he knows it. 'Cigareets and whisky and wild wild women –'

DOREEN: Excuse me . . .

[COL *looks at her and says nothing.*]

Are you the new people that's come next door?

[COL *makes an uncouth noise which she takes for affirmative.*]

I've done ever such a soft thing, I went out to work this morning and left my key behind. Dad's not in while seven o'clock tonight, and it don't look like my mum's in, neither. So I shall have to wait in the garden.

COL [*rudely*]: Ah?

DOREEN: You're not very friendly, are you?

COL: Take it one gate, take it t'other. Here's your garden, here's ours. Can talk your head off.

DOREEN [*offended*]: Well I don't know, I *must* say – [*She turns away.*] I think I'd better go and wait round the back.

COL: Hey.

    [*She pauses.*]

Come here.

    [*She comes, carefully.*]

Here's a song for *you*. [*He puts on the record again, and lifts off the needle after a few lines.*] It's a true song, see. I can tell you.

    [*The baby howls.*]

SALLY: There's that Geordie again.

COL: Go in and stay in, kid. God's sake shut him up.

SALLY: Col, I want to hear records . . .

COL: Go on.

    [SALLY *goes.*]

'Drive you crazy, drive you insane' . . . it happens, you know. This kid's dad, he used to –

DOREEN: She's your little sister?

COL: Ach no, Rosie's kid, she is. It's like her dad, he goes right crazy some days. He gets out after six month, eighteen month, or whatever, and then, boy, it's the cigareets and these women, and (hoo hoo) the whisky. Then he comes for Rosie. 'Away out of it,' she says. 'For me, you're a dead damned man and that's all.' And she won't take him these days – not since wee Geordie, nowise. So he goes crazy like the song. Wild crazy. Then inside again. Six month, two year. It's a true song, that.

DOREEN [*disparagingly*]: It's an old song, isn't it? Must be all of nine or ten years old. Don't you have no up-to-date discs? It's awful corny, that song is.

COL: Corny? It's truth of life, *I'd* say. I tell you, experience. What it is, you see, them kids' dad, he's half of a Romany.

DOREEN: A Romany? You mean, you're gipsies?

COL: *We're* no gipsies. But *he's* half of a Romany, you see. What we say – it's: they stink like foxes, them Romanies ... What's your name?

DOREEN: Doreen. Doreen Jackson. What's yours?

COL: Col.

DOREEN: Col what?

COL: Just Col. They call us Sawney, cos of old Sailor, see. While Big Rachel's with Sailor, we're all of us, like, Sawneys. But that's not to last. You call me Col.

DOREEN: Oh.

[*There is an awkward pause.*]

COL: Hey, how do you live?

DOREEN: What?

COL: I say how do you live?

DOREEN: Well just like anybody else, I suppose.

COL: Here?

DOREEN: Why not here?

COL: We come here last evening, just.

DOREEN: Well?

COL: Look at it. You got a house you got a house. Then you got a bit of garden. Then there's a house and house. Then you got a bit of garden. A house a house a bit of garden. Then you got the concrete bloody road and two blue coppers thumping up and down it. I'll tell you, I'm going off me nut already ... You work all the day, don't you?

DOREEN: Yes.

COL: *Then* what d'you do?

DOREEN: Well we watch the telly sometimes. Or we go to the flicks. Or Sheila and me (Sheila's my friend at the shop, nylon counter, you see – I'm lingerie) we might go to the Pally Saturday nights. Do you like dancing?

COL: The way *we* dance – I've been at one of them Pallies one time – 'Away out with you!' he says: and we'd not been in

117

the place five jumps . . . Here's to dance, judy! Way *we* go dancing, hey? [*He puts on another record – an old-fashioned ragtime tune. He dances to the music in a very strange barbarous fashion, flinging out his legs and arms and whooping. The general effect is almost as though an unskilful person were trying to do a Highland reel to the wrong accompaniment. Suddenly glancing at* DOREEN *to see her reaction, he discovers that she is laughing. Immediately he knocks the gramophone needle off and recoils, stung.*] You think it's to laugh at, do you?

DOREEN: I'm sorry, I didn't mean to –

COL: All right! But there's more of us than me – *we* don't think it's to laugh at.

DOREEN [*upset*]: Oh look, I *didn't* mean, honestly –

MRS JACKSON [*from the street*]: Doreen!

DOREEN: Here comes my mum. Dad's with her, and all. She must have gone to meet him at the Co-op. I wonder –
  [MR *and* MRS JACKSON *enter.*]

MRS JACKSON: Doreen, come inside at once.

DOREEN: But mum . . .

MRS JACKSON: You heard what I said.

DOREEN: Oh, O.K., mum . . . [*she whispers to Col*] So long, See you again, soon, eh?
  [DOREEN *and her mother go indoors.* JACKSON *comes round to the Sawneys' door.* COL *bends over the gramophone, adjusting it; and ignores him.*]

JACKSON: Her-hum. My name's Jackson.

COL [*without looking up*]: Get out of it.

JACKSON [*embarrassed and pompous*]: I believe my wife was round here this morning. She was talking to the lady of the house.

COL [*startled*]: The what's that?

JACKSON: Mrs er Mrs Sawney, ent it? Is she in?
  [COL *shakes his head.*]
  Oh. Have you any idea what time –
  [COL *gets up with the gramophone and takes it into the house.*]

JACKSON [*in vain*]: I say have you any idea what time she *will* be in . . . .

[COL *shuts the door in his face.*]

JACKSON: Oh. Well *I* don't know.

[JACKSON *raises his hand to knock on the door; thinks better and turns away.* RACHEL *has entered from the street and is looking at him.*]

RACHEL: You ringing at that door?

JACKSON: I – I was thinking of it, aye . . .

RACHEL: He's not in.

JACKSON: Who's not?

RACHEL [*who is somewhat flushed with liquor, and speaks bitterly*]: Sailor the gaily Sailor. He's voyaging to Archangel on the wave-tops of *my* money, mister. And he turns me home from the boozer while he spends it. What sort of a man, what sort of a man.

JACKSON: Are you Mrs Sawney?

RACHEL: So?

JACKSON: My name's Jackson.

[RACHEL *laughs.*]

Now look here, Mrs Sawney.

RACHEL: Look here, Johnny Jackson mister. Hold out your hand.

[*He does so automatically.*]

Cross the tall tart's palm with silver and who'll tell you your fortune, will she? I'll tell you *yours* without. You wor sent to tell me your wife tells you we tell her the dirty road to go today.

JACKSON: Why as a matter of fact –

RACHEL [*she takes his hand and caresses it mockingly*]: Oh, you're a strong big man, you shouldn't worry what the ladies say, Johnny. You know what they did? They put us in this house the last day. And they're holding us in it and all. They've even put a bathroom for us, to be certain sure we're clean for their snow-white garden paths. I don't go for baths regular. It's not my common life. But I'll strip me down one day for this one, and you can be there to see me do it. Then you tell the copper and the Council that Big Rachel's had her bath, all like they like it. There's a pleasure for you, mister. I'll tell you the day ... So *let* him go to Archangel, I'll tilt his keel, his bloody keel, I will.

[*She sits down on her doorstep.* MRS JACKSON *opens her door a crack and calls softly to her husband.*]

MRS JACKSON: Ben? Ben? What did she say?

JACKSON [*going over to her, bewildered*]: Oh – she must be drunk. Couldn't get any sense out of her at all.

MRS JACKSON: Well, I call it a right disgrace. If it goes on I shall make a complaint. They've no right to send people like that to live here.

JACKSON [*dubiously*]: They may settle down. They're like gipsies or summat ...

MRS JACKSON [*significantly*]: Our Doreen, Ben ...

JACKSON: She'll be all right. I don't reckon –

MRS JACKSON: Well I do. Anything might happen. Come on in.

JACKSON: Aye aye, love.

MRS JACKSON: Kettle's boiling. [*She goes indoors.*]

JACKSON: Aye, aye, I won't be a minute, I'll just sort these milk bottles for you.

MRS JACKSON [*inside*]: What?

JACKSON [*making a clatter with the bottles on the step*]: Milk bottles, love. I'll not be a minute. [*He tiptoes over towards Rachel.*] I say, Missus ...

[RACHEL *turns and grins at him like Burt Lancaster.*]

JACKSON: It's just come to me. I've seen you afore.

RACHEL: Huh?

JACKSON: In the passage outside the Earl Fitzwilliam, selling matches and that ... More than matches, and all, aye ... [*He laughs nervously. Change the subject.*] Look, about my Missus, I dunno who started it this morning, but she *does* let things sometimes get a bit, like on top of her – if er well – I'm all for being neighbourly, you know – are you still around over at the Earl Fitz?

[*She shakes her head.*]

Aye, well, maybe, some other time, er, some other er – now and again, eh? er –

MRS JACKSON [*inside*]: Ben!

JACKSON: Be with you! 'Night, Missus – er, 'night . . .
  [*He laughs nervously. He goes into his house.* RACHEL *sits brooding in the doorway. The night darkens in.*]

Scene Four

SONG

Good rest and warm inside the house
For all who come along:
Here's a piece of meat, and there's drink, me boys,
And set you up with a song.

Interior. Night.

RACHEL *is lying on a pile of bedding in the big bedroom.* ROSIE *is in the living-room feeding the baby.* SALLY *is with her, eating out of a tin bowl.* COL *and* SAILOR, *fairly drunk, are on the stairs with bottles. Also on the stairs is the gramophone playing the third record – a military march by a brass band.*

SAILOR: They call me Sailor Sawney. They call me a killer. You know why they call me that?

COL: You tell me why they call you that.

SAILOR: They gave me that name. Times I sail the sea they gave it. So take you one look at 'em: forcsle, deck, or captain's bridge – 'Watch out for that boy, he's a killer.' That's the word they'd use. True?

COL: You say so.

SAILOR [*savagely*]: I say so. I say it: and it's true. [*He grabs* COL *by his neckcloth.*] Killed a Finn one day. Puts a witch on me, does he, a witch's curse. I knew him. Third mate, but a bloody Finn he was. *What* did I do to him!

COL [*breaking loose*]: Killed him. You killed him. O.K.

SAILOR: A witch's curse. In there – [*He points to the closed door of the big bedroom.*] In there. She'd turn your eyes to charcoal, that one – you look at her straight. *Rachel!*

COL [*laughing stupidly*]: Rachel . . .

SAILOR: Rachel. [*He batters at the door with his fists, and* COL *beats on the wall – both shout 'Rachel!'* RACHEL *gets up, listens to them a while, then suddenly opens the door.* SAILOR *staggers into the room, and kicks the door shut in* COL's *face.* COL *returns to his bottle.*]

SAILOR: Go on, go on then, witch me, you power of fury – you!

[*He goes at her passionately and they wrestle. They fall down together and they roll on the floor, biting one another and howling in their throats.*]

SALLY: Mam, mam, what's happening?

ROSIE: It's Sailor and it's Rachel, that's all it is, lovey.

SALLY [*gleefully*]: He'll break her heart, won't he, mam, Old Sailor will, eh? Break it, eh?

ROSIE: He'll have his try. He'll have it one time or the last.

[*The front door opens and* BLACKMOUTH *comes in cautiously. The gramophone has now ceased playing.*]

BLACKMOUTH [*to someone outside*]: Here's the place. Wait while I make sure. [*He comes into the hallway proper.*] Hey ey!

COL [*looking down the stair and recognizing him*]: Hey ey!

BLACKMOUTH [*enthusiastically*]: Col, me boy, me little Colly-O ...

[ROSIE *hears him and listens tensely.*]

COL: We've had a few jars tonight.

[RACHEL *forces* SAILOR *off her and he falls with a crash against the door.* BLACKMOUTH *looks questioningly at Col.*] Sailor and Big Rachel.

BLACKMOUTH: Rosie with you? Eh?

COL [*jerks thumb at living-room door*]: Rosie.

BLACKMOUTH: In there? Away hey, then, let's have a look at her. [*He flings open the door and stands gaily on the threshold of the room.*] Ah me bonny Rosie, here I stand in the door!

[SAILOR *comes out of the bedroom and stands at the top of the stairs.*]

ROSIE [*hostile*]: I'm giving these kids their suppers. We don't want you.

BLACKMOUTH [*very charming*]: You don't?

ROSIE [*trembling*]: No I bloody don't.

SALLY: Mam, is that my dad?

BLACKMOUTH [*taking some toffee out of his pocket*]: Aye Sally, it's your dad. Here, look, I've got a bit of spice for you. All the road from London it comes. D'ye want it, d'ye want it, all the road from London and here it is for Sally ... [*He dangles it in the air and she jumps after him trying to reach it.*]

SALLY: Give it, give it, give.

BLACKMOUTH: You've got to catch it first. Come on, kid; jump now jump; whoop where's it gone?

[SALLY *succeeds in seizing the toffee.*]

SALLY: Ah! I've beat you, I've got it. Eh I do like it when my dad comes.

ROSIE [*bitterly*]: Do you? Begod you're about the only one as does.

[SAILOR *comes down the stairs, followed by* RACHEL, *who goes across the hall to glance out of the little window beside the door.*]

SAILOR [*at the living-room door*]: Is he here? Is that dirty dog-fox Romany here, is that black-mouthed bastard –

BLACKMOUTH [*smiling*]: Aye I'm here. Good old Sailor, always the same. Come on, man, you've drank three jars already, Col's drank two of them, I've not been offered none yet. Let's be having some warm in us, hey?

SAILOR [*hard*]: What are you doing here, Blackmouth?

BLACKMOUTH: Wah wah wah, spit on the hearthstone, always the same. Friendly faces *I* get, don't I?

SAILOR: We thought you was still Inside.

BLACKMOUTH: Wah wah wah, what's Inside? Well I'm outside now, aren't I; and I've not eat for nigh half a week. Go on: she feeds my kids all right. Liverpool lobscouse she gives for *them*; but not for bloody Blackmouth. Oho. He's only their dad.

RACHEL: Why don't you give him eating? He comes in from the road. It's foul cold outside, he's not had nowt. Give him it. Go on, Col.

[COL *goes into the kitchen.*]

BLACKMOUTH [*jovially*]: Ah me old Rachel –

RACHEL [*hard*]: Who did you bring with you, Blackmouth?

BLACKMOUTH: Eh?

RACHEL: I says: bring with you. You left two outside in the dark. Who are they?

BLACKMOUTH [*embarrassed*]: Oh aye, them.

[COL *brings in a pan of stew, which* BLACKMOUTH *takes.*] Here's the stuff, Col, here's the eating for a man. Aha! [*He eats greedily.*]

SAILOR [*watching him closely*]: Who are they?

BLACKMOUTH [*with affected ease*]: Ah, you're a grand cook, Rosie. . . . Them two, you see: it's only the Old Croaker. I picked her up at Macclesfield. [*He eats with an eye on Rosie.*] There's Daffodil with her.

[ROSIE *knocks the pan out of his hand, and hits him on the side of the head.*]

BLACKMOUTH [*parrying the blow*]: Eyey, ey, Rosie, steady your heart now . . .

ROSIE [*white with anger*]: You bring that Daffodil here?

BLACKMOUTH [*reasonable and pleading*]: Well now, what else? Look: they wor after her in Macclesfield, see. So I meet up with them, chancy, on the road, the Old Croaker's half-daft: where are they going, what are they to do? See, Daffodil: like, poorly – I don't know what, she's *poorly*. And then there's some of them Scotchmen we met, you know, Jocky Faa with the one eye, his lot – through here Tuesday with their wagon, he says they've been giving to you Sawneys a right living house here, warm and roof and all. . . . You're not going to turn us out now. Why, Daffodil's gone all wrong. And with travelling nights and all. We come here on a lorry. Spewing sick every mile.

SAILOR [*still hard*]: Bring her in.

BLACKMOUTH [*relieved*]: Ah well, you've room enough – I knew it.

SAILOR: Blackmouth clever-mouth, aren't ye? Go on, bring her in.

BLACKMOUTH [*opens the front door and goes out calling them*]: Hey ey there, come on in!

COL [*with lecherous anticipation*]: It's that Daffodil, is it? I've heard a word or two of *her*, me boys. Heh heh heh.

SAILOR: She'll try no turnings here, and that's for certain. Oh, not in Sawney's place.

RACHEL: Let 'em all come. If they put us here off of the roads, why not us bring the rest from the roads: who're *wanting* to come?

[BLACKMOUTH *brings in the* OLD CROAKER *and* DAFFO-DIL, *all carrying bundles.* DAFFODIL *seems weak and sick.* RACHEL *greets them.*]

Here's the Old Croaker, she's daft and she's dizzy, but she can shovel in the scouse, me lovely, can't you?

ROSIE [*cold*]: You're Daffodil, they tell me. You're feeling poorly, they tell me.

DAFFODIL: Who are you?

ROSIE: Oh don't mind as to *my* name. I'm no one as counts. That's so, ent it, Blackmouth?

BLACKMOUTH [*vexed*]: Don't talk so soft. She's Rosie, Daffodil. You've heard of her.

DAFFODIL: Rosie. Oh aye, Rosie. [*She laughs venomously, and turns upon Blackmouth.*] You never tell me *she* wor going to be here!

BLACKMOUTH: Ah, now, now, Daffodilly –

DAFFODIL [*hysterical*]: You never tell me! You smarty bastard, aren't you. Look, I'm proper poorly. I'm all shaking like a west wind. Get me somewheres to lie down, Blackmouth, I'll pass out on you again.

[*She huddles down on the floor shuddering.* CROAKER *is eating the stew from the pan.*]

BLACKMOUTH: Let's get her to a bed, eh. Where can we kip her down?

RACHEL: Upstairs. There's a room over the front. Col's in it. He'll not mind that, I daresay.

[COL *laughs.*]

BLACKMOUTH [*in mock admiration*]: Upstairs begod. We've got an upstairs! Come on, Daffodil. Give us a drain for her, Col. You can sleep in the passage, boy. [*He seizes a bottle from Col, and gives it to Daffodil.*] Swallow this lot down, eh? [*He leads her upstairs and takes her into the small bedroom.*]

CROAKER [*sings*]:

> Tom Tom the piper's son
> Plays his pipe when he was young
> And all the tunes that he could play
> Was over the hills and far away.

Where's Blackmouth?

RACHEL: You eat your scouse and shut up.

CROAKER: That's my girl, that Daffodil. Eh she's a bold one. Do you know what she went and did? In Police Station. I saw it. She did. She said: '*I'll* wash your nasty floor for you,' she said, and she stood and – he he he, she did it –

SAILOR: She'll try no turnings here.

CROAKER: Right there on the floor in front of all them female coppers. He he he. Eh she's my girl, my lovely girl.

BLACKMOUTH [*tucking Daffodil up in the bedding on the floor*]: Here you are now, kip you down. You'll be a right dragon-fly by morning eh? Bright and lively.

DAFFODIL: You never tell me she wor –

BLACKMOUTH [*fervently*]: O begod, now Daffodilly. Rosie, Rosie – it's over two year since I wor in ten mile of Rosie – what you worry about *her*, God help us?

DAFFODIL: Now you listen to me, Blackmouth. I know your goings, I do. You can't nancy me, you know. You come here for that Rosie. If I warn't so bloody poorly I'd have known of it afore.

BLACKMOUTH: Well *I* didn't know of it, neither.

DAFFODIL: Don't you tell me! You only brought me with you because I hung on to you like a flaming padlock –

BLACKMOUTH: There's more to it than that.

DAFFODIL: Aye, there's more. We'd seen you: that's what's more. And how to keep us quiet except you bring us with you, eh? I know.

BLACKMOUTH [*sourly*]: If you think like that, I'm off downstairs. Let's have that bottle.

DAFFODIL: I need it. I'm shivering, I tell you.

BLACKMOUTH [*going to door*]: All right.

DAFFODIL [*earnestly*]: Look, Blackmouth. I'm over poorly to do owt about it now; but remember: padlocks bites tight. [BLACKMOUTH *snarls, leaves the room, and comes downstairs. At the living-room door he finds* RACHEL.]

BLACKMOUTH [*with a parody of courtesy*]: Upstairs and downstairs and under me lady's armpit. The Sawneys at home. 'May I make so free, ma'am, as to come for to go for to pass beside you into your commodious apartment? Thanking you in anticipation, ma'am' – [*He passes her and enters the room.*] Hi Rosie.

ROSIE: Ah no. You don't touch me.

BLACKMOUTH [*giving her up and turning to Sailor*]: She ought to have a doctor, you know.

SAILOR: What's wrong with her?

BLACKMOUTH [*shrugs*]: Fevered and that. Christ, I don't know …

SAILOR [*confronting him strongly*]: Laugh or not laugh over it, it's Sawney's place is this place. It's long time since you was with Sawneys, Blackmouth.

BLACKMOUTH [*airily*]: Ah well, I'm on my road, soon. I didn't *want* her with me, you see. Nor the Old Croaker neither, but –

CROAKER [*sings*]: All round his hat he wears the green willow.

CROAKER ⎫ [*singing together*]: He wears it for his true-love
SALLY ⎭ who is far far away.

BLACKMOUTH: But what to do about 'em, you tell me. Besides, you don't know *who* she goes talking to.

CROAKER: Meet all the old folks, tell 'em the old tale. Packet o' chips and a bottle o' stout and all o' that too – eeh, lovely days.

[*She starts to tear up a piece of cloth she has found on the floor.*]

RACHEL: Hey, you leave that alone.

CROAKER [*complacently*]: I tear it all up, don't I?

BLACKMOUTH: And then the other thing. They look for me on the roads. I'm always on the roads, eh? eh? They'd never look in a house, would they? [*He starts beating the walls and floor with his hand.*] Walls, you see? Roof, you see? Floor. Clench you close and safely.

RACHEL: Who *should* be looking for you? Anyplace?

BLACKMOUTH [*showing signs of unbalance*]: They had me Inside all of for two year, this go. But I showed 'em. I came out of it. God-quick: this go. Rah bah rah! [*He goes through the motion of kicking, stabbing, and punching low.*] There's one blue screw to bite no padlocks on to no poor boys no more. Look at his two eyes all smoking hot tar, they are, black full of the blood. Ss. Ss. Set to look at *me*, eh? I showed him where.

COL [*delighted*]: Oh, ho ho, you did him proper, didn't you, Blackmouth?

SAILOR [*dangerously*]: Are you calling yourself killer?

BLACKMOUTH: Eh?

SAILOR: *My* name, Blackmouth. And I ain't no reeking fox, ye know.

RACHEL: *Easy, Sailor.*

SAILOR [*brushing her off*]: Let alone, will ye! So ye're in my place, Blackmouth. Then watch it how ye go. And mind your work with Rosie, my Rosie. You mind.

[BLACKMOUTH *meets his challenging glare with another one, but thinks better of it, and slides aside from the defiance.*]

BLACKMOUTH: O.K. O.K.

RACHEL [*to Sailor*]: What if they come after him?

SAILOR: No one comes after no one into Sawney's place. No one. I'm the killer here and all the rest they clap their gobs afore I clap 'em for 'em. Rachel, ye bloody leprosy, come up to the bed.

[*He lurches upstairs to the big bedroom and* RACHEL *follows.*]

BLACKMOUTH: Rosie –

ROSIE: Get out of here. Me and the kids is going to sleep. And take her with you. [*She indicates the Old Croaker.*]

BLACKMOUTH [*calm but menacing*]: Aye aye, me old Rosie. Go on, Croaker, there's your place. [*He pushes her into the kitchen.*] Aye aye, me old Rosie. Come on, Col boy, what about a drain.

[*He and* COL *go and sit on the bottom of the stairs with a bottle.*]

CROAKER [*singing in the kitchen*]:

He wore it for his true-love for a year and a day
And when they come to hang him on the gallows
He cried 'Where is my true-love? Oh, so far so far away.'

Scene Five

SONG

They build a wall to keep you in,
It serves to keep them out.
So when they set their feet on the wall
Beware what you're about.

Exterior. Morning.

COL *is sitting on the Sawney steps.* BLACKMOUTH *leans out of the window beside him.* DOREEN *comes out of her front door on her way to work. Her mother appears in the doorway behind her.*

DOREEN: 'Bye, mum.

MRS JACKSON: Doreen, you've forgot your plastic overshoes.

DOREEN: I don't need them today, mum, it's not raining.

MRS JACKSON: It said on the forecast –

DOREEN: Oh the forecast –

MRS JACKSON: Well. If it's wet tonight you might be ten minutes waiting for a bus, catch your death of cold, you never think on what I try to tell you –

DOREEN: Eh mum, all right then – come on, I'm going to be late for the shop, Mr Holroyd's been on to me already twice last week – [*She snatches the overshoes and hurries away.* MRS JACKSON *shuts the door as* DOREEN *turns to call.*] Goody-bye-ee!

BLACKMOUTH [*rudely*]: Good-bye-ee!

COL [*shutting him up*]: Tst! Hey, kid . . .

DOREEN [*nervously*]: Look, I'm late –

COL [*coming down to her*]: Don't you take no note of him – he's a dirty jumper, all he is – eh, Blackmouth?

E

DOREEN: Mustn't let my mum see you talking to me, Col –
she's been on and on about it –

COL: Ah what the hell –

DOREEN: Please, Col, you mustn't –

COL: It's tonight, ent it, dancing, you said –

DOREEN: Well, but Col –

COL: At the Pally.

DOREEN: I don't know.

COL: I'll be there. You *said* you was going. You said with your
friend – Sheila, ent it, eh?

DOREEN: Col, I'm going to be late for the shop.

COL [*turning back towards the doorstep*]: Pally, right, I'll see you?

DOREEN: I don't know . . .

[*She hurries off down the road.*]

BLACKMOUTH [*appreciatively*]: Take that one up in a barn
loft, she'll learn ye some places for the straw to scratch you,
heh heh heh.

COL [*considering it*]: Why not, eh? What d'you reckon,
Blackmouth?

BLACKMOUTH [*sings*]:

> If you want to be a soldier
> You must learn to carry your gun,
> Learn to march and to encounter,
> And to turn you around and run.

But go for her, Col boy.

> The route is for the land of Flanders
> The route is out for Germany
> Tow-ri-ah the doodle addy
> Tow-ri-ah-di the doodle-ay.

She'll swerve you fair and nicey.

COL [*with admiration*]: *You* can tell 'em, can't you, Blackmouth? I dunno though. You ever been to these Pallies, like,
dancing?

BLACKMOUTH: Aye, sure.

COL: She's not like the sort I went with ever . . . Ah – I
dunno . . . It's time I was to work. What time is it?

BLACKMOUTH: I dunno.

COL: I can't get the time at all, living in this dump. All times of day looks the same round here. He says last week, 'If you're late again, you're off of this job.' He says, 'Ain't you got no clock to look at?' I says, 'Bloody no we aint.' He says, 'Don't you tell me.' I says – where's me snap tin?

[BLACKMOUTH *passes him out through the window a sandwich tin, which* COL *puts in his haversack, together with a bottle of cold tea.*]

BLACKMOUTH: And your cold tea, boy. A man's drink for the good work!

COL: O.K. O.K. See you, Blackmouth. Is that doctor still upstairs?

BLACKMOUTH: Aye.

COL: She takes her time, don't she? I thought you said your Daffodil wor getting better.

BLACKMOUTH [*shrugging*]: I dunno.

COL: O.K., O.K. See you.

[*He goes out down the road, leaving* BLACKMOUTH *at the window.*]

Scene Six

SONG

The Doctor's trade's a very good trade
To raise the dead to life:
But some of them no man should raise
For they died of a needful knife.

The Doctor's trade's a dangerous trade
For who can know for sure
If dust and bones that stand and walk
Will walk where they walked before?

Interior. Morning.
SAILOR *and* RACHEL *are sleeping in the big bedroom.*
BLACKMOUTH *is lounging moodily in the hall. In the small bedroom the* DOCTOR *is taking the pulse of* DAFFODIL (*who is in bed*

with a thermometer in her mouth). CROAKER *is squatting in a corner moaning and tearing up a sheet of newspaper. The* DOCTOR *takes and examines the thermometer.*

DOCTOR [*to Croaker*]: I asked you please to leave the room if you can't be quiet.

CROAKER: Quiet?

DOCTOR: If you can't be quiet.

CROAKER: That's my girl, you know. Her.

DOCTOR: So you told me.

CROAKER: You're the doctor, aren't you? Doctor.

DOCTOR: I'm the doctor.

CROAKER: Ee ee, a female doctor. Female coppers and female doctors. You don't know where you are these days. I think I'll go for a soldier meself – how about it? You give her physic.

DOCTOR [*writing a prescription*]: She can take two of these every four hours.

CROAKER: Physic.

DOCTOR: Two of these. They're tablets.

CROAKER: He give it in a bottle, afore, he did. He didn't give her none of them things.

DOCTOR: Who didn't?

CROAKER: Doctor didn't.

DOCTOR: What doctor?

[CROAKER *sucks her teeth and sways on her haunches.*]

DAFFODIL: Macclesfield it was.

DOCTOR: Well, I wouldn't know about that –

DAFFODIL: But it wor after that I got took, on the road, see; got took sick, doctor.

DOCTOR: There's nothing seriously wrong with you that a few days in bed won't cure.

CROAKER: Eh but she's proper poorly, doctor.

DOCTOR: A few days in bed.

CROAKER: Proper poorly. Spewing sick. You should have seen her.

DOCTOR [*to Daffodil*]: But you ought to be looked after. Are you married?

[CROAKER *cackles.*]

Well, who do you live with? Who else is in the house?

CROAKER [*in great delight*]: Blackmouth, she means. Married. Eee, Blackmouth.

DOCTOR: Please be quiet.

DAFFODIL [*urgently*]: Here, doctor, here ... The way they are in this house, they'd throw me on the street, give 'em a quarter chance of it. They would, you know. Aye. You tell 'em I'm proper poorly. Go on, you tell 'em. Tell 'em if they make me move I'll die.

DOCTOR: I shan't tell anybody anything of the sort. You've only had a mild chill. Stay in bed for a couple of days and then you can get up. Come and see me in my surgery on Monday if you're still not feeling right. [*She goes out on to the stair-head.* CROAKER *stands aside at the door for her. She speaks to Croaker.*] This house is appalling, you know, the condition of it: appalling. Look at the state of this room. Supposed to be a sickroom, filthy. [*She goes down the stairs and* BLACKMOUTH *accosts her obsequiously at the bottom.*]

BLACKMOUTH: She all right doctor?

DOCTOR: Who are you?

BLACKMOUTH [*evasive*]: Oh I'm just – She all right, doctor?

DOCTOR: She would be if she was properly fed. There's no reason why not, these days. Does she work?

BLACKMOUTH: Oh aye. Now and then.

DOCTOR: What at?

BLACKMOUTH [*greasily*]: Oh – not to give it a name, doctor. *You* know ...

> Up the lane behind the wall:
> Lying down or standing tall ...

Ah you know: we've got to live, doctor.

DOCTOR: Do *you* work?

BLACKMOUTH [*still evasive*]: Is it me? We all have our lives, like. Like: you're a doctor, make folk well. She'll soon get better. Won't she, doctor?

DOCTOR: I have no doubt.

SAILOR [*waking up*]: Who's that – there's someone in the house!

RACHEL [*waking too*]: Go to sleep, it's the doctor.

SAILOR: Doctor for that Daffodil.

RACHEL: That's right. It's time she was bloody better.

SAILOR: Time she was better and out. [*He shouts loudly.*] Make her better, doctor!

DOCTOR [*taking no notice*]: Filthy. I was appalled by the bathroom, appalled. This is quite a new house. You ought to know how to treat it properly.

[SALLY *comes out of the kitchen and looks at the doctor.* ROSIE *appears nervously in the kitchen door, carrying the baby.*]

SALLY: She the doctor, dad?

DOCTOR: Yes, I'm the doctor.

SALLY: Ee-ooh.

DOCTOR [*to Blackmouth*]: She's your child?

BLACKMOUTH: Aye. Oh aye.

DOCTOR: Is it her mother upstairs, then?

BLACKMOUTH: Oh no. No.

ROSIE: No, it's not. I'm her mother and so what's that to you?

DOCTOR [*looking closely at Sally*]: How long has she had these sores on her face?

[*They are silent.*]

Hasn't the school doctor seen them? ... You do see the school doctor, don't you, little girl? ... She does *go* to school? You do *go* to school?

[*They are still silent.*]

Why doesn't she *go* to school?

ROSIE: Why should she go to the school? They'd not learn her nowt there. They'd knock 'em about there. *I've* heard of it. Hurt her. Keep her book-reading at night when she ought to be having her play and her sleep. We'll not let them take my Sally for the school. Oh no, no, we don't.

DOCTOR [*giving her up*]: Well it's none of my business –

ROSIE: And that it's not.

DOCTOR: But you can be made, you know. Brought before the courts. I don't understand your attitude. Present day and age. House in this condition, child needs attention – what do you imagine the Health Service is for? Why don't you take her to the children's clinic? Here's the address: look. [*She gives Rosie a card.*]

ROSIE: Why should we?

DOCTOR: Oh good heavens. Well ... well ... if that's the way you want to – Good morning.

BLACKMOUTH [*politely*]: And to you, doctor.

[*The* DOCTOR *leaves, and shortly after we hear her car start up outside.* ROSIE *looks at the card irresolutely and then drops it to the floor.*]

SALLY: Mam, have I to go to the school?

ROSIE: No lovey, you've not.

SALLY [*frightened*]: I'm not going, I'm not going.

BLACKMOUTH [*indulgently*]: Hey hey Sally, *who's* off to send you to school? Anyone to send you to school, they've to sort wi *me* first: let 'em sort it with your dad, what about it?

ROSIE [*sardonic*]: Aye, what about it?

BLACKMOUTH: Away to the back room, Sally, I want to talk with your mam.

SALLY: I'm not going to the school.

BLACKMOUTH [*fiercely*]: Off away with you, kid. Go on! [SALLY *goes into the kitchen unwillingly.*]

BLACKMOUTH: She says Daffodil's getting better.

ROSIE: She does, eh?

BLACKMOUTH: Aye ... Ye see what it means, don't you? Old Sailor'll want to put us out. The killer, he. Ss...I dunno about Rachel.

ROSIE [*sardonic*]: Ach Rachel.

BLACKMOUTH: Well. She don't know her mind one day into the next, Rachel. She takes us in to spite her Sailor, that's all.

ROSIE: So.

BLACKMOUTH [*passionately*]: Look, what the bastard hell, Rosie – I don't want that pinchy tart of a Daffodil! Not any more begod, anyhow. I want you.

ROSIE [*bitterly satirical*]: Ohoho, you do? The third time he says it. First time's for Sally, next time's wee Geordie, so for your third time – O.K. Here on this hard house floor just like you cry for . . . And then what?

BLACKMOUTH [*rather puzzled*]: Well and then we –

ROSIE: Well and then we get up again; and you wipe yr dirty gob wi' the back of yr hand and you say: 'Aye aye me old Rosie, never tell 'em Blackmouth don't know how to love you.' And then there's two years, and then you come back; and begod here I am with another little Blackmouth set puking on me knees. And so we start again. And so we start again for number *four*!

BLACKMOUTH [*trembling and shaken*]: You didn't ought to talk to me like that. That's the road you send men off their nuts, I'll tell you. You remember the last time.

[*She turns away.*]

Look, now look; Rosie! We get out of here, now. You come with me. Afore there's Daffodil on her feet again we're out and travelling, and she nor nobody never knows where. Come on, come on, Rosie, *now*.

[SAILOR *comes out and stands on the stairs.*]

ROSIE [*doubtful despite herself*]: You don't mean it true . . .

BLACKMOUTH: I do so. I want you. I'm bloody starving for you.

ROSIE: You don't mean it. Besides, there's coppers chasing.

BLACKMOUTH [*violently*]: I don't care a donkey's hiccup for any o' that. Rosie, will you come?

SAILOR: Blackmouth!

BLACKMOUTH: Hallo?

SAILOR: I hear ye, ye letchy polecat. Now you hear *me*. You say you're wanted by the Polis: right. Now let there stand one more word atween you and my Rosie and you go bang away out o' this without her: and run your own chances with every flatfoot in the land!

BLACKMOUTH [*shaking even more*]: You didn't ought to talk to me like that, Sailor.

SAILOR: I talk how I want to who I want.

BLACKMOUTH [*in a vicious whisper*]: I'm not afraid of no blue coppers. You say Go – all right all right . . . [*He moves*

towards the front door.] Sawneys, eh? Good friends to all, eh?
I'll tell the boys along the road, I'll tell 'em. Ss ss. Good
friends, good friends. *I'll* tell the bloody boys –

[*He slips out, trembling and jerky.*]

RACHEL [*who has also come on to the stairhead*]: Off into the
sunshine; or is it raining today?

[SALLY *comes out of the kitchen.*]

SALLY: Where's my dad gone?

ROSIE: He's gone off, lovey.

SALLY: I want him back, mam.

ROSIE: Shut up, will ye. Sailor, maybe he comes back, you
know.

SAILOR: Ach, for that . . . He's only a dirty Romany, so.

ROSIE: He makes me scared.

[CROAKER *comes out of the small bedroom.*]

CROAKER: Ee ee? she wants her dinner.

RACHEL: What's that?

CROAKER: Her dinner. She wants it.

RACHEL: Dinner?

CROAKER: Dinner. My Daffodil, my girl. She does. Oo hoo
hoo hoo . . .

Scene Seven

SONG
Oh why do you laugh and why do you cry
And why do you walk alone?
I'm hunting down a tall woman
To make her all my own.

Interior. Afternoon.

DAFFODIL *is asleep in the small bedroom with* CROAKER
crouching beside her, eating a crust of bread. RACHEL *and* JACKSON
are discovered coming out of the kitchen towards the stairs. JACKSON
is nervous and trying to hide it by being boisterous. RACHEL *is quiet
and saturnine.*

JACKSON [*in the middle of a story*]: Well, of course, I could see he wor pulling his rank on me, and that, you know. Coming it proper strong he wor – bags of bull. I said, 'Sergeant Hipkinson,' I said. 'You may be carrying more of it up here [*He touches his upper sleeve*] but there's other places,' I said 'where us Privates carry '– No; no, that's not right, I said it sharper than that – By, I told him proper – I said, 'There's other private places,' I said, 'where some of us carry' – Nay that's not it neither. Eh, I've forgot what I *did* say, now; but By, it wor strong, any road. And you know what he did? – He said, 'Fetch me a bucket,' he said, 'I'm going to be sick!' He said, 'Fetch me a bucket.' In that French tart's room and all. She wor just sat there on the bed, you know, humped up like a hedgehog and looking at him. He said, 'Fetch me a bucket,' he said – Eh –

[*He laughs uproariously, holding on the stair-rail for support.* CROAKER *comes out of the bedroom.*]

CROAKER: Ssh-ssh-ssh, ssh-ssh! She's asleep!

[*She pops inside again.*]

JACKSON [*alarmed*]: Who's that?

RACHEL: That's the Old Croaker, that is.

JACKSON: You said there warn't anybody in.

RACHEL: No more there is, mister. Only her and her Daffodil.

JACKSON: Her what?

RACHEL: Christ, don't be feared, man. Who cares at all? One of 'em's daft and the other's asleep. Come on, come on, man.

[*She goes upstairs and he follows apprehensively. She leads him into the big bedroom and sprawls out on the bedding.*]

JACKSON: I hope nobody saw me at your kitchen door. If I'd known you wor going to bring me back to this house I'd not have come. I mean it's damn dangerous – of course my job on the van, she doesn't know where I've got to all day, and of course she's out this afternoon, but –

RACHEL: Let's have a fag.

JACKSON [*finding one for her*]: Here. [*She takes it and he lights it for her clumsily. She sticks it in the corner of her mouth and drags at it crudely. He watches her and his excitement begins to grow again.*] By, you're a right strider, I'll bet you are – I could tell it as soon as I saw you. Like this bint I knew in Naples – I wor in the old Headquarters Group in them days – ah we had some times there. She used to wear this red dress, you know, busting out at the corners of it like a pan of milk boiling over –

[CROAKER *suddenly cackles with laughter.*]

JACKSON: What's that!

RACHEL: That's the Old Croaker, that is.

JACKSON [*relieved*]: Oh aye, so it is ... Ah, the old H.Q. in Naples. We had a time there. By, you're a right strider, you are, lovely ripe and striding – By!

Scene Eight

Interior. Afternoon.

RACHEL, *half-dressed, sprawls on the bedding in the big bedroom. She is smoking the butt of a cigarette.* DAFFODIL *is asleep in the small bedroom.* CROAKER *is in the living room tearing up some paper.*

CROAKER [*sings – the tune is the same as the link songs between scenes*]:

> When I was a girl to dance and sing
> Little I thought upon
> How soon my youth be rooted out
> And my pleasuring all torn down.

[*There is the noise of a lavatory chain being ineffectually pulled once or twice.* JACKSON *comes out of the bathroom, buttoning his jacket.*]

JACKSON: Fair shocking disgusting.

[*He starts to go down the stairs.*]

RACHEL: Hey! Come here, mister.

[*He halts and goes in the bedroom reluctantly.*]

You just walk out on me like that? Why, Johnny Jackson, you've got a sauce, eh?

JACKSON [*sourly*]: How much do you want?

RACHEL: You tell me, you tell me, mister. Put a value on it. I'll wait.

JACKSON [*bitterly*]: Value. You're a beauty, aren't you? I didn't come up here, you know, to be – What the hell you think you are, anyroad? Bloody animal, I'd call it.

RACHEL: You don't find much o' my sort of loving up and down *this* town, likely?

JACKSON [*in outrage*]: No and it's a damn good thing we don't – what you want a lump of raw meat shoved in the bars of the cage to tear at, *you* want. By, I've never met the like. You bloody animal. What do you want to carry on like that for? We could have had us a right nice time this afternoon if you'd only – Well I didn't expect it like that, I can tell you.

[RACHEL *laughs nastily.*]

It's all right laughing. All right. But if I want a tart again – it's the last time I come to *this* house. I've had my lot of you, and that's for truth. I'd sooner spend my afternoons rolling in a muck tip! It'd smell a bit sweeter, anyroad. . . . Three quid. That do you? It'd better bloody do you.

RACHEL: You make it five, mister. And we'll not let on to your wife.

JACKSON: You'll not *what*?

[RACHEL *laughs.*]

[*Very angry.*] Oh none o' that, you know, none o' that. You'd better watch it. I'll have the police after you. There's more than the police I could have, and all. I could call this house a Public Nuisance, you know. I could tell the Sanitary Department a thing or two about this house. Aye and I could tell . . . I'll make it four pound ten and there you are. I want nowt more to do with you. I'm fair bloody disgusted. [*He thrusts the money at her and goes downstairs. She spits after him. He turns angrily back at her, but then thinks better and carries on down. As he reaches the bottom the* OLD CROAKER *appears at the living-room door. He turns on her with a snarl.*] And you. You mind to your own affairs. Keep yer old nose out, aye.

[*He goes out furiously through the kitchen.* DAFFODIL, *awake, sticks her head out of her room.*]

DAFFODIL: Is that Blackmouth downstairs?

RACHEL: No, it's not and bedamned.

DAFFODIL [*querulously*]: It's time he wor back. Why don't he come back? Eh I do feel bad. Why don't he come back, the dirty devil?

> [*She goes back to her bed.* CROAKER *tears up paper and hums her song.*]

Scene Nine

SONG

> Oh why does he laugh and why does he cry
> And why does he walk alone
> Along the roof and over the wall
> And underneath the moon?

Exterior. Evening.

MRS JACKSON *appears on her doorstep with a saucer of milk.*

MRS JACKSON [*calling*]: Choo-choo choo-choo choo, puss puss puss! Choo-choo-choo! Pussy! Pussy! Tea time!

> [CROAKER *comes out from the Sawneys' door and watches her.*]

CROAKER [*mimicking*]: Choo-choo choo-choo-choo, choo-choo choo-choo-choo. Come for his milk. He likes his sup of milk.

MRS JACKSON [*taking no notice of her*]: Choo-choo-choo, pussy-pussy, where are you! Where are you . . . ? [*She at length agrees to notice Croaker; and speaks to her coldly*]: You've not seen our little cat, I suppose.

CROAKER: Eh, nay, I don't know. He's a strong tom, I'll bet he is, eh; makes 'em spring and yo-ow-owl—

MRS JACKSON [*sharply*]: She's not a tom, she's a tabby. I said have you seen her?

CROAKER: Them tom-cats they know how to lead their jolly lives, they do. [*Beckoning mysteriously*] Here, come here. Ssh-ssh. Come here, lady. You don't take to our Rachel, do you? I know. She tells you the dirty road to go. But I tell her, and I tell her, and –

MRS JACKSON [*interrupts in vain*]: Look, I've not got all
  evening . . .

CROAKER: – do you know what they're at? Them Sawneys?
  They want to put, us, on, the road. Put-us-on-the-road!

MRS JACKSON: Yes, well, I dare say –

CROAKER [*detaining her*]: My pretty girl, proper poorly,
  grudged her the drops of water for her thirst, they took the
  very shoes off her feet. There's more nor that they've took,
  ooh – don't go, don't go yet, gentle lady, lovely lady – you
  see, Old Croaker knows where your tom-cat went up this
  afternoon!

MRS JACKSON [*startled*]: What! Where?

CROAKER: Ssh-ssh, they'll hear us . . .

MRS JACKSON: She's not a tom: she's a tabby. I knew it. That
  woman took her.

CROAKER: He was strong and squalling, but he ran away from
  her. Hoho yai! Down the stairs and out.

MRS JACKSON: Where is she now?

CROAKER: Nay nay nay, lady. How could Old Croaker tell
  you that?
    [*She sings:*]
      Come all you little black cats.
      He chases the dirty rat
      The rat is sharper than the cat
      And fetches the blood right out of his back . . .
  I'd sooner love a biting rat, I would, than any day with our
  Rachel; ee-ay-yai –
    [COL *enters from the street and goes towards the Sawney door.
    He has his haversack on his shoulder and is eating fish and chips
    out of the paper.*]

COL [*to Croaker*]: What you gabbing over the fence, you old
  haystack? How's our chirping Daffodil today?

CROAKER [*in a sort of trance*]: Eh? Who is it? Col?

COL: You know me as well as your own toe nails, you do.
  Where's Blackmouth?

MRS JACKSON [*to Croaker*]: I asked you where's my cat
  gone.

CROAKER [*hopelessly*]: Miaow, miaow? Croaker doesn't see no cats, no more tom-cats now . . .

MRS JACKSON: But you just said –

CROAKER: Oh no no, all tore to little bits and gone.

[MRS JACKSON *goes into her house in disgust.*]

She's proper poorly.

COL: What?

CROAKER: My girl is. Aye-yai.

COL: I says where's Blackmouth?

CROAKER [*shakes her head*]: Ooh, chips, eh?

COL [*crossly*]: Ach – where is he? I've a thing for him to see.

CROAKER [*chants*]: Old Sailor turns him out

turns him out

turns him out

Old Sailor turns him –

You haven't got a bit of fish, have you? Like, with the chips?

COL: Achtcha to that, you know: there's no man to turn *Blackmouth* out . . . Our Rosie, hey?

[CROAKER *laughs.*]

Ahahaha. Aye . . . Hoy there–[*He is looking down the street*]– Sally! Here –

[*He tosses the remnant of his fish and chips to Croaker, as* SALLY *comes running in from the street excitedly.*]

SALLY: Col! Col! I done it, Col. I done it like you told me, Col.

COL: You give them tools to Charlie?

SALLY: Snotty Charlie.

COL: You give 'em?

SALLY: He warn't going to let me have more nor a quid, Col; but I says to him, I says: 'Col says my dad Blackmouth's home and he did a Screw right dead and if you don't give me more nor two quid he'll do you too, good and proper,' I tell him. So he give me thirty bob for 'em. Here, see. [*She gives him the money.*]

COL [*vexed*]: T't' t't – not much, wor it? O.K. kid, you buy you some spice. O.K. [*He gives her a couple of coins back.*]

SALLY [*in delight*]: Eee Col! . . . Is my dad back?

[CROAKER *laughs and shakes her head several times. Having finished the fish and chips she is now tearing up the paper.*]

Ent he coming back, Col?

COL [*carelessly*]: Aye, he'll be coming.

CROAKER: I tear it all up, don't I? [*She laughs again and goes into the house.*]

COL: Hey, Sally, you go to Charlie, next time; you take him this.

[*He produced an electrically powered carpenter's drill from his haversack.*]

SALLY [*her eyes wide*]: Oooh.

COL: There's all of ten quid here. [*He runs around with the drill, presenting it like a Tommy Gun.*] Brrr-brrr-brrr . . .

SALLY: Brrrr-brrrr . . .

COL [*seeing the Jacksons' front door opening*]: Oy-oy. Here, kid, fetch it inside. Quick.

[*He thrusts the drill back in the haversack and* SALLY *runs indoors with it.* DOREEN *leaves her house, calling back.*]

DOREEN: 'Bye, mum.

COL [*slyly, to her*]: Hey – up!

[JACKSON *has entered from the street and meets his daughter – who, watching Col, does not at first see him.* JACKSON *looks at Col.*]

JACKSON [*sourly*]: You calling me?

COL [*taken aback*]: Eh?

JACKSON: You calling me?

COL [*recovering himself, continues to call, but looking upwards*]: Hey – up! . . . No: I warn't. Calling the birds.

JACKSON: Birds.

COL: Give 'em a holler, down they swing down; sit on your head. Hey – up! tweet-tweet.

[*He turns his back on Jackson and walks about pretending to signal to birds.*]

DOREEN: You're a bit late tonight, dad?

JACKSON [*in a foul temper all round*]: Shut up, can't you? I've had a bad day. Where are you off to, anyroad?

DOREEN: Going dancing. With Sheila.

JACKSON: Oh are you? Well you watch yourself. Them young Teds at the Pally ...

DOREEN: Oh, dad –

JACKSON: All right. I'm telling you.

DOREEN: 'Bye, dad.

[JACKSON *snorts and goes in to the house.* DOREEN *glances at* COL, *who does not appear to notice her, and then hurries off down the street.*]

DOREEN [*offstage*]: 'Byee.

COL [*looking after her*]: Hey-up! Sally!

[SALLY *appears at ground floor window.* DAFFODIL *at the same time looks out of an upper one.*]

COL [*to Sally*]: I'm off out away. You take care of what I have given you, while morning. O.K.?

[SALLY *nods.*]

COL: O.K.

[SALLY *goes away from the window.*]

DAFFODIL [*plaintive*]: Col. Col. He run out when I wor sleeping, Col.

COL: He'll be back, eh.

DAFFODIL: Don't you go too, boy. You come up here.

COL: See you, my lovely ... Hey-*up*.

[*He goes out down the street in the same direction as* DOREEN. DAFFODIL *shuts the window and retires inside.* JACKSON *comes out of his house, shouting back at his wife.*]

JACKSON: All right. All right. If I can't get a civil word in my own house, 'Cat's lost, cat's lost' – all you can say. I told you before what you could do with that cat. I'll be back while closing-time and you'll be lucky if it's no later.

[*He stamps off down the street.*]

Scene Ten

SONG

At half past ten they turn you out
And bar the bar-room door.
The night is dark and the road is cold
But why should you despair?

> For if you have no home to go
> Nor wife to hold you dear
> Then draw your sweet and naked knife
> And murder all your fear.

Interior. Night.
In the living-room ROSIE *and* SALLY *are sitting making clothes-pegs. The baby sleeps in the pram. In the small bedroom* DAFFODIL *lies sleeping and* CROAKER *squats in the corner.* COL *comes in through the front door in a bad temper, slams the door, and starts upstairs.*

SALLY [*running out of the living-room*]: You back from dancing, Col, already?

COL: Aye, I'm back.

SALLY: You warn't at it long, wor you?

COL: No I bloody warn't.

[*He goes into the small bedroom and slams the door behind him. The* OLD CROAKER *starts up. He stands looking at Daffodil while* CROAKER *makes signs to him to be quiet.*]

SALLY [*going back into living-room*]: He warn't at it long, wor he, mam? I say, mam, eh, he warn't at it long –

ROSIE: Get making them pegs and shut your noise.

SALLY [*rudely*]: Owowow –

CROAKER: Don't wake her up, Eee. She do sleep beautiful, oh look at her, tender, tender my little duckey.

DAFFODIL [*waking*]: Who is it? Blackmouth? ... Oh. [*She lies back disappointed.*]

COL [*with a quiet smile*]: No it's not. It's me. You says: come up. Well: I come.

[*He flicks his fingers towards the door and looks at Croaker. She giggles. He gestures again, more imperiously, and she hurries obediently out and downstairs. As she passes the living-room door, she pops her head in and says 'clothes-pegs!' – then she goes out into the kitchen.*]

DAFFODIL [*putting on a seductive languor*]: Oh sure you come climbing, Col ... You seen Blackmouth out in the town, did you?

COL [*coming closer to her*]: Na.

DAFFODIL [*mockingly*]: Eh you'd never see him. All you'd be seeing's that daisy from next house, ent it? Ent it?

COL [*in a practised insinuating voice*]: I know *you*, Daffodil, don't I? Heard of you, you see, all of us heard. Old Croaker's little Daffodil. Kind and right to the boys. Takes 'em and gentles 'em. Is truth of life is that. Why, you'd never be like – this dancing-and-warm the one way, knives-in-the-eyes the next, crying-and-scared the third – that's never *you*, is it? You tell me it's not you. [*He strokes her body and she relaxes to him as if of old habit.*]

DAFFODIL: No. Oh no. Not me.

COL [*suddenly*]: What the hell is Blackmouth anyroad? Old Sailor Sawney, *he* throws that boy. A limping sailor throws him.

[*They embrace.* BLACKMOUTH *comes quietly in through the front door. He looks white and haggard and is talking mechanically to himself in a low mutter, maudlin.*]

BLACKMOUTH: Hey killer, are you at home? No, he's not at home. Who's at home? No one's bloody home. Home of friends gentle and kind. But for Blackmouth, but for Blackmouth – only one killer in Sawney's house allowed. Poor devil Blackmouth, let *him* try to set up his horn – where's the friends gone then?

[*He has been rummaging vaguely around in the rubbish in the hall, and picked up one or two possessions of his. Now he goes upstairs.*]

SALLY [*in a whisper*]: It's my dad.

ROSIE [*holding her*]: Sssh.

[BLACKMOUTH *goes into the small bedroom and continues to rummage, without taking the slightest notice of the two sitting on the bed.*]

BLACKMOUTH: I left my bundle, so. [*He picks up his bundle from the floor and collects other oddments.*] Poor Blackmouth, on the road. Set up his horn in Scunthorpe, aye or Doncaster. No killers hold the road in Nottingham. Why not Nottingham? I never see Sheffield a long time. All right:

Sheffield. [*He moves to the door. For the first time he appears to understand what Col and Daffodil are doing. They have lain petrified since his entry.*] In her bed. In her bed. Ss ss ss. [*He picks out a flick-knife and jerks it open.*]

COL [*leaping to his feet*]: Oh-oh. Knives.

[*He has no weapon, so he snatches up a garment and hangs it over his forearm as a shield. He and* BLACKMOUTH *revolve slowly round each other,* COL *looking desperately for something to fight with. He sees a frying pan and grabs it just in time to parry a dangerous thrust by his enemy.*]

DAFFODIL [*sitting against the wall*]: Kill him, Col; kill him, Col, kill him, Col Col Col Col Col. [*She suddenly starts to scream like a lunatic, without moving her body.*]

BLACKMOUTH [*hissing at her*]: Shut up!

[*Distracted by the noise, he relaxes his guard sufficiently to permit* COL *to jump past him and so down the stairs. At the bottom of these* ROSIE, SALLY, *and the* CROAKER *have collected fearfully.*]

COL [*pushing past them*]: Get out of it!

[*He goes into the living-room, drops the pan, picks up a large clasp knife Rosie was using for the clothes-pegs, and backs to the farthest wall of the room.* BLACKMOUTH *has stopped half-way down the stairs, undecided.* DAFFODIL *comes out into the landing. She has stopped her screams.*]

COL [*taunting*]: Are ye coming, Blackmouth? Are ye coming down? I'm not Old Sailor, ye know: *I* never killed no witches at sea – oho no, but I'll do *you*, Blackmouth, any man can do *you*, a limping sailor can do *you* – you fox-tailed Romany. Hey ey they can smell you to the top of Halifax, they can!

[BLACKMOUTH *gives a moan of despair and rage and comes down the last stairs with a run. He trips over* SALLY *at the foot, raises his knife as though to strike her; and then stands looking at her with a silly smile.*]

SALLY: Eh dad –

BLACKMOUTH: Sally. My Sally.

SALLY: Eh dad, what are you doing to Col –

BLACKMOUTH: Ss ss. Come on, kid. Come with your dad. Get ye some spice, eh? Right spice for you to suck, just like you like it, eh?

[*He backs to the front door, still holding his knife at the ready.* COL *cautiously advances to the door of the living-room.*]

ROSIE [*as Sally seems to be about to go with Blackmouth*]: Sally, you stay here.

BLACKMOUTH: Are ye coming, Sally?

COL: You not take the kid, Blackmouth. Don't you go with him, kid. I'm *telling* you, Blackmouth.

ROSIE: Sally.

[SALLY *stands a moment irresolute. Then she makes up her mind and runs to Rosie.* BLACKMOUTH *moans again, makes a hopeless gesture, and ducks backwards out of the front door, moaning, and still holding the knife ready. Outside his voice rises to a howl like a dog's; and then dies away.*]

COL: Ach, it's always the same, ye match yourself again a Romany man, and he runs out of the door! Don't he, Daffodilly?

DAFFODIL: Fast as a ferret, Col boy.

COL: Hey ey, let's have the old gramophone. *I* showed him where.

[*He goes into the living-room again, winds the gramophone, and puts on the 'Cigareets, etc.' record.*]

SALLY: My dad's gone all runny, ent he, mam? Eh with his knife and all?

[CROAKER *laughs.* COL *mounts the stairs carrying the gramophone, with the record playing and he singing along with it. As he reaches the landing,* BLACKMOUTH *howls again outside. He pauses; then goes into the small bedroom with* DAFFODIL.]

ROSIE [*weeping*]: Now you've gone and woke up Geordie.

[*She goes back into the living-room and rocks the pram.* SALLY *and* CROAKER *dance in the hall to the music.* SAILOR *and* RACHEL *enter through the front door.*]

SAILOR [*imperiously*]: Col! Col!

COL [*in the bedroom*]: Oh-oy?

SAILOR: Cut that music off and come down here.

COL [*coming out on to the stairs*]: What's for yelling about, ye old –

SAILOR: I said cut that music off, or I'll bloody cut *you*. D'ye hear me?

[DAFFODIL *stops the music*.]

Now then. There's that bloody Blackmouth raging in the street. Has he been here, has he?

COL [*sulkily*]: He came and he went. *I* showed him where.

SALLY: He wor going for Col with a knife, you know – ooh.

SAILOR: What did he want?

COL [*shrugs*]: Said he wor after his bundle. Took it with him, O.K.

ROSIE [*shouting from the living-room*]: He tried for to take my Sally, that's what. I'll *kill* him, he does that again. Oh, oh, I will so.

[CROAKER *is edging slyly to the kitchen door*.]

SAILOR [*seeing her*]: Don't you try to slip it out the road – I see you. Now is that smarty lass o' yourn better, or ent she? Hey?

CROAKER: Oh my Daffodil –

SAILOR: Hey?

CROAKER: Proper poorly. She takes it terrible hard, Sailor. She takes it –

SAILOR: She takes it nothing. I know 'em poorly, I know 'em dying, she ain't neither. Daffodil! [*He climbs the stair.*]

COL: Now wait, Sailor –

SAILOR [*pushing past him into the bedroom*]: Daffodil! Let's have a look at ye. [*He seizes her by the wrist and holds her at arm's length, looking her up and down. Then he bites her on the forearm. She gives a yelp and aims a furious swipe at his head.*] Aye aye, there's nowt the matter with you. So away out on the road; and take your Croaker with you. And that's the lot and the last.

COL: You're not turning her off, you know.

SAILOR: Ah?

COL [*backing down the stair as* SAILOR *comes down*]: Na na, Sailor. I'm telling her, she can bide.

DAFFODIL [*bitchily*]: He likes me, don't you, Col? He wants I should bide.

SAILOR: Oh I know two o' that.

[*He pulls a beer bottle out of his pocket and offers to hit Col.* COL *presents the knife which he is still holding.*]

RACHEL: Let him be, Sailor. He wants his tart – he can have his tart, why shouldn't he? He's my lad, he's a mind and rights of his own.

SAILOR [*after a pause, lowering the bottle*]: Ah, so. The young man cries for his rights and the old man carries the load. Well, live and let live. I'm asking nowt more nor that for *me* – so I'm as well to serve it to *you*, I dare say. Go on, Daffy, you bide. Till he breaks your neck. Heh heh. [*He comes downstairs, with sardonic resignation, and* COL *goes up. At the bottom,* SAILOR *turns and calls jeeringly*]: I say, Col!

COL [*on the landing*]: What, then?

SAILOR: You're a quick-change dancer, aren't ye? Call it the April weather. I thought your tart she lives in *next* house. Pally of dance and oho the right young lady! What happened to *her* tonight?

COL [*a little abashed*]: Aye, well . . .

RACHEL: Aye well what? Did you do her?

COL [*defiant*]: No, I didn't. [RACHEL *laughs.* COL, *no longer abashed, continues*] All right and be damned. There's some windows have glass in, and there's others as don't.

[*He goes back into the bedroom with* DAFFODIL *and puts on the gramophone.*]

SAILOR: Sally, go to your mam.

[SALLY *goes into the living-room.* CROAKER *starts dancing again to the music.* SAILOR *turns on her.*]

Ah yah, dance away, dance the bloody roof down. [*He sits and drinks from his bottle.*] Ye know what, Rachel? They used to call me a killer. When I sailed the water, they would put that name on me. Ye know what, Rachel –

[BLACKMOUTH *howls outside, and they all freeze, listening.*]

Scene Eleven

Exterior. Night.

BLACKMOUTH *howls in the distance.* MRS JACKSON *comes to her door.*

MRS JACKSON: Ben, Ben, is that you, Ben? ... Eh dear, I wish you'd come home. [*She picks up the cat's saucer of milk and puts it down again, then calls without much hope.*] Puss puss puss? [BLACKMOUTH *howls. She shudders and clutches herself with worry.*] Doreen? Doreen?

BLACKMOUTH [*quite close offstage*]: Ow – yow, friends, good, good, good, friends to all –

MRS JACKSON [*to herself, in great fear*]: Oh listen to it, it's been going for hours ... What's that?

[JACKSON *enters from the street, surly.*]

JACKSON: *I'm* that. Me. Mister, the Boss, Lord and Gaffer, ha-ha. What are you talking about – 'what's that'?

[BLACKMOUTH *howls.*]

MRS JACKSON: That. I mean *that.*

JACKSON [*vaguely and with irritation*]: Oh. It's the rising moon, the wolves of Russia – I dunno what it is; what the hell do you *want* to know for?

MRS JACKSON [*angrily*]: Ben, where have you been? Do you know what the time is?

JACKSON [*savagely satirical*]: Aye, I know what the time is. It's time your cat came home ... oh such a, such a sweet companion, and pretty little feet, and, and –

MRS JACKSON: I've nowt to say to you! Come home in this state. It's not like you, Ben!

[BLACKMOUTH *howls.*]

Listen. Ben, oh *listen.*

JACKSON [*sobered with alarm*]: That's not the moon ...

MRS JACKSON: I'm frightened, frightened to death.

[BLACKMOUTH *howls.*]

JACKSON [*sharply*]: Get in the house. Godsake, what are we doing here listening to a –

MRS JACKSON: Doreen.

JACKSON: Eh? [*Pulled up short.*] Eh?

MRS JACKSON: Doreen, Ben. She went out dancing. She's not back yet.

JACKSON: She'll be all right. Some young lad'll be bringing her home.

MRS JACKSON: I don't know as she's got a young lad though . . . Of course, there's Sheila . . . Ben, please, will you go and find her?

JACKSON: Eh don't be daft . . .

MRS JACKSON [*grimly*]: Then *I'll* go.

JACKSON [*futile protest*]: Go, go where?

BLACKMOUTH [*in the distance*]: I'll tear it in strips out of your bellies, I'll tear the yellow stripes out of you –

MRS JACKSON: Ben, I've got to go . . .

[DOREEN *enters from the street.*]

Doreen! Oh, *Doreen!* You get straight upstairs, young lady, how *dare* you come in all hours of the night out of our *wits* with worry –

DOREEN [*in a sob*]: Mum. Oh mum . . . [*She pushes past them both and goes into the house.*]

JACKSON: What, what's she –

MRS JACKSON: You stay down.

[*She goes into the house.* BLACKMOUTH *howls.* JACKSON *kicks over the cat's saucer, on purpose, and leans glowering against the porch.*]

JACKSON: Cat's milk. Huh. Little pitter-pat feet. Huh. *Claws.* [*He growls unintelligible profanity and kicks away at the doorstep. Sawneys' door opens and* SALLY *peeps out, with* ROSIE *behind her.*]

ROSIE: Lovey, you get in and sleep.

SALLY [*as* BLACKMOUTH *howls*]: He's still out there in the streets, do you think he's come back, mam, eh?

ROSIE [*shrugs*]: He might, maybe.

SALLY: He went off though, right off, didn't he, eh?

ROSIE: He did.

SALLY: He said he'd do us all with his knife, he reckoned. Ooh. Will he, mam, eh?

ROSIE: No, lovey, no. Now shut it, can't ye. Sleep.

BLACKMOUTH [offstage, beginning quite close, then fading away]: You didn't ought to talk like that, oh no, not where Blackmouth shows his horn. Poor Blackmouth on the road. He knows his friends. Ow-yow. . . .

ROSIE: There, he's going. Lovey, lovey – [She beckons SALLY in and closes the door on them.]

MRS JACKSON [inside the house]: Ben!

JACKSON: What is it?

MRS JACKSON [inside]: Ben! [She comes out.] Do you know what's happened to our Doreen? It was Mrs Atkins's Len, he found her and gave her a lift to the end of the road. Do you know where he found her, Ben? She wor up by the allotments at the corner of Honeywell Lane, and that young lad was with her.

JACKSON: Len Atkins?

MRS JACKSON: No. Them ruffians, there. The young one.

JACKSON [ominously]: Eh?

MRS JACKSON: He'd been trying to interfere with her, Ben!

JACKSON: Wait while I get up to her!

MRS JACKSON: Ben! She's all right. She's a bit shook-up, and of course, her blouse and that are all torn, but she's all right. Len Atkins brought her home. He's a good boy, Len is.

JACKSON: Wait while I get up –

MRS JACKSON: Leave her till morning, Ben. It's not her fault at all. It's a matter for the Police. Come on in. [She goes into the house.]

JACKSON [in alarm]: What, Police! Now wait, wait – eh, Police – [He follows her, protesting.]

BLACKMOUTH [far away]: He knows his friends. He knows his friends. Oh Blackmouth knows his friends . . .

Scene Twelve

O Sailor Sailor love me close
I don't know where you go:
You set your foot on the gangway plank
So long long time ago.

Interior. Night.
The household are all in bed and asleep, so in each room nothing is to be seen except shapeless huddles under the bedding. In the big bedroom SAILOR *and* RACHEL *lie snoring.* SAILOR *tosses and groans.*

SAILOR [*talking in his sleep*]: Stand by to cast off!
    [RACHEL *grunts.*]
    Cast off forrard!

RACHEL [*aroused and irritable*]: Oh shut up.

SAILOR [*loud and emphatic*]: Cast off astern! What's fouling her up? Will ye get them moorings sorted or have I got to – wah wah wah . . . I'll bloody learn you gawp at *me*!

RACHEL [*shaking him*]: Hey, Sailor, hey –

SAILOR [*still asleep, but quieter*]: All cast off forrard and stern. Half-speed ahead both engines. Port five. Mid-ships. Mid-ships! Wah wah wah, mid-ships . . .

RACHEL [*shakes him again*]: Hey, wake up, you old –

SAILOR [*waking*]: Ah, huh, ah – what's the – what – what are ye at?

RACHEL: You're gabbing in your sleep again.

SAILOR: Oh no I warn't.

RACHEL: Oh aye you was and I don't stand it. Ach, if I've not got enough to do with you on a day without you're to holler out like a foghorn half the night. What's the matter with you?

SAILOR [*grumpily*]: It's my bad leg.

RACHEL: What is?

SAILOR: It's bad. It hurts: so. Night-times, it hurts me.

RACHEL: It's been better all of six month. Why don't you get some work?

SAILOR: What likes of work?

RACHEL: Ah you tell me. You do most likes o' work, don't you? Digging, building, drive horses. What else? Why don't you go back to the sea, you growl about it all night?

SAILOR: I don't go to sea no more. You know that.

RACHEL: That was your Rosie's man fetched you from the sea.

SAILOR: Well?

RACHEL: Why don't your Rachel send you back, then? What do you do for me? What do you do for *me*?

SAILOR: Is it work? *I* can work. But what for, work? I've had my glories. On the sea. Aye aye. I've seen the lands of glory. and the gold and the fishes and the beasts. And the brown women, so.

[RACHEL *laughs*.]

SAILOR: More nor that, I've seen. New York. Archangel, Hard iron towns and they kill in them towns. Oh aye I've seen 'em die . . . A man can work and he gets glory, right?

RACHEL: He gets the lolly too, boy.

SAILOR: But after that – but after that – where is it, his glory? It's in the folk around him and his sweet liberty to hold *their* lives and glory, and stand no man's work against it. So Sawney holds the road; and he takes his woman and he takes her boy, and he takes his daughter and hers.

RACHEL: Ah go to sleep.

SAILOR: I can't now. You've woke me up: and my bad leg.

RACHEL [*mockingly*]: Your bad leg. Cut it off and get a new one. Chair-leg, table-leg – serve you better. Cut it off of a telegraph pole. Strength there, boy . . . Go on, now, go to sleep.

[SAILOR *hunches himself up to sleep.*]

SAILOR [*muttering*]: Aye, it's always how it runs. Talk till your mouth breaks out to your lugs, and she says go to sleep. Uh. She says go to sleep. Uh.

[*He snores.* RACHEL *continues sitting up and talking aloud to herself.*]

RACHEL: Glory ... *I* got glory ... Like, glory of choice. Take: when I want. Choose one, choose 'em all. And the last one is the old one with the bad leg, and what'll *he* do?

SAILOR [*from the bedclothes*]: He'll last you out, that's what. *And* he'll have his laugh at it, bad leg for ever!

RACHEL [*still apparently to herself*]: Then that's my glory too ... Oh, work, has he had? Folk around him, has he got? Then let him have his laugh. I can carry up with it, marry along with the broke ghost of some tattery ship full of brown women. Or stuck in the ice. Or a sinking ship? Ah, sunk, and all ... There's choices I've had. I've made 'em. They've gone. Like, nowt. But all *mine*. Take that little bastard at Northampton. Blue eyes. Yellow hair. No nose on his face. What about *him*? Hoopla stall at the fair he had. Choose your prize and toss your silver ring:

[*She sings:*]

> Oh who's throwing my way
> Or who's throwing yours
> Or who'll throw the other way
> And crawl out on all fours?

What does it matter which way, so you make your true own choice of it? Hey?

SAILOR [*stirs round and looks at her*]: True choice at Northampton got you a dandy job, I don't think. Under the skirts of Tony Piazza's roundabout, warn't it?

RACHEL: Ah so, he shaped his little time, and I gave him glory for it.

SAILOR: He gave you more than glory, dearie.

RACHEL [*fiercely*]: *And* I'd sooner take that from some than I'd take bloody fish and chips from others, I would: in cartloads and all. Hot. Aye, and with a sink-full of red sauce and that's the truth. For all the trouble and pain, and death. If I took it, I took it.

[*She sings:*]

> Oh had he but warned me before he disordered me,
> Had he but warned me of it in time –

I'd have pulled him down to me there in the mud, just
same like I did ...
There's other words to the tune and all:
[*She sings:*]
For I was as free as a bird on the mountain,
For I was as free as a swallow so high.
And that time I made it his time. For a while. Or –
[*She sings:*]
I was as free as a bloody great eagle –
Biting out me dinners for anyone's paunch as comes. From
all of them. Biting and biting. Left tooth, right tooth. And
what do I bite out of *you*? Hey?

SAILOR [*snapping his jaws at her*]: Ah-arrh.

RACHEL [*triumphantly*]: Ah, spite and warfare! *There's* the
meat to feed: cos when you've et that, so you can sick it
back again; yet always you're in liberty! Which I've *got* to
be, boy. *Got*. Northampton wept and cried when I left him.
I know well *you'd* not do that. And that's good.
[SAILOR *laughs.*]

RACHEL: You'd never, would you? Northampton ran around
his wagon, bawling for me: 'Bide wi' me, Rachel!' Just like
lovely Blackmouth. But I went from him, so. To an old
raving ghost with a warp in his keel and a half of a split mast,
voyaging God knows where. Where is it, Archangel? God
knows, you see. Cos Rachel don't.
And red eyes: and a bad leg, too ... Hey then, hold it out.
I'll rub it till it's better. Oh me poor old horse. [*She massages
his leg, singing.*]
  Poor old horse, poor old horse.

SAILOR [*sings*]:
  Poor old horse, poor old horse.

COL [*waking up in the small bedroom and shouting*]: Shut the
bloody row!

SAILOR
RACHEL } [*sing together*]: Poor old horse, poor old horse, *etc.*
  [COL *beats on the wall.*]

Scene Thirteen

You angry man, you rage away
Against the women's game:
But you served them your best part of you
Without a wink of shame.

Exterior. Morning.

MRS JACKSON *is on her doorstep, sweeping it.* JACKSON *comes out of the house.*

MRS JACKSON: Not a sign of her, Ben. I've called and I've called.

JACKSON: Ah. She's run off on you. Gobbling food, stinking out the kitchen, they fill your upholstery with fleas. So who cares? *They* don't. Puss puss puss. Where's Doreen?

MRS JACKSON: Doreen! Hurry up then. Your dad's wanting to be off to his work. You'll make him late.

DOREEN [*appearing at an upper window*]: Well, all right, let him go. I can get to the shop by myself.

MRS JACKSON [*angrily*]: I'm not having you walking out alone, my girl, not after last night! Now don't argue.

JACKSON: Come on. I'm telling you.

DOREEN: All *right*, dad. I've got to go to the bathroom yet. [*She shuts the window.*]

MRS JACKSON: It wouldn't surprise me if they'd not eaten her, the poor little thing.

JACKSON: Now who'd eat a cat? You're talking soft.

MRS JACKSON: *They'd* eat a cat. We wor better off with them black Americans in the war and that's no story ... Yelling in the streets twelve o'clock at night. And besides – I think we ought to go to the police.

JACKSON [*angrily*]: Now look. We had all that out.

MRS JACKSON: Well I'm not convinced. If our girl can't even –

JACKSON [*violently*]: Do you want the police? Do you really want the police?

MRS JACKSON: It's not what I *want*, Ben –

JACKSON: Cos look: how long have we been on this Housing Scheme?

MRS JACKSON: Two year.

JACKSON: Well! Where did we live afore that?

MRS JACKSON: You know where we lived.

JACKSON: Then you don't need me to tell you. Balaclava Row, a lovely place *warn't* it? I'd enough of it at work, I can tell you. 'Hello Ben, how's the thieves' kitchen this morning?' 'I see there wor another Grievous Bodily Harm up your way last night, Ben – ooh you'll have to watch it, Ben – Yer getting too well known to the coppers!' Ha ha. Funny jokers. Huh.

MRS JACKSON: Well. It wor as bad for me.

JACKSON: Aye. And when at last Corporation's good enough to let us get out up here and *get* a new house, what then? 'I think it's perfectly disgraceful the way they put those people from Balaclava Row into such nice new places. They tell me they even use the toilet seats for framing pictures with' – *and* the rest of it. Blah blah blah. You want to start all that again?

MRS JACKSON: No Ben.

JACKSON: *Well!* If you fetch the coppers up, you *will*. Doreen!

MRS JACKSON: Doreen! Whatever are you at up there?

[*She goes into the house.* JACKSON *hangs moodily about on the doorstep.*]

JACKSON: *And* it's washing day. God help us. Cold meat for us dinners and bloody underwear all over the kitchen.

[RACHEL *comes out of her house to throw a pan of bones out on the garden. They look at each other.* RACHEL *spits on the ground and then laughs.*]

JACKSON [*ominously*]: All right. But I'm warning you.

RACHEL: Warning us what, mister?

JACKSON [*going towards her and lowering his voice*]: It's one thing wi' *me*, you know: but I'm not standing your games with my lass.

RACHEL: Games?

JACKSON: Aye, games. There's a young lad in your house, you ask *him* what games.

RACHEL: Col, is it?

JACKSON: Is that what he's called? Well you tell him he'd best not walk where I walk, that's all.

RACHEL: And what'd you do if he did?

JACKSON: I'm not that old I couldn't learn him summat – *oh* no – it's a fair while sin I last took my jacket off, but by God if I –

RACHEL: He's *my* boy, is Col.

JACKSON: Eh? Oh, he is, is he? Well that just about caps it. That just about sets the blasted roof on it, that does. Your boy. I might have known. Well, I can't say I'm surprised neither. It's clear to see what nasty puddles he sucked *his* manners out of. Huh. Your boy!

RACHEL: So? There's not only my boy's manners sucks out of them puddles, is there, mister?

JACKSON: What do you mean?

RACHEL: You like to have your lick at a puddle or two, yourself, now and again, don't you? Johnny Jackson, Johnny Jackson – you ought to take better care of yourself when you wander the stairs of the town without a guard or guide, boy. You don't know *what* you're going to pick up, do you?

JACKSON [*taken aback*]: Pick up?

RACHEL [*enjoying herself*]: You see, now; take puddles. There's all sorts of feet can tread in the puddles, you know. Some clean, some mucky. Didn't they learn ye *nowt* in the Army, Johnny, all them foreign tarts you had?

JACKSON [*terrified*]: Here, what are you getting at –

RACHEL [*sings*]:
Oh had she but warned me before she disordered me – and all for lovely Rachel's love. Oh Johnny Jackson, you poor bloody animal, you . . .

[*She goes into her house again, laughing.*]

JACKSON [*frantic*]: Hey, hey, wait a minute, wait a minute –

[DOREEN *hurries cheerfully out to him.*]

DOREEN: Hello dad, here I am ready at last. Eh! I *am* a slow-coach.

JACKSON [*turning on her in his terror*]: Eh? What? Wait half the bloody morning for you: what d'you think you're playing at?

DOREEN [*dashed*]: Dad!

JACKSON: Blah blah blah, you stupid –

[RACHEL *comes out again, carrying a lump of dripping on a bit of newspaper.*]

RACHEL: And another thing, mister. You tell them pair o' bitches of yourn to stop squealing in the streets at night. Driving our sleep away – what kind of way to live is that?

[MRS JACKSON *comes out.* RACHEL *hands the dripping to* JACKSON *and, as tho' in a trance, he takes it.*]

Here, I've brought you a bit of dripping. Cool and soothe you. I say I've brought him a bit of dripping missus. Good for him, ent it? Like, soo-oothing ... Howl about the bloody streets all night ...

[*She goes inside and slams her door.*]

MRS JACKSON: What did she want, Ben?

JACKSON: Eh?

MRS JACKSON: What did she want?

JACKSON: I don't know.

MRS JACKSON: Did you speak to her about Doreen?

JACKSON: Oh – like, like kind of.

MRS JACKSON: Well what did she say?

JACKSON [*violently*]: Well you heard what she said! You've got a pair of ears, haven't you? She said you wor howling in the street last night.

MRS JACKSON [*in bewilderment*]: Me?

JACKSON [*turning on his daughter*]: Or you were: *I* don't know – I – what's *this*?

DOREEN: Dripping.

JACKSON [*stupidly*]: She give me dripping.

MRS JACKSON: Why?

JACKSON [*throwing it down*]: Tach! It's time you started on your wash-day!

MRS JACKSON [*firing up also*]: And it's time *you* started on your road. What's the matter with you?

DOREEN: What *is* it, dad?

JACKSON: What's what? Bloody women.

MRS JACKSON: You'd best take Doreen to the bus-stop, hadn't you?

[*She goes indoors.*]

DOREEN: Look, dad, you don't have to come with me, you know.

JACKSON: Well I'm coming.

DOREEN: You don't really mean to meet me off the bus this evening, do you, like me mum said? You don't *need* to, dad; and look, I'll be with Sheila.

JACKSON: You were supposed to be with Sheila last night – ah find your own road. I'm sick and tired.

DOREEN: Well, I'll go with you to the bus-stop now.

JACKSON: Come on then. Why you didn't let that lad lay you, while he was about it, and make a proper job of it; instead of just –

DOREEN [*appalled*]: *Dad!*

JACKSON [*confused*]: Oh you know what I mean. Or *I* know what I mean. Or, God, I don't know; who knows what, anyroad? Come on. I'm late.

[*They go off down the road.*]

Scene Fourteen

SONG

It's whether you come or whether you go
Or whether you bide at home:
They're always right behind you, Jack,
And never leave you alone.

In your footsteps they will plant their feet
For every step you tread,
They trample on your shadow, Jack
They trample on your head.

Live Like Pigs

Interior. Afternoon.

The stage is empty. Two letters fall through the letterbox in the front door, and there is a pair of raps on the knocker.

RACHEL [*from the kitchen*]: What d'ye want then?

> [*She comes out of the kitchen, eating. She picks up the letters and looks at them dubiously.*]

SAILOR [*from in the kitchen*]: Who is it? What's he after?

RACHEL: It's more of them letters.

SAILOR: Oh?

> [*He appears in the kitchen doorway.* SALLY *runs out into the hall underneath his arm.*]

SALLY: Is it letters, is it? Who's sending us letters, eh? Eh? Eh?

RACHEL: Get out of it.

> [SAILOR *takes the letters and looks at them.* ROSIE *comes out of the kitchen.*]

ROSIE: Sally, come here.

SALLY: Who sends us letters, mam?

ROSIE: I don't know, lovey. It's not so good, whoever it is. Now you bide quiet and don't make Sailor mad while he's thinking on what to do.

SAILOR: It's second lot this week.

RACHEL: Maybe we ought to open *these*, y'know.

SAILOR: Why?

RACHEL: I don't like to burn things always. Jocky Faa once tell'd me he burned a whole quid in a letter one time.

SAILOR: Aye, aye. But what a daft bloody trick that, put a quid in a letter. Am I opening these, or not?

RACHEL [*uneasily*]: It'd be better so.

SAILOR: All right then. Let's have a look. [*He opens the letter and looks at them uncomprehending.*] There's one is printed and there's this other is type-wrote. I don't like it. Read 'em. [*He hands the letters to Rachel.*] What do they say?

RACHEL: This printed one. It's a form. For filling-in, see.

SAILOR: Then burn it. We've never had it.

RACHEL: Ach, I dunno. It's the National Insurance.

SAILOR: What about it? Those bastards'd chase ye from New-castle to Cornwall. They're worse nor the bloody Peelers.

RACHEL: There might be an Entitlement, though. Like, you and your bad leg.

SAILOR: Na na. I said burn it . . . What's the typewriting all about?

RACHEL: I can't make it clear yet. It's from the Corporation.

SAILOR [*in alarm*]: Oh . . . It is, eh? That's not so good, neither. Go on read it.

RACHEL: He says, 'Complaints relating to condition of – of aforesaid residence. And gardens appertaining.' Ach, all that it is – words.

ROSIE: They send these words at us under the door all the time. It's not right. What can *we* do when we get them? They put us, it's like a dog in a box, you can stick spikes through every corner at him and he's no place to turn at all.

[*There is a knock on the door. They look at one another. There is another knock.* RACHEL *opens the door. The* OFFICIAL *from the Housing Department comes in.*]

OFFICIAL: Good afternoon, Mrs Sawney . . . Mr Sawney . . . er, Mrs er . . . Hello love . . . I dare say you remember me, eh? aye, well . . . You had a letter last week from the Department, didn't you? And you should have had another today. Aye there it is, you've got it, I can see. Have you read it yet?

RACHEL: We've opened it. So what?

OFFICIAL [*embarrassed*]: It's a bit awkward for me, is this, missus: you see, after all, I'm only the bottle-washer in the department – I mean.

SAILOR: What have you come for, mister?

OFFICIAL: The fact is, Mr Sawney, you've hardly been in this house two months, have you? And it's in a shocking state. I mean, look at it . . . Eh dear. There's been complaints, that's all. And what are we going to do about it, eh?

SAILOR: Aye. What *are* we going to do about it?

OFFICIAL: Well. My instructions, Mr Sawney, are to tell you that unless something *is* done, steps will be taken, Mr Sawney, by the Department, to put you out; and that's that. I'm sorry. There it is.

SAILOR: And where will we go? The institutions, isn't it? Cos you've burnt the tram-car we used to live in. We can't go on the road, we've two little kids with us. We've not got money for a wagon. So what do we do?

OFFICIAL: If you take my advice, you'll clean the house. Hang some curtains up. Tidy the garden. And get rid of your lodgers.

RACHEL: We ain't got no lodgers.

OFFICIAL: No?

RACHEL: No.

[*She has moved round behind him till she is standing between him and the closed front door. The others close in on him a little. He looks round nervously. A car is heard driving up outside.*]

OFFICIAL: It's no use you trying to intimidate me. I told you before, *I'm* not responsible. If you lot get evicted, you've only yourselves to thank –

[*There is a sharp double knock on the door. They look at one another.*]

OFFICIAL: Aren't you going to see who it is?

[*The knock is repeated, very loudly, and a voice shouts:* 'Police!' *The* POLICE SERGEANT *opens the door and comes in abruptly.*]

SERGEANT: You're very ready to answer, aren't you? Sawney's house?

SAILOR: It is.

SERGEANT: Are you Sawney?

[SAILOR *shrugs.*]

SERGEANT: Proper mucky hole you've got here, and all . . . [*He sees the Official.*] Who are you?

OFFICIAL: Oh I'm from the Town Hall, Officer. Housing Department.

SERGEANT: Ah . . . Sawney's, eh? You were down on the old caravan site, weren't you; before they sorted you out?

SAILOR: We were.

SERGEANT: They were none too soon in shifting you, neither.

[*He is wandering about the ground floor of the house, looking at*

everything, and throwing his comments over his shoulder at them.]
There was a Police Constable wounded last night. At
approximately twelve forty-five a.m. Near the junction of
Market Hill and Princess Adelaide Street. Know anything
about it? Nasty dark place, that, middle of the night. So,
you see, he couldn't see who stabbed him. Could he?

SAILOR: It wasn't none of us, now.

SERGEANT: Not? You see, our lad couldn't see who stabbed
him, but he could hear. It was a man, probably drunk, shouting out the name of Sawney. Shouting out your name.
There aren't many Sawneys are there, in this town;
specially ones as go stabbing policemen. Come on, then.
Who was it?

SAILOR: It wasn't none of us.

ROSIE: We was all in the house, middle of the night. *You* can't
prove no different. No.

SERGEANT: You know who did it. I been fifteen year at this
game. You can't play it clever with *me*, so don't think you
can. Very well. We'll try it another way. [*He picks up the
gramophone from the living-room floor.*] Where did you get
this?

RACHEL: That's mine. I bought it fair. *You* can't prove no
different.

SERGEANT: Not? You've got a receipt for it, have you?

RACHEL [*taken aback*]: A what?

SERGEANT: A receipt. I'll bet you haven't. Now an instrument
like this seems to me an unlikely item for folk in your sort of
circumstances to possess. Don't it? So I am now going to
Take you In – suspected In Possession of Stolen Property.
Come on. And you – Sawney – you can come too. You
live with her, don't you? Aiding and Abetting. Come
on.

SAILOR: Wait a minute; you can't go taking us like this –

SERGEANT: Not? Who are you to tell me what I can do? [*He
puts his whistle to his mouth.*]

[DAFFODIL *comes in through the kitchen. When she sees the
Sergeant she recoils in terror.*]

SERGEANT [*sprinting at her*]: And who are *you*, young lady?
... Well? Another Sawney? Are you?

RACHEL: She's with us. So?

SERGEANT [*pinning Daffodil in a corner*]: What's your name?
... Eh? What? Can't hear you!

DAFFODIL: What – what –

SERGEANT: Now then. *You* tell me. Who knifed the Constable
last night down Adelaide Street, shouting the name of
Sawney?

DAFFODIL: Why Blackmouth did. Least, I suppose, he did –

SERGEANT: Who's Blackmouth?

DAFFODIL [*now recovering herself*]: Oh don't you know who
Blackmouth is? Ooh, you want to go for *him*, Captain. He'll
give you promotion, he will!

SERGEANT: Blackmouth? ... *I* know. Wait a moment ...
[*He takes a notebook out and thumbs through the pages.*] Blackmouth ... Aha! What about this: William Lewis, otherwise known as Blackmouth. Escaped from Strangeways
Gaol, thirteenth of last month, after severe assault upon
Prison Officer. Age twenty-eight, five foot ten tall, black
hair, swarthy features, general gipsy-like appearance. That
the lad, is it?

[DAFFODIL *nods and smiles.*]

SERGEANT: Where is he?

DAFFODIL: Sheffield.

SERGEANT: How do you know?

DAFFODIL: He said he wor going. He went, see. Last night.
You catch him, Captain. Ah.

SERGEANT: All right, I will. [*He goes to the door.*] Now you
behave yourselves. I'm warning.

OFFICIAL: Er – Officer. I wonder could you give me a lift to
the Town Hall, if you're going that way.

SERGEANT: Oh, I don't mind, sir. I'll take you as far as the
Station, anyroad ... I'm warning. [*He goes out.*]

OFFICIAL: And bear in mind what *I* said, too. And *don't* let's
be finding you've got lodgers here. I know. [*He goes out
with a meaning look at Daffodil.*]

ROSIE [*furiously, to Daffodil*]: What you tell him that for?

DAFFODIL: Why shouldn't I tell him? What's Blackmouth done for *me* I shouldn't tell him? Or you neither?

SAILOR: Shut up. He's no loss, is Blackmouth. But it's a fool's lark telling owt to them devils. You ought to know it be now.

[SALLY *has collected Col's haversack* (*with the drill in it*) *from the living-room floor, and is on her way out of the house with it.*]

RACHEL: What you got there, kid?

ROSIE: You leave her alone . . . Come here, lovey. Where are you off to?

SALLY: Taking it to Charlie's. Col said.

SAILOR: Na na. We're none on us walking the town with that like o'load for a day or two. Put it back where you found it. I'll talk to Col.

DAFFODIL: It's nowt to do wi' you what Col does with his work. You let the kid sell it for him, if he wants.

[SAILOR *turns angrily on her. She retreats backwards up the stair.*]

[*Childishly rude*] Ah wah wah – [*she pulls her tongue out and, going up the stairs, sings:*]

> The dirty old man
> Fell into the river
> The dirty fishes ate his liver
> Quack quack a dirty duck
> Bit the end off his dirty –

[*Angry knocking at the back door in the kitchen.*]

MRS JACKSON [*off*]: Let me in. Let me in. [*She storms into the hall through the kitchen, very angry indeed.*] The last straw. Oh I've stood enough. Stood enough. But By, I'm not taking this. Where are they?

SAILOR: What the hell are you on about?

MRS JACKSON: My washing. All my washing hanging out on the line in the back garden and it's gone! I want it back, I tell you, I want it back!

SAILOR: We don't have your bloody washing. Now you get

out o' here and keep out. It's not your place, no, and never will.

MRS JACKSON: I'm going to find my washing. And my little cat. My little cat. Took her and eaten her. Took her and eaten her. . . . [*She hurries about the ground floor rooms, routing about in the piles of junk.*] You'll not stop me. I'll find my washing. I know you've got it here.

[RACHEL *tries to stop her, with an angry shout; but* SAILOR *holds her.*]

SAILOR [*restraining Rachel*]: Let her rummage if she wants. We've nowt o' hers. Can't ye sees she's – [*He taps his forehead.*] Let her be. She'll soon be tired of it.

MRS JACKSON: Where is it? Where is it? [*She goes upstairs into the big bedroom.*]

RACHEL: You keep out o' there!

SAILOR: Let her be. We're wanting no more trouble *this* day.

[MRS JACKSON *goes into the small bedroom.* DAFFODIL *follows her in.*]

DAFFODIL [*quietly*]: My room, this is.

MRS JACKSON: I don't care.

DAFFODIL: Is it your husband: red face, hairy legs? Eh?

MRS JACKSON [*briskly*]: Don't you talk about my husband's legs. There's enough and all to talk about without that like o' rudeness. I want my washing!

DAFFODIL: My mam the Croaker, she saw his legs when he wor with Big Rachel. She says, hairy.

MRS JACKSON [*taking it in*]: Eh? . . . When he wor with –

DAFFODIL: Big Rachel? Oh aye. [*She giggles.*] Last afternoon. In *there*. Croaker knows what they did. I wor asleep though. I thought he wor Blackmouth, but he warn't.

MRS JACKSON [*stunned*]: With Big Rachel . . .

DAFFODIL: In that room: *there*. They lay down. Lovely.

MRS JACKSON: That's not true.

DAFFODIL: Ent it?

MRS JACKSON: You're wanting to frighten me.

[DAFFODIL *grins.*]

MRS JACKSON [*in a whisper*]: Oh no. It's not right. Ben

wouldn't do that. Never. No. [*She comes down the stairs, and meets Rachel in the hall.*] Are you – are you – you're Rachel.

RACHEL [*nods*]: Have you found your washing yet, missus?

MRS JACKSON: He wouldn't do that? Would he? Would he? [*She looks at Rachel, then turns and runs out of the house, through the kitchen door.*]

[RACHEL *laughs.*]

DAFFODIL [*laughs*]: That sent her, didn't it? Oh –
[*She sings:*]

> Up and down the road we go
> He comes fast and she comes slow
> Slowly slowly wait for me –
> Oh – I'm so blind that I can't see.

What can't you see?

> Twenty fingers holding tight
> Twenty toes in the middle of the night
> Four lips. Four eyes. Four ears.
> And all the rest as goes

SALLY: With his long red nose.

DAFFODIL: With his long red nose.

SALLY
DAFFODIL } : With his long red *nose!*

[*The* OLD CROAKER *cautiously puts her head in at the front door.*]

CROAKER: I tear them all up, don't I?
[*She comes inside. She has her arms full of washing, all in rags and tatters, and streamers of it are trailing behind her. She continues to rip the fabrics up.*]

SAILOR [*strides furiously towards her*]: Why, you old –

CROAKER [*terrified*]: Oh *no*, Sailor, don't.
[*She throws the washing at his feet and cowers away. He looks at it and her, then bursts into laughter.*]

SAILOR: By God. Her bloody washing! Let 'em all come. We've got the washing –
[*They all start in, tearing the washing up and shouting:* 'We've got the washing.' *Up and down the house they dance throwing the washing all round and over each other.*]

Scene Fifteen

The rage of angry wives awaits
No trumpet-call nor drum:
When once it breaks, like thunder it breaks
And they run around the town.

For their hearts are hurt and their houses hurt.
Their houses are their heart.
And those within their houses are
The least important part.

At their left-hand lip they hang out their tongues,
Their teeth hang out at the right:
Their fingers' nails are red-hot coals
And their nostrils flaring white.

Exterior. Afternoon.
DOREEN *comes home from work, goes up to her door, and takes her key out to let herself in. As she prepares to do so, she looks off-stage along the street, and quickly drops her key back into her handbag.* COL *comes in from his work, and goes to the Sawney door without more than the merest glance at Doreen. He sits before the door.*

DOREEN: Eh, I've gone and I've lost my key again.

COL [*casually wounding*]: Hello there, hinny. So they're letting ye out alone in the street again, are they? Phoo – they didn't ought to do that, y'know.

DOREEN: I'm not having anything to say to you – you know why ... What do you mean: they didn't ought to let me out alone?

COL: Ach, just what I said, so. Dancing and laughing, you. But let a man stand at ye just one half minute, and ye're off hollering like one o' they curlews; playing at the broken-wing game, isn't it, so?

DOREEN: Col, I don't know what you mean. Last night I was enjoying it all honest, until you began trying to –

COL: I warn't trying no more than what you'd like it from me; least, I'd *say* you'd like . . . You're not telling me you never wanted it, now. I mean, are you, hinny?

DOREEN: Well, of course, Col, I suppose all girls would like –

COL [*abruptly*]: Ah so, then! . . . Well, come away round the wall there, and I'll give it you now. What d'ye wait for?

DOREEN [*on the verge of tears*]: Oh but, but, Col –

COL [*disgusted*]: Ach, ye're still the same, and it's all true I said it: y're not fit to be loosed outside of houses alone. [*He goes to the Jacksons' door and beats on it.*] Hey, missus, hey hey missus, come here!

[MRS JACKSON *opens her door in amazement.* COL *jumps back a few paces into the garden, behind Doreen.*]

MRS JACKSON: What's all this about? What do you want?

COL [*pushing Doreen forward*]: She's yourn, ent she? Your little daisy flower? Then take her and water her and keep her away from beehives. Bzzzz. [*He goes back to the Sawneys' door and sits down before it again, ignoring the others.*]

MRS JACKSON: Doreen! Why aren't you with your –with your dad, Doreen?

[DOREEN *bursts into tears and hurries away from the house.*] Doreen. Doreen. Where are you off to? Lovey! Lovey! Come here – [*She runs after Doreen and catches hold of her arm imploringly.*]

DOREEN [*with passion*]: Always on to me. You're always on to me. I never had a chance –

[JACKSON *enters from the street; and intercepts his daughter as she breaks clear again of Mrs Jackson.* MRS JACKSON, *at the sight of her husband, withdraws a little.*]

JACKSON: Here, what is it now? [*He sees Col.*] Has *he* been up to his fancy larks again, has he?

DOREEN: No, he's not. And what if he has, anyroad? I'm old enough. I can take care of myself, can't I? Can't I?

JACKSON: No!

DOREEN: Well I'm going to have a try. I don't want to stay in this house any longer. I – I mum, I'm *going* –

MRS JACKSON: Doreen, lovey, *where* are you going?

DOREEN: I'm going to Sheila's. That's what. And don't try and stop me. I'm going to Sheila's house. *Her* mum doesn't treat her like a, like a daisy flower! Nor beehives, beehives, neither! [*She runs off weeping.*]

MRS JACKSON [*trying to follow*]: But lovey –

JACKSON [*checking her*]: Eh, don't chase her now ... Or she might go somewhere worse nor Sheila. Now take it easy.

MRS JACKSON [*looking at him for the first time*]: Take it easy ... So you thought you'd come home, did you?

JACKSON [*puzzled*]: Eh? Why shouldn't I come home? It's tea-time, ent it?

MRS JACKSON [*bleak and deadly*]: You can get your tea where you got your dripping. *And* the rest of what you got. [*She goes in and slams the door.*]

JACKSON [*astonished*]: Here, Emmy! What's wrong?
   [*The bolt is heard drawn on the inside of the door.* JACKSON *becomes frightened.*]

   Emmy! I say Emmy, let me in! [*He beats on the door.*]
   [COL *laughs, and opens the Sawney door.*]

COL [*calling indoors*]: Hey, Daffy!
   [DAFFODIL *comes to the threshold.*]

DAFFODIL: Ai-oo?

COL: Locked out. Look at him.

DAFFODIL: Ooh.

JACKSON [*frantic*]: Emmy, look. I don't know what you've heard, but it's not true ... I mean, Emmy, you can't believe what folk like that'd tell you – I mean ... Emmy, *will* you let me in?

COL: She won't let him in, y'see, till the milkman's got hisself dressed and away out the back ... Ach, who's for the boozer? Come on.
   [*He and* DAFFODIL *come downstage and walk across past* JACKSON, *who ignores them and bangs on his door.*]
   [*Shouts*]: Let him in, missus, he's clamming up wi' cold! [*He makes a snatch at Daffodil's haunches. She shrieks and runs off. With a roar he follows her. Offstage, she gives a yelp as he catches her, and then a soft giggle.*]

JACKSON: Emmy! ... [*He suddenly stands away from the door and shouts.*] All right, then, if that's how you're going to take it, you might as well have the lot and be damned. Tell 'em *all* about it! Let the whole Housing Scheme hear! Aye, I did go with that bloody tart next door, and a *right* time I had of it and all! Do you want to know what she did and how?

[MRS JACKSON *opens the door again in horror.*]

MRS JACKSON: *Ben!* Ben! *Shut up*, Ben!

A WOMAN'S VOICE [*offstage, calling*]: Mrs Jackson, Mrs Jackson!

MRS JACKSON [*calling back*]: Hello! Is that you, Mrs Atkins!

WOMAN'S VOICE [*off*]: Is all your washing all right, love?

MRS JACKSON [*surprised*]: No, it's not

WOMAN'S VOICE [*off*]: I thought not. She's been up and down all the gardens tearing it to shreds and all.

MRS JACKSON: Who has?

WOMAN'S VOICE [*off*]: It's her, the old crooked devil out o' next door to you!

MRS JACKSON: No!

ANOTHER WOMAN'S VOICE: It's true.

MRS JACKSON [*leaning against the doorpost as though faint*]: Then that's the lot. That's it. That's it. My cat, my Doreen, fat as a pig they called me – he said a right time he had of it and all, do you know that the bloody bitch she ate my little cat ...

[*Her voice trails away and she stands in a sort of trance, gasping. JACKSON looks at her in concern. DAFFODIL, offstage, giggles and squeals. MRS JACKSON stares after Col and Daffodil, breathes heavily, talks in gasps.*]

There's a pair of them *now*, it's time we showed 'em what we thought of 'em in this town. [*Suddenly she roars in her throat like a bull and sets off at a run down the street after Col and Daffodil.*]

1ST WOMAN'S VOICE [*off*]: That's it. That's it. Right. Right.

2ND WOMAN'S VOICE [*off*]: Right. Right.

[*There is sudden yelping, offstage, as of hounds worrying.*

JACKSON *backs into his doorway, staring after his wife in the direction of the noise. His eyes are wide and horrified, and he shakes his head.*]

Scene Sixteen

Interior. Evening (immediately after Scene Fifteen).

DAFFODIL *bursts through the front door, shouting:* 'Sailor, Sailor!' *She is hysterical. She hangs on to the stair-rail and screams.* SAILOR, RACHEL, ROSIE, SALLY, *and* CROAKER *crowd into the hall.*

DAFFODIL: Sailor, they're tearing him to bits, they've all set on to him, they've all set on to him, listen!

[*Shouting and screaming can be heard from outside.*]

RACHEL: Col?

DAFFODIL: They're tearing him to bits –

RACHEL [*setting to rush out of the door*]: Let me get at 'em! Sailor –

SAILOR [*catching her back and slamming the door*]: It's his own bloody lookout. Now you bide in here, ye great crocodile, and use your bloody top. You know who was at this house today and you know what they said. If Col and her want to dance yelping on the doorsteps of the street, then they can look to the cows in the street to trap them. And be damned. We start killing 'em for it, and we get the Peelers in again, we're really for the nick, girl, I ent joking.

SALLY [*looking out of the hall window*]: Col's coming, Col's coming, Col, Col, Col.

[*The shouts outside grow louder.* COL *bursts in.* RACHEL *flings the door open for him and shuts it smartly behind him.* COL *is in an alarming state. His clothes are half torn off his back, and his face and body (where it shows through the ripped garments) are clawed and streaked with blood. He leans against the wall panting.*]

COL: By – by – I got away.

[RACHEL *seizes him and shakes and slaps him.*]

RACHEL: You got away. Oh you got away. But not from me

you don't get away, bringing 'em all on to us, you blasted
young –

COL [*breaking away from her*]: Hey, hey on, now. What have *I*
done, you set on me like that?

RACHEL: They've been here today. Coppers –

COL [*stupidly*]: Coppers?

ROSIE: Aye, and they're turning us out of the house and all,
they said they give us warning, Col, they said –

SAILOR [*dominating*]: Now wait, the lot of ye. Be easy . . .
What did they do to ye, boy?

COL: Well look at me, for God sake . . . Women are they? I'll
tell you, Daffy. They've near finished Col for *your* pleasur-
ing, the next half-year.

SAILOR: How many were there?

COL: Twelve, fifteen, I dunno – three of 'em begin it, then they
run out of every doorway at me . . . Women? Bloody
leopards!

SALLY [*at the window*]: They're all outside the garden fence.

SAILOR [*sharply*]: Come away from that window, kid.

[*He pulls her away, just as a brick crashes through the hall
window.*]

A WOMAN'S VOICE [*outside*]: *And* any more of you, we'll serve
'em the same!

[*Outside is a constant noise of voices – not too many; there are
only a score of women at most, at this stage.*]

SAILOR: See what I mean? [*To Rachel who has her hand on the
latch.*] *Don't* open the door.

RACHEL: I'm going to –

SAILOR: I said: wait. They'll clear away soon. Most likely they
will. There aren't that many.

COL: Teeth, nails, feet, everything. Half a bloody brick. Look
at my fingers. They held 'em flat on the causeway and –
there wor three of 'em got me down and the rest they – I
tell ye, they're –

[*Another brick is thrown at the window.*]

A WOMAN'S VOICE [*outside*]: Come on out of it, we'll show
you!

RACHEL [*furiously*]: I'm going to talk! [*She flings open the door; and, standing on the threshold, screams out her defiance. As she goes on, she seems to become possessed by her rage, and her words are interspersed with sheer animal noises.*] You want us out o' here? I tell you, you want more'n you know you want, you darling lovely girls! We'll come out, oh we'll come out, you'll not forget us when we come. I tell you: we live like bloody animals, you don't know what animals are! You hide in your hutches in your good warm straw and you think you got thirty-two teeth in your heads; but we carry fifty three, ohoho-rho – and there's blood for each one of 'em between the leg and the neck, when *we* come, when *we* come blooding, ohoho-*rho* – who wants us now? [*She steps back, foaming at the mouth. Then she starts laughing quietly to herself, and says: 'Ohoho-rho,' to herself and shuts the door. The voices outside are silent.*]

SALLY [*at the window again*]: They're going off. You've *feared* 'em, Rachel, ooh, terrible feared.

SAILOR: Are they going? [*He goes to the window.*] Looks like it, so.

RACHEL [*quietly*]: Why not? They know I tell 'em true. I say it: and they run.

SAILOR: Aye aye, But it's not the first time.

RACHEL: What?

SAILOR: You been telling 'em it since we come here, right?

RACHEL: All right.

SAILOR: Each time you tell 'em louder. So each time they run from not so far. And each time after, they get madder. Eh? The loudest time you tell 'em, they don't run at all.

RACHEL [*scornfully*]: Don't give me that.

SAILOR [*he sounds depressed*]: I'm giving you what I can see. You don't know this bastardy-like of folk like I do. I've lived longer, girl, so listen. Aye, aye, they belong inside their hutches, their houses and all. And they don't fight strong. But when they're out and calling *you* out, they don't run home soon, neither. They're in their crowd and they'll swarm you and you'll drown. Live and let live, I say. But

that's been broke into two by this lot and we don't know
where we are. They maybe look like they've run. I'd say
different.

ROSIE [*frightened*]: Then what'll happen, Sailor?

SAILOR [*shrugs*]: Huh ... There's just us, and there's *all* o'
them. That's what'll happen. They're feared o' Big Rachel,
O.K. Begod they're that feard of her, they'll kill her. All of
us. Just cos we live.

ROSIE: What are we going to do?

SAILOR [*shrugs*]: I'll tell you what *I'll* do now. I'll get out the
back door of the house, over through the gardens, see are we
clear that road. If we are, I'll stop in at the Beer-off, get us
some bottles; give you the whistle; then we can *all* go.

RACHEL: Go where?

SAILOR: You tell me. Or if you're right, and they've run, we
can bide. But I'll have a see, first.

RACHEL: I'm coming, too.

SAILOR: Na na. You can wait. And one of you go out. D'ye
hear me?

  [*They grunt assent.*]

Right then: I'm off. Lock the doors till you hear me give the
whistle. I'll take some o' the empties while I'm on the job.
There's money on 'em. [*He gathers up some bottles and goes out
through the kitchen.*]

RACHEL: You heard what he said. Col, go lock that door
behind him.

DAFFODIL [*piteously*]: No Col, you stay wi' me.

ROSIE: I'll do it.

  [*She goes with Sally into the kitchen.* RACHEL *bolts and
  chains the front door.*]

ROSIE [*from the kitchen, in fear*]: Rachel!

RACHEL: What is it?

ROSIE: I can't lock this door!

RACHEL: Why not?

ROSIE: Old Croaker took the bolt off of it, Tuesday, and
there's one of the hinges broke!

RACHEL: Oh God, I'd forgot. There is and all! Well, shove

summat again it. The gas-stove, that. Wait, I'll help you. [*She goes into the kitchen. Then calls from thence:*] Col!

COL: Ah?

RACHEL: See all them windows is fast for God-sake. We don't want 'em climbing –

COL: O.K. You done yet, have you – [*to Daffodil.*]

DAFFODIL [*who has been wrapping a rag round his injured hand*]: Oh it's not tight, Col, it'll come off you again –

COL: Ah, leave it so.

[*The* OLD CROAKER *suddenly comes running down the stairs, at the top of which she has been sitting throughout the scene.*]

COL: Where d'you think you're off to, you silly old tortoise?

CROAKER: Fish-and-chip shop!

COL [*angrily*]: Fish-and-chip – You heard what Sailor said, din't you? Din't you?

CROAKER: Sailor. Ooh, Sailor's all afeared.

COL: Aye and so am I. And so ought you, you old –

CROAKER: Oh, *I'm* afeared. Ooh. Daffy. Where's my girl? Daffy?

DAFFODIL [*impatient*]: What is it she wants now?

CROAKER: Ah, Daffodil. She's my girl, she is. Daffy, are they coming for us – what he said?

COL: Coming, is it? They've bloody *come*!

DAFFODIL: Near tore him in bits, they did.

[RACHEL, ROSIE, *and* SALLY *come in from the kitchen.*]

RACHEL: That's the door done. What about the windows?

COL: Doing 'em now. [*He secures the windows, upstairs and down.*]

CROAKER: Will they come in through windows?

COL [*in disgust*]: Will they come in through windows.

CROAKER [*as if remembering something with a great effort*]: I know it – I know it –

DAFFODIL [*quickly*]: Now you don't know nothing.

CROAKER [*stubbornly*]: I know it how to do with windows. Close them up, fast. Feared of them, through the windows. Feared. Where's my Daffodil? You come do it with me.

DAFFODIL: No oh no, we're not having that. That's old rubbish, you don't want that.

CROAKER: Daffy, I'm feared. You do it with Croaker.

DAFFODIL: No, I'm not doing it with you. We're not having it.

RACHEL: Not having what?

DAFFODIL: All her old rubbish. Words and that. She says rhyming, see. It's not –

RACHEL: If she wants it, let her do it.

CROAKER: Who's do it with me? it's for two to do – one says, one follows – or it's not good.

RACHEL: Let the kid do it.

ROSIE: Hey, no –

RACHEL: Ach, it's all right. Let her help her.

CROAKER [*taking Sally*]: Little Sally, eh? Little lovey, we go to the window. This keep them out, the time they come. [*She flattens her palms on the glass of the hall window's unbroken pane.* SALLY *copies her, standing beside.* CROAKER *recites:*]

> Window close and window true
> In and out and who comes through?
> Mary and Jesus and the Twelve Tall Riders
> Nobody else nobody else nick nack noo!

Now you say it:
> Nobody else –

SALLY: Nobody else nobody else nick nack noo!

COL [*laughs*]: Eh that ought to hold 'em. If you'd told us that the first place, there'd have been no coppers here today!

DAFFODIL: It's all rubbish, I won't let her do it.

RACHEL: It don't do no harm. Go on, Croaker, do it all the windows, and the bloody doors and all, why not? [CROAKER *and* SALLY *go from window to window, reciting the rhyme.* ROSIE *goes into the living-room and rocks the baby in its pram. There is a knocking on the back door.*]

SAILOR [*offstage*]: Aaah! [*They all look at each other in fear.*]

181

Live Like Pigs

RACHEL: It's Sailor. Come and let him in.

[*She and* ROSIE *hurry into the kitchen.*]

SAILOR [*off*]: Quick, quick, open up! Aaah. [*After a moment, he comes in through the kitchen door, staggering. He has a wound on the side of his head. He drops a number of new bottles on the floor.*] No good. No good at all.

RACHEL: What's no good?

SAILOR: They're in the streets still. I got as far as the Beer-off, come out with the bottles, they see me in the street.

RACHEL: Hey hold up, what's the matter?

SAILOR: Let fire a stone at me.

ROSIE: Who did?

SAILOR: Oh, one o' them – out o' the dark – God knows. Stones. Yelling at the corner. It's no good us to try to run out again. They're all round the streets.

ROSIE: But what'll we do?

SAILOR [*shrugs*]: Huh . . . I know now what I'll do. [*He knocks the head off a bottle of spirit.*] All around in the streets. [*He swills a great gulp of the spirit; and then another.*] Ha ha, they don't know.

COL: Who don't know?

SAILOR: They don't know. That I'm a killer. *Do* they?

COL: Oh God, *that*.

SAILOR [*laughs bitterly*]: Aye aye, that. [*He sees Sally and Croaker still reciting, at the living-room window.*] What's *she* doing?

DAFFODIL [*nervously*]: It's like rhyming-words, she says it at the windows, Sailor.

SAILOR [*starting up*]: Ah na na, none o' that. Damned Finmark witching. That's the end of *that*, so leave it!

CROAKER [*as he drags her away from the window*]: Oh no, no –

SAILOR: Ah, so. You're feared, eh? But never mind, though. I'm a killer. [*He passes the bottle round.*]

RACHEL [*drinking*]: So we're in, and we wait.

[SAILOR *laughs bitterly. The baby cries.* ROSIE *sits and rocks the pram. It is now dark.*]

ROSIE [*sings*]:

Sleep, O sleepy babby, now
They sow the corn is after the plough
They reap the corn when it grows green
And grind the corn to make the bread
To grow the golden hair on your head,
Sleep, O sleepy babby, now.

Scene Seventeen

SONG

Afeared and waiting all the night
And never go to bed.
They've trampled on your shadow, Jack,
They'll trample on your head.

The morning comes, they all of them come,
Now fight them for your life:
They'll have you out and down and dead,
So fight fight fight for your life.

Before the Scene is discovered, as the song is ending, we hear the sounds of the house being attacked – shouts of a mob (much larger than in the previous scene) composed of both men and women – broken windows, etc.

Interior. Morning.
All the Sawneys are clustered together in the hall. The gramophone is playing the ragtime record. RACHEL *is leaning against the wall in exhaustion.* SALLY *is clutching Rosie's skirts, terrified.* ROSIE *holds the baby in her arms.* DAFFODIL *is huddled down in a corner beside the* OLD CROAKER, *whimpering.* SAILOR *sits on the bottom of the stairs, holding his head in his hands.* COL *screams through the letter box.*

COL: What are you trying to do at us? What are you trying to do at us? What are you trying –

MAN'S VOICE [*outside*]: We're going to get you out o' that house –

WOMAN'S VOICE [*outside*]: We're going to show you, by God, we're going to show you! What are you trying –

MAN'S VOICE [*outside*]: You bloody gipsies, we'll chuck you in the canal.

COL [*hopelessly*]: He's calling us Romanies. [*He shouts.*] Look, there's kids in this house –

ANOTHER WOMAN'S VOICE [*outside*]: Aye, and *we've* got kids and all. What about Mrs Jackson's lass?

[*There is an angry growl from the crowd outside.*]

COL: There's scores of 'em outside. We can't do nowt if they make a rush. [*He has a knife in his hand.*] I've got this, though. *I'll* let 'em know aren't I better nor any Romany with it.

SAILOR: He comes to me and he says – 'Sawney, who killed that Finn? There's only one man on this ship,' he says, 'has the strength to strangle that one. And I'm glad,' he says. 'He was the death of this ship.' Aye aye. Sawney has the strength . . .

ROSIE: It's his head still, where the stone hit him. Hey Sailor, wake up, it's *Rosie* – don't you know me –

SAILOR [*vaguely*]: Eh? What's that?

MAN'S VOICE [*outside*]: Chuck 'em in the canal.

COL: I think they're coming.

RACHEL [*taking deep breaths like a tired runner*]: Ah ah ah . . .

[*The noise outside grows, fitfully – as though the people were approaching the house a little, then withdrawing, then making a short rush – a gradual crescendo, cut into by the sound of the arrival of a Police-car with bell clanging.*]

COL [*runs from letter box to window*]: It's the coppers – look! The *coppers* coming –

RACHEL [*defiant*]: Let 'em come.

COL: Hey but no, they're in among the crowd. Eh begod, boys, I never thought I'd be glad for no damn coppers. Heh, I say, it's the coppers, for *us* – they're saving *us*, they're chasing them off! Eh Daffy, they're chasing 'em off –

[*Loud knocking at the door.*]

SERGEANT [*outside*]: Police!

[COL *moves to unbolt the door.*]

RACHEL [*checks him*]: No.

[*More knocking.*]

COL: Come on come on, we *got* to let 'em in now.

[*He opens the door and the* POLICE SERGEANT *comes in.* RACHEL *stops the gramophone.*]

SERGEANT [*looking round grimly*]: Well? . . . Once here, soon back again, eh? What's all this going on?

COL: They wor going to do us, that's what.

ROSIE: We're glad to see you, oh God, we're glad to see *you*, mister.

SERGEANT: Oh aye? They wor going to do you? And what were *you* going to do with that piece of ironmongery? Peeling onions I suppose. Were you?

[COL *drops his knife.*]

Aye. I should think so.

[*The* SERGEANT *turns in the doorway and calls to the crowd.*] Go on, clear away now, get moving! Saunderson, go round the back of the house and break up that mob in the garden. I've got summonses, you know, for anyone obstructing Officers! [*He turns back to the Sawneys.*] Now then. What's it all about?

MAN'S VOICE [*outside*]: They're bloody Gipsies, Sergeant. They've been mucking about with our lasses –

SERGEANT [*to the crowd*]: Go on. Go home!

[*He shuts the door.*]

Well?

SAILOR: Who is it? What does he want? . . . Why, he's a Peeler, stood there; he's a tall Bobby Peeler inside of Sawney's door! . . . [*He stands up, very tottery; but pertinacious.*] This is a house. They made me have a house and they put a door on it, and you can't come past that door without you're warranted. Right?

SERGEANT: Now don't you talk what you know nowt about, Sawney. *I'm* the one to say who's warranted. There's been a Breach of the Peace here this morning: I've reason to believe you've provoked it. So let's have no back-answers. You're now living in a law-abiding neighbourhood. Least, it has been for the last year or two, once the folk got settled down; and we don't want your lot stirring it up again.

RACHEL: Who stirs it up? They all but gelded my poor boy last evening – you don't stand and tell us –

SERGEANT: That'll do, missus. I'm going to have a proper look around this place for once. I ought to have done it yesterday, but there was other things was more important.

[*He goes upstairs.* SAILOR *follows him up.*]

SAILOR: You're not warranted. You got no right for this.

SERGEANT: I know my rights, old man: I don't need you to tell me.

[COL *goes into the living-room and starts hunting among the clutter.*]

COL: Here, where's my haversack – by –

SAILOR [*on stairs as the* SERGEANT *prowls in the bedrooms*]: I've got rights. I've got a house and I've got rights. I say you can't come here without you're warranted.

[SALLY *runs out of the kitchen with Col's haversack containing the drill.*]

SALLY [*whispers*]: Col, Col, here it is, Col.

COL [*runs out of living-room to her, whispering*]: Get that out of here –

[*They involve themselves in an awkward little huddle and the haversack drops on the floor. The* SERGEANT *sees them over the banisters.*]

SERGEANT: Hey hey, lad, what are *you* up to? Stay where you are.

[*He starts coming downstairs, but* SAILOR *gets in his way.*]

Let me past, will you –

[*The* SERGEANT *pushes past;* SAILOR *falls back down the stairs and lands at the bottom with a cry of pain.* ROSIE *runs to him.* DAFFODIL *snatches up the haversack, thrusts it at Col.*]

DAFFODIL: Col, Col, run boy, run!

[COL *gives a yelp of excitement, runs through the living-room, flings open the window.* DAFFODIL *comes after him, having tripped up the* SERGEANT, *who is not fully disentangled from Sailor.* COL *jumps through the window and pulls* DAFFODIL *after him. The* SERGEANT, *obstructed by* RACHEL, *follows as quick as he can. Instead of jumping out of the window, he leans out of it and blows his whistle, then calls to the Policeman in the back garden.*]

SERGEANT: Saunderson, hold that man! *Hold* him! Aah! . . . Well, get after them then! [*He hurries through the house and throws open the front door to call.*] Williams! There's a couple got away across the gardens with some sort of swag. Drive down to the main road. Try and cut 'em off. Saunderson's after them.

POLICEMAN [*outside*]: All right, Sergeant!

[*The Police-car is heard starting away.* SAILOR *lies writhing and groaning on the hall floor.*]

ROSIE [*to Sergeant*]: You've killed him, you have.

SERGEANT: Eh, what? Rubbish. Now come on, Sawney, stand up again, you're not hurt.

SAILOR [*hopelessly*]: My bad leg, it's my bad leg, done for me with my leg . . .

SERGEANT: Let's have a look at it. [*He handles Sailor's leg.* SAILOR *gasps and cries in agony. The* SERGEANT *seems rather disconcerted.*] H'm. Ha-h'm. Aye, well. There does seem to be some damage there. Your own fault, you know.

[*He goes to front door and calls out into the street.*]

SERGEANT: Hallo there, somebody! You, missus! Will you go and ring for an ambulance, please? There's a police-box on the corner. Say it's an old man with a broken leg. And tell 'em to look sharp. Right. [*He comes in again.*] It'll not be long. They'll have you in hospital, so lie still while it comes.

SAILOR [*sobbing his heart out*]: He's done for me. Rachel, he's done it, he's broke my leg and he's broke my life. He's broke my life, Rachel, it's all my glory, Rachel, it's all drank up and dry, it's all dry, it's all dry. Oh – oh – oh . . .

SERGEANT [*in a tired voice*]: I could take the lot of you in, you know – Obstructing Police, Stolen Goods, Breach of the Peace – but I doubt if it'd be worth while. You'll be getting a summons on the last of them charges, anyroad.

CROAKER: Where's my girl?

SERGEANT: Why you people can't live decent, I can't think.

CROAKER: She went off out of window. *I* know. Old Croaker,

she goes after . . . [*She giggles and moves towards the living-room.*]

SERGEANT: Oh shut up, mother, and stay put. She'll be fetched back soon enough.

CROAKER: Oh? Oooh. Copper.

[RACHEL *moves towards the front door and picks up a bundle from the floor.*]

SERGEANT: Where are you off to?

RACHEL: Northampton.

SERGEANT: Oh no you're not. I said there's summonses waiting.

RACHEL: Then they can chase me to Northampton, and that's all about it.

ROSIE [*fiercely*]: You bloody bide with Sailor, you!

SAILOR [*imploringly*]: Rachel –

RACHEL: Heh! An old man with a broken leg. He says 'Bide with me, Rachel!'

[*She laughs and goes out of the house. As she leaves she meets the* OFFICIAL *on the threshold.*] Come on in, Mister, I'm just out! [*She leaves, laughing.*]

SERGEANT [*to the Official*]: Good morning.

OFFICIAL [*who is carrying a little cat in his arms*]: Oh hullo, Sergeant. What's been happening here, for Goodness' sake?

SERGEANT: You might well ask. What can we do for you?

OFFICIAL: I, er, I'd come about this question of unauthorized lodgers, but –

SERGEANT: We're waiting for the ambulance.

OFFICIAL: Oh . . . You know, it's a nice little cat, isn't she? I found her in the road outside, she wor frightened to death by all them stamping women. I wonder who she belongs to? Timid, she is, eh? [*In a confidential tone, to the Sergeant.*] They'll *have* to go now, you know. I mean it's not just a question of lodgers, is it?

SERGEANT: H'm.

OFFICIAL: We don't *like* doing it, but –

[CROAKER *comes over to Sailor and crouches down beside his head.*]

CROAKER [*chants*]:

> Old Sailor's fallen down
> fallen down
> fallen down –

ROSIE: You leave him alone.

CROAKER: Ah, it's you and me, Sailor, we're the old bones, aren't we? They tear us all up, you see.

[*She sings:*]

> Old, old and thrown on the road,
> Washed away with the rain:
> Dig a hole and put them in
> And never come out again.

SALLY: Mary and Jesus and the Twelve Tall Riders.

CROAKER ⎱
SALLY ⎰ : Nobody else nobody else nick nack noo.

[CROAKER *laughs. The ambulance bell is heard approaching.*]

The Happy Haven

Written in collaboration with
Margaretta D'Arcy

First produced at the Royal Court Theatre, London, on 14 September 1960, with the following cast:

DR COPPERTHWAITE	Peter Bowles
MRS PHINEUS	Susan Engel
MRS LETOUZEL	Rachel Roberts
MR GOLIGHTLY	Barrie Ingham
MR HARDRADER	Nicholas Selby
MR CRAPE	Frank Finlay
ROBINSON LORD MAYOR	James Bolam
SMITH SIR FREDERICK HAPGOOD	Edward Fox
NURSE JONES LADY MAYORESS	Mary Watson
NURSE BROWN LADY FROM THE MINISTRY	Rosalind Knight

Directed by WILLIAM GASKILL

Author's Note

The play is intended to be given a formalized presentation. This involves the use of masks, which are worn as follows – the Five Old People wear character masks of the *commedia dell' arte* type, covering the upper part of their faces only. The Doctor does not wear a mask, except at the very end, when he is shown in one that covers his whole face, and represents himself as a child. The Nurses and Orderlies have their mouths and noses covered by hospital antiseptic masks.* The Distinguished Visitors wear masks similar to those of the Old People, but less individualized.

The Setting should suggest a Hospital atmosphere, not too clinical and rectilinear. The scenes are not localized to any particular rooms.

The Dog is to be imagined by the audience, but must be understood to be seen by all the characters on the stage – it is not a 'delusion'.

The stage directions are those used for the original production at Bristol University, when the play was presented on an open stage, following roughly the Elizabethan model. There were two doors opening from the back wall of the stage, with between them a recess closed by sliding doors, which accommodated the Doctor's laboratory equipment. Above this recess was a small upper stage. At the Royal Court, the play had of necessity to be played within the proscenium arch. This is a necessity that will doubtless be imposed upon most productions of *The Happy Haven* in this country, but it is none the less a regrettable one. The unsatisfactory organization of the English theatre in general and the archaic design of its buildings continually hamstring any attempts on the part of dramatists and directors to open out the conventions of the drama; and I must record my gratitude to Bristol University and its Department of Drama for making it possible to prove to myself that the leanings I have long had towards the open stage and its disciplines were justifiable in practice as

* It may be found more convenient if they only wear these in specifically 'clinical' scenes: otherwise, they are bare-faced.

Author's Note

well as in theory. I would urge anyone who wishes to produce this play to do so, if at all possible, on an Open Stage. Structural limitations may prevent the use of the upper stage: but it is not an essential part of the setting, and the scenes set on it may be brought down to the main acting level without undue difficulty.

Act One

Scene One

[DOCTOR COPPERTHWAITE *enters on upper stage and addresses the audience directly.*]

DOCTOR: Ah-hum. Good evening, ladies and gentlemen. First, let me say how glad I am to see you here and to extend a cordial welcome to the Happy Haven. We are, as you know, as yet only a small institution and our grant from the revenues of the National Health Service is alas not as generous as it might be – but, well, I dare say you'll know the old proverb – Time mends all. I'd like you to meet some of the old people who are in our care. As the phrase is, the evening of their lives – well, I've more to say about that later – but at present sufficient to indicate that this hospital for the amelioration of the lot of the aged is situated in pleasant rural surroundings, almost self-supporting – own produce, eggs, butter, and so on – within easy reach of London, and, I am happy to say, the most up-to-date facilities for both medical treatment and – most important of all from my point of view – research. I'm the Superintendent, my name's Copperthwaite, I've been here five years, and – er, yes, well, you want to meet the patients, don't you Nurse Brown, Nurse Jones. We're ready to meet the patients.

[*The* NURSES *enter and remove a screen on the main stage, which reveals the* OLD PEOPLE *all enjoying their party. The Old People have entered through the doors of the recess, which are closed before the screen is taken away.*]

We call them patients, but you'll understand they're not really ill, they're just old, you know, the passage of time, the gradual declension – it's a physical fact, you look at it scientifically, it all fits the picture – above all things in an establishment of this nature, *must* preserve the clinical approach: can't be too often stressed. We might say today is really an auspicious occasion for meeting these five old people. You see, the old lady in the middle is enjoying her ninetieth birthday, and, of course, there's a bit of a celebration. Shouldn't there be a cake, Nurse?

[NURSE BROWN *exits*.]

Right. Well, she's going to cut the cake and they'll congratulate her. She's our oldest, Mrs Phineus her name is, and she's been a widow for twenty years.

[*Enter* NURSE BROWN *with cake. She carries it to Mrs. Phineus, and puts the knife into her hand*.]

Now here's the cake, and here's the knife to cut it: and Mrs Phineus is just about to cut it; and she's *cut* it!

[*As* MRS PHINEUS *cuts the cake, the* NURSES *and* OLD PEOPLE *all clap*.]

Now they're all about to congratulate Mrs Phineus in the traditional fashion.

OLD PEOPLE [*sing*]:

> Happy birthday to you
> Happy birthday to you
> Happy birthday, Mrs Phineus,
> Happy birthday to you.

[*The cake is cut up by* NURSE BROWN *and a piece handed to each patient*.]

DOCTOR: And the party is in full swing. While they're all enjoying themselves, it would perhaps be appropriate if I were to give a brief resumé of their names, ages, and case histories.

[*He refers to a sheaf of notes*.]

We'll start with Mrs Phineus – not much to be said about her, general condition remarkably promising considering her years. Some obstruction recorded in the condensers, sandbox apertures require occasional overhaul, but by and large answers very well to her regulator. Now then: number two. On Mrs Phineus's right we have Mr Golightly, seventy-five years old, bachelor, very good state of preservation. Fitted six years ago with improved Walschaerts valve-gear replacing original Stephenson's link motion, and injectors also recently renewed. Latent procreative impulses require damping down on the firebox, but less so than formerly. Next one, number three, on Mrs Phineus's left, you will observe the only other female member, Mrs Letouzel. Aged seventy, all moving parts in good condition, cross-head pins perhaps slightly deteriorated, and occasional trouble from over-heated bearings when financial gain is in question. General report, extremely favourable. Now next to her we have Mr Hardrader, number four, our best running specimen. Very firm original design in smokebox and blast pipe has resulted in continual first-class steaming conditions. Age eighty-eight on the thirteenth of next month. Finally, on the extreme left, you will see Mr Crape. There has been here an unfortunate case history of overall deterioration, but last year was given a complete refit, including elongated smokebox, revised cylinder-head design, and replacement of obsolete perforated splashers. Age is now seventy-nine. There is still a tendency to over-exceed the power-potential beyond nominal capacity, but provided this can be overcome – well, I think we can say, further outlook quite hopeful. This is about all I can usefully tell you at the moment. Their little party is well under way, though they mustn't be allowed to get too excited –

OLD PEOPLE [*sing*]:

> Knees up, mother Brown
> Knees up, mother Brown
> Knees up, knees up, don't get the breeze up,
> Knees up, mother Brown.

DOCTOR: I think we'd better tactfully put an end to the evening now, a little kicking over the traces goes a long way at this age.

[OLD PEOPLE'*s song repeated.*]

Ye-es, I think so. Nurse. I think that had better be all, Nurse. Off to bed, boys and girls, you're half an hour late as it is, burning the candle at both ends, y'know, have to go easy, don't we, that's the way, off to bed now, Nurse. Good night, good night, boys and girls. If you've not ate your cake yet, you can take it to bed and finish it there. That's right.

OLD PEOPLE: Good night, Doctor.

DOCTOR: Good night.

[*Exeunt* NURSES, *taking in* OLD PEOPLE – *each one holding half-eaten slice of cake.*]

And for the time being, that's that. Now the next thing, ladies and gentlemen, is my laboratory. I dare say it would be of interest if I were to give you some short exposition of the type of research I'm at present engaged in? Smith, Robinson.

[ORDERLIES *enter on main stage.*]

Get the lab ready, will you? Thank you very much.

[*Exeunt* ORDERLIES, *into recess.*]

If you'll just wait one moment, ladies and gentlemen – I'll be with you directly.

[*Exit* DOCTOR. ORDERLIES *re-enter on main stage, wheeling out from the recess the lab bench with its equipment. As they place it in position, the* DOCTOR *enters on the main stage.*]

We can call it the next morning now, and this is my morning routine – every morning, very early, before the patients have their breakfast, just about the time they're beginning to be washed. This is also, I suppose, how shall I call it, well, you will no doubt best understand me if I say, that this is the one true 'Ratio Operandi', the 'Reductio ad Quem', the – oh I don't know – the overriding purpose and ambition of my work in this hospital. My research. My project. My daily work for the full five years I've been Superintendent here. To quote, somewhat tentatively, a literary example as being perhaps most appropriate for this audience, you can call me if you like, a Doctor Faustus of the present generation. It's not an exact parallel – Faustus sold his soul to the devil, I believe. I'm selling mine to nobody. But what I have here or what I shall have here, ladies and gentlemen, is nothing less, or will be nothing less, than the Elixir of life – of Life, and of Youth. I haven't got it yet. Now I'm near, I'm extremely near, oh I can tell you that, in certainty. Perhaps this very morning will prove the last of all the mornings I've had to stand in this lab, and calculate, and attempt, and slowly progress, experiment by experiment, formula by formula. Those five old people you saw go to bed last night are to be the raw material upon which I shall work. They don't know it yet, but they are. If I am successful, and the Elixir is found – *Copperthwaite's Elixir* – or might I call it the Happy Haven Elixir – the institution is greater than the man – *if* I am successful; then those five old people will not be at the end of their established term of years, but at the beginning! They will be able, they will be able, to be completely reborn! To any age we may see fit to lead them. Think of that. Think of that! . . . But let us preserve our professional detachment. The experiment, ladies and gentlemen, is by no means over yet. [*He turns to his bench.*] We'll have a look at it now. Notebooks please.

[ORDERLY SMITH *hands him books as he names them.*]
Number thirty-two, thirty-three, thirty-five-A, and the current one. Thank you. Experiment Number One; two-eight-six, Stage Four. Are you all paying attention, I want you to take particular note of the equipment mounted here, and containing, in the vessel, the solution derived from yesterday's work, reading nine-by-three by four-and-a-half scantlings, ledged braced battened and primed. This solution is now cool, yes, it's cool, and it has been allowed to stand for twenty-two hours. I term this the secondary or tensile state of leading. To it I am about to add nought point three-double-six degrees of *this* [*He holds up a second retort, also with liquid in it*] – which is a five-eighth screed, three parts three-sixteenth aggregate, one-and-a-half parts plastic terrazzo. The resulting precipitate will then be heated for three hundred and twelve seconds, all headers, stretchers, and squints removed by oxidization: and then I – and *then*, why perhaps *then* – ah, well, we'd better take it as it comes, hadn't we? [*He pours the second liquid into the first.*] Bunsen burner, please.

[ORDERLY ROBINSON *lights the burner.*]
I want absolute quiet. This is very tense, very delicate.

Thank you. Before heating I add the necessary trimmers and binding members. Number four.

[ORDERLY ROBINSON *hands him a test-tube of liquid which he pours into retort.*]

DOCTOR: Number eight.

[*Similar business.*]

Twelve-B.

[*Similar business.*]

Eighteen. Eighteen ... where's number eighteen? Come on, come on! God's sake, Robinson, have these things ready –

[*Similar business, rather flurried.*]

Now then, timing dial. Thank you.

[ORDERLY SMITH *hands him large stop-watch.*]

DOCTOR [*reads the seconds off stop-watch*]: Three-twelve. Three-ten. Three-eight. Six. Four. Two, one, three *hundred*.

[ORDERLY ROBINSON *has taken the retort and is holding it over bunsen while* DOCTOR *calls the time. Every twelve seconds – indicated by* DOCTOR *jerking up his arm – he whips retort away from flame and agitates rapidly in the air, then holds it back again above bunsen.*]

This is done every twelve seconds exactly, to prevent coagulation of sediment. After the first hundred seconds, we do it every five. Two-nine-four. Two-nine-two. Two-ninety. Two eighty-*eight*.

[*Mixture agitated again.*]

All right so far. Seems to be all right. This is the most dangerous part though. ... Two eighty-four. Two-eight-two. Two hundred and eighty –

[CRAPE *enters.*]

CRAPE: Er, excuse me, Dr Copperthwaite –

DOCTOR [*whirling round, startled*]: Eh, *what*! What is it, what are you doing here –

CRAPE: Excuse me if I interrupted. Doctor –

DOCTOR: *Interrupted!* You bloody dog, get out! [*He looks at the retort.*] Oh my God: coagulated. The whole damn thing's coagulated. It's no damn good at all. Clear it out, clear away, it's three weeks' consolidated work, oh no, it's nothing, no –

it's all the luck of the game, *isn't* it, you interfering old – [*He pulls himself together.*] Eh, what's the use. I'm sorry, ladies and gentlemen. I'm afraid you're disappointed. We didn't reach it after all. But we will. Very shortly. It's a long road that has no turning, as they say. We all find these little set-backs. Don't we?

[*The* ORDERLIES *have wheeled away the bench, etc., into the recess.*]

Cleared away, Smith? Good. I'm not doing any more this morning. Tomorrow we'll start again at Number One-two-eight-one, Stage two. All right? And tell Sister that I want all male patients to be given an enema before this evening. I'm a little alarmed about the state of their blood-streams. There seem to be symptoms of mortification. . . . Thank you.

[*Exeunt* ORDERLIES.]

You know very well I am never available to patients when I am working in the laboratory, Mr Crape. So what do you want?

CRAPE: I do beg your pardon, Doctor, if I in any way intruded – of course we're all of us aware how important your work is –

DOCTOR: Are you? There are rules in this hospital, you know, and they're meant to be obeyed –

CRAPE: Oh naturally, naturally, Doctor, I do indeed apologize yes – but this is as you might say special, as a matter of fact, a delicate question, you see –

DOCTOR: And why can't it wait till a more normal time? There are stated hours for making complaints about the other patients, as you know perfectly well, Mr Crape – you take advantage of them often enough.

CRAPE: But Doctor, in these cases, one is often impelled to, well, like, to break with decorum, on account of the im-portance of imperceptibility – I mean, I don't want to be seen here, do I? I mean, bad for the value of our little talks, Doctor – after all it *is* only out of loyalty to the hospital, eh?

DOCTOR: All right, all right . . . So what has Mrs Letouzel

been up to this time? I hope it isn't more pilfering. I told them to see that the collecting box for the spastic children had a padlock put on to it. Hasn't it been done?

CRAPE: Oh yes, yes, I think so, Doctor, yes – it's not about Mrs Letouzel really this morning. Mr Hardrader.

DOCTOR: Well?

CRAPE: He's still got it, you know. He takes it for walks.

DOCTOR: In the hospital?

CRAPE: Not exactly, no . . . but –

DOCTOR: In the grounds then?

CRAPE: Well to be quite frank, Doctor, I am not entirely sure –

DOCTOR: Mr Crape, I see nothing whatever to prevent Mr Hardrader possessing a bull-terrier or any other sort of dog, provided he does not infringe my regulations by keeping it on the premises. If you can't bring evidence to show that that *is* what he's doing, then you can please stop wasting my valuable time! Is there nothing else? Are they satisfied with their diet? There's far too much of a tendency for grumblings and grumblings and nobody ever tells me – one has to know these things – Well?

CRAPE: I think Mrs Phineus sometimes gets into the larders when there's no one about – Mrs Letouzel said she keeps a pot of strawberry jam under her bedclothes, but I don't think it can be very likely –

DOCTOR: I suppose a pot of jam won't do her any harm: but it could be a dangerous precedent . . . all right, Mr Crape. That'll do for now. Off you go to breakfast.

CRAPE: Oh, but Doctor, I've just thought –

DOCTOR: Off to breakfast, Mr Crape, I've a great deal to attend to this morning –

CRAPE: You asked about Mrs Letouzel. There *is* something, you know. It's about what she is, Doctor. That old woman – she's a Spy.

DOCTOR: Spy?

CRAPE: That's right.

> Ooh, Doctor, she's a greedy Spy
> Ooh, Doctor, she's so sharp and sly!

And what she wants to find out, Doctor, find out, here ...
[*He makes a series of gestures around him and towards where the bench, etc., have been taken out.*]

DOCTOR: Now please, let's have it in English.

CRAPE: Sh-ssh ... I'll whisper it. She wants, to find out, what it is, you're at!

DOCTOR: I dare say she does. Anything else?

CRAPE: Isn't that enough? Of course we all know the importance of your work –

DOCTOR: How?

CRAPE: How?

DOCTOR: Yes, Mr Crape. *How* do you know my work is so important?

CRAPE: Why ... it stands to reason, Doctor. I was saying to Mr Golightly only the other day – 'Dr Copperthwaite, Mr Golightly, is what they term an Intellectual – he's a real scientist,' I said. 'And what he does in his Laboratory, I'll wager you nor I couldn't come near comprehending it, not if we tried for twenty years.' Could we, Doctor? It stands to reason.

DOCTOR: H'm.

CRAPE: Now you and me, Doctor –

DOCTOR: Mr Crape, you have been talking for nearly ten minutes, you have told me absolutely nothing: and you *ruined* my experiment! I don't want to see you again for a very long time.

[*Exit* DOCTOR.]

CRAPE: Ah, disappointing. What we might term a disappointing devolution? But they aren't all, you know – oho no. There's times when I've been able to learn that Doctor some most remarkable things, yes: *he* knows my value. [*He sings:*]

The darkening age of James J. Crape
Yet burns with one surviving fire:
To see the old fools all a-shiver and a-quiver
At the secret probings of my power!

Oi-oi, what's this? [*His eye falls on a loose leaf which has fallen from the Doctor's notebook at the time of the interruption, and has lain unnoticed on the floor. He picks it up.*] The Doctor's dropped his – hey, Doctor! Doctor! Doctor, you've dropped your – he doesn't hear me, I'm too late. Good. [*He has called in a careful diminuendo, ending in a whisper.*] Not but what there's much advantage to be gained out o' *this*, I don't imagine. Signs, calculations, arithmetics, algebras, squared paper, crossing out – real Doctor's handwriting, too – I can't hardly read it. . . . 'Optimum ages and reduced minimum of estimated reductions – thirty years, forty years, fifty –' A list of names – oho . . . 'Letouzel, Phineus, Hardrader, Golightly – *Crape*.' Well: I don't know what it is, and I don't like it. But it's got *their* names on, as well as mine. Forewarned is forearmed. I'd call it worth preserving.

[ORDERLY ROBINSON *enters.* CRAPE *whips the paper into his coat.*]

Oh, Mr Robinson, er, looking for something? Left something behind? No . . . no, nothing here . . . but I'll keep a sharp eye – ha ha, good morning . . .

[*Exit* ORDERLY.]

This place isn't safe. I'd better make meself scarce. I'll go and find Letouzel – see what the old nutmeg-grater's plotting today. Maybe something there to advantage? Ha ha . . . maybe . . . [*He goes out singing.*]

      All a-quiver and a-shiver

      At the secret probings of my power . . .

Scene Two

[*A* VOICE *over the loudspeaker.*]

VOICE: Mr Golightly, please. Mr Golightly to report to Sister's office. Mr Golightly, if you please.

[*Enter* MRS LETOUZEL *pushing* MRS PHINEUS *in her wheelchair.*]

PHINEUS: Yes . . . I think I do, yes.

LETOUZEL: No, dear, no.

PHINEUS: Yes.

LETOUZEL: It comes more expensive.

PHINEUS: No.

LETOUZEL: Oh yes it does, dear, much more expensive. Besides, it's better to drink Indian. Not so much tannin.

PHINEUS: I beg your pardon, Mrs Letouzel?

LETOUZEL: I said Indian tea, dear, does not contain so much tannin. The China tea is very corrosive, you see.

PHINEUS: Corrosive?

LETOUZEL: To the intestines, dear. It corrodes them.

PHINEUS: Yes . . . I spoke to Dr Copperthwaite. He said I could have China tea if I asked for it. He said so. I want it.

LETOUZEL: It's much more expensive.

PHINEUS: Yes.

LETOUZEL: I'll see about it. Next week. . . . Oh, by the way, dear, I wonder if you wouldn't mind putting your name on this. [*She produces a document and a fountain-pen.*]

PHINEUS: Oh dear . . . what?

LETOUZEL: Your usual signature, you just write it *here*. We have to make sure that your Anglo-Ethiopian Copper Shares remain well consolidated, don't we?

PHINEUS: I don't quite understand . . .

LETOUZEL: Consolidated, dear. If we are to spend so much more on having China tea, we must preserve for our investments a degree of consolidation, you know. Sign here, dear.

PHINEUS [*signing*]: Yes . . . yes . . .

LETOUZEL [*sings to the audience*]:
One thousand pounds she thought that she could save.
For no true need, you see:
Indeed for naked greed.
The State will pay to dig her narrow grave.
[*She takes the document back.*] That's right, dear . . . thank you. I shall send it to the Solicitor's by the afternoon post. Here is the letter to go with it. [*She produces a letter.*] Would you like to read it over? It refers to your quarterly payments to Dr Copperthwaite, you know he has put his fees up this summer, don't you?

PHINEUS: Has he? Oh dear. I expect it will be because of the extra cost of the tea. . . . No, no, I don't want to read it, Mrs Letouzel, I'm afraid it might perturb me . . . must I put my name?

LETOUZEL: If you don't mind, dear. Here.

PHINEUS [*signing*]: Yes . . . yes . . .

LETOUZEL [*sings as before*]:
> One thousand pounds she thought that she could save.
> For no true need, you see:
> Indeed for China tea.
> A marble teapot should adorn her grave.
>
> [*She takes the letter back and puts it together with the other document into an envelope, closes it, but does not seal.*]

PHINEUS: Is Mr Golightly coming to see me this afternoon, do you imagine?

LETOUZEL: I've no idea, I'm sure. He usually contrives to. So I expect he will today. . . . Oh by the way, dear, you've forgotten your contribution for the Spastic Children Fund, haven't you? Dr Copperthwaite wants all of us to be regular contributors, you know. [*She produces from the recesses of her clothing a small oblong collection box which she presents.*] Half a crown, dear.

> [MRS PHINEUS *finds a coin after much fumbling in her huge knitting bag.*]

LETOUZEL [*sings to the audience during the fumbling*]:
> One thousand pounds she thought that she could save.
> The children's need, you see,
> To me is dear indeed.
> This narrow box more fruitful than the grave.

Thank you, dear. Tired? Yes. Why don't we have a nice rest, that's right, close your eyes, dear, a nice rest . . . yes . . . [*She wheels her away.*]

Scene Three

[*Enter* GOLIGHTLY.]

GOLIGHTLY: Ah, well, thank goodness that's over for today.

206

Undignified, yes, but alas, you will tell me, necessary. Dr Copperthwaite says necessary, a good working bowel is the foundation of a good working life. Even in the evening of our days the heart may – may it not? – beat its wings a little, unencumbered by the more brutish obstructions. It will shortly be time for my cup of tea with Mrs Phineus. You understand that most days she condescends to receive me, and – a cup of tea, a Bath-bun, or Eccles-cake, a few mild words of tender and respectful intercourse, and if she is so minded – a little sport or game, a gay twenty minutes. Sometimes dominoes, sometimes spillikins, sometimes halma – *today* – ha ha – [*He produces a small dartboard from under his coat*] I have obtained permission, with some difficulty, for this. Darts, in a hospital, may be said to be hazardous. But I pressed the point. I emphasized to the Doctor that my skill was considerable and there would be no damage. Mrs Phineus can't play darts. But if I can teach her, shall I not in some manner be putting her in my debt, and is not that an enviable state for a yearning heart? Hey? Let's hang it up. [*He hangs the board on the rear wall of the stage.*] Now then: three darts – let's see what we can score. [*He throws the darts. They all miss the board.*] Oh. Never mind. Practice makes perfect. Try, try again. [*He throws them again. They all hit the board but with a very low score. He quickly takes the two worst and improves their position.*] Ye-es. Well, we'll call that one bull, one twenty – oh, we'll allow this one, a five – not so good, but it *got* there. [*He now pretends to talk to his opponent.*] Your turn, Mrs Phineus – no, no, dear lady, hold it so, the helping hand, the tentative touch on the shoulder – ah dear, dear dear, balance, above all, *balance*! Splendid! Splendid! Next time they'll *all* be on the board. Remarkable progress for such a beginner. . . . Perhaps we're a little tired? Tea? Oh, *tea*, Mrs Phineus – how very kind, certainly, dear lady, or may I use a more familiar name? This tender moment, Margaret, this – oh Margaret, all my life, all my life I have waited for such a – Margaret, I melt, I weep, forgive me, my presumption, so sweet, so tender, oh so very vulnerable and in need of my protection, dearest love, my heart, my chick, my chuck, princess of pulchritude – oh love, dear love –

[*In his emotion he is now kneeling at an imaginary pair of feet.* MRS LETOUZEL *enters wheeling* MRS PHINEUS *in her chair.* MRS PHINEUS *is asleep.*]

GOLIGHTLY: Oh, good gracious, how do you do, dear lady – Mrs Letouzel – I seemed to have broken a shoelace. Careless, but undaunted, I should wear elastic-sided boots, should I not?

LETOUZEL: Ssh, she's asleep.

GOLIGHTLY: Oh.

LETOUZEL: Do you think I could have a word with you, Mr Golightly? Now, quickly, before she wakes up? She'll be asking for her tea.

GOLIGHTLY: Ah, yes, her tea –

LETOUZEL: How does it go?

GOLIGHTLY: I beg your pardon?

LETOUZEL: You: her: how does it go? Let's play the Truth game – we're old enough, aren't we?

> Truth or Lie, till the day I die
> Strike you dead if you tell me a lie.

Come on, Mr Golightly, oho come on, rogue, *I* know the tickling heart. Who's the discreet one – you or me? Who sends her tea in every day and always asks the nurse for two cups? Who contrives the Eccles-cakes or Bath-buns on her plate and sees that always there's an *even* number? Who's your fairy-godmother, Mr Golightly? Dr Copperthwaite – or me? Oh come on – come on, you rogue –

GOLIGHTLY: You put me to a confusion, Mrs Letouzel, I had not realized that I was so apparent. . . .

LETOUZEL: The tender heart calls to the tender heart, you know. Yes: but: ah no: no, no: yet, but: I *do* wonder . . .

GOLIGHTLY: You wonder?

LETOUZEL: If perhaps I haven't been a half-inch stupid, a quarter-inch too easily swung, by sentiment maybe – she will eat you up.

GOLIGHTLY: Eat me?

LETOUZEL: What happened to *Mister* Phineus?

GOLIGHTLY: Mister? Why, post-operative complications following an appendicectomy, I understood.

LETOUZEL: Yes. But complications; not always organic, are they?

GOLIGHTLY: What? but –

LETOUZEL: I am saying not a thing. Only reflecting. I see you: and I see her, and ah, it's not always so good to be too warm and trusting. The trusting heart, the fallen fledgling.

GOLIGHTLY: Mrs Letouzel, really, I must protest. These are insinuations, yes, that is what they are, dear lady, I'm sorry, but there is no other word. And in fairness to Mrs Phineus I must ask you either to keep them to yourself, or at least not behind her back, or in the long run to establish evidence, madam, but not just to *toss* – this broadcasting, this subversive, this cruel undermining – I must insist, madam: *no!*

[MRS PHINEUS *wakes.*]

LETOUZEL: Ssh, she's awake.

PHINEUS: It is now half past four.

LETOUZEL: Not quite yet, my dear. Twenty past.

PHINEUS: Eh.

LETOUZEL: Twenty past. Twenty past four, dear.

PHINEUS: No. Half past. I never make a mistake about the time. When I wake up I know to the moment the exact hour of the day. Your watch must be slow, dear Mrs Letouzel. Ten minutes. Yes.

GOLIGHTLY: You are quite right, Mrs Phineus. It *is* half past four.

PHINEUS: I beg your pardon – I am a little hard of hearing – ah, Mr Golightly, how very agreeable to see you this afternoon and what a pleasant surprise. Yes. You're quite right, it is half past. Dear Mrs Letouzel, as you go out, perhaps you would be so kind as to ask nurse to bring in my tea. Mr Golightly, will you join me? I do hope so. Two cups, my dear. You just ask the nurse. Yes.

[*Exit* MRS LETOUZEL.]

The Happy Haven

PHINEUS: Sit beside me, Mr Golightly.

GOLIGHTLY: Shall we have our little game, before tea, my dear lady.

PHINEUS: I beg your pardon? I'm a little hard of –

GOLIGHTLY: I said would you like to play our –

PHINEUS: Oh no, I don't think so today, I am very tired of dominoes. Dr Copperthwaite says that the black and white, so often repeated, must eventually affect my eyes. Yes.

GOLIGHTLY: Not dominoes today.

PHINEUS: No, no, not dominoes. Dear Mrs Letouzel will send in the nurse and she shall bring us tea.

GOLIGHTLY: I thought you might prefer to play –

PHINEUS: I have asked this week for neither Bath-buns nor Eccles-cake, but a small tomato sandwich. One has to consider the intake of protein. Dr Copperthwaite does not seem very aware of the danger of starch in my diet. I have spoken to him about it. Yes. Twice.

GOLIGHTLY: To play *darts*?

PHINEUS: I beg your pardon?

GOLIGHTLY: Darts? You see, there is the board all ready for us. Three darts and they're very light and easy to throw. Perhaps if I could demonstrate –

PHINEUS: No no. Not dominoes today. Hopscotch.

GOLIGHTLY: Hopscotch?

PHINEUS: Yes. You see, you must mark out the floor – and then – oh we're neither of us too old to jump here – and then there. Are we? No. Dr Copperthwaite says I must leave my chair for a good half hour every day. Give me a piece of chalk.

GOLIGHTLY: Oh, chalk? Well I should have a piece –

PHINEUS: I have a piece. [*She takes a huge piece of chalk out of her enormous reticule.*] Mark out the squares.

GOLIGHTLY: I don't think I quite remember how –

PHINEUS: I do. [*She jumps out of her wheel-chair and points out the position of the squares on the stage for him, moving with surprising agility, and always being a couple of moves in front of him.*] One there.

GOLIGHTLY [*drawing hastily*]: Here?

PHINEUS: Then two. Here.

GOLIGHTLY: Here?

PHINEUS: There.

GOLIGHTLY: Oh. Here.

PHINEUS: Then three. Three there.

GOLIGHTLY: Here.

PHINEUS: Three more. More.

GOLIGHTLY: Yes.

PHINEUS: Two.

GOLIGHTLY [*puffed*]: Oh ha hoo – Two.

PHINEUS: And one. And one. And one, here. Here. Here. One there. There.

GOLIGHTLY: And one and one and one ... would you like first turn?

PHINEUS: No, you.

GOLIGHTLY: Are you quite sure you wouldn't –

PHINEUS: Go on. Go on. Hop!

GOLIGHTLY: But shouldn't there be a stone, or a tin, to – to kick?

PHINEUS: What have you got?

GOLIGHTLY [*produces a matchbox*]: This?

PHINEUS: No.

GOLIGHTLY [*produces spectacle-case*]: This?

PHINEUS: No. No.

GOLIGHTLY [*produces gold cigarette-case*]: Well, all I have left is –

PHINEUS: That one. Yes.

GOLIGHTLY: But, dear lady, it's real gold –

PHINEUS: Very pretty. That one. Yes. Now hop.

GOLIGHTLY [*hopping with difficulty*]: One: and two: and – [*He rests on both feet.*]

PHINEUS: No no no! Not to rest yet. One foot, only. *This* square, you can rest.

GOLIGHTLY: Oh dear. Yes. Ah ... Ah ... Oh dear. [*He falls down.*] I don't think I can quite –

PHINEUS: My turn. The rules are strict, you see. Not to rest

except in the outside square. *My* turn now. [*She hops.*]
One. Two. Oh . . . Oh . . . Three! I'm allowed a rest. [*She rests.*]

GOLIGHTLY: No.

PHINEUS: Yes. The second time, you see. This is the *second* hop. So we have extra rests. Yours was the *first* hop, wasn't it?

GOLIGHTLY: But this is the first hop *you've* had.

PHINEUS: No. In the whole game: the *second* hop. Now then: [*She hops farther.*] One two three. Ah . . . Ah . . . A little rest, here. Yes. Now then: one two three. I'm allowed another rest. Here. Yes. This is the second hop. Now then: one two three – [*She accidentally kicks the cigarette-case out of play: but picks it up and puts it in the final square.*] Home! I won. I won. I won. I won. Yes. I won. I won. I won. Yes. I won. I won. I won. Yes. I won. I won. I won.

GOLIGHTLY: No!

PHINEUS: I *won*.

GOLIGHTLY: But you used your fingers. Picked it up with your fingers. It has to be *kicked*.

PHINEUS: No. No. The second hop: you see. Those are the rules.

GOLIGHTLY: Oh? Are they? Oh. I didn't quite remember them like that, I must say, but –

PHINEUS: Shall we have tea? Yes.

[*Enter* NURSE JONES *with tea-things.*]

Here it is. I thought it would come now. Thank you so much, Nurse. So very kind.

[NURSE JONES *helps her back into her chair, and then leaves.*]

I'm mother, am I not? Yes. So while I pour the tea, dear Mr Golightly, perhaps you would sing to me? It would be so kind. Yes. The melancholy song, perhaps.

GOLIGHTLY: Oh, please, not that one – I had really rather not . . .

PHINEUS: The melancholy one. It begins, you know how it begins – about the Sea Captain who steers his ship in vain,

and then about the whales. You remember, don't you?
Sing it. Yes.

[*She attends to the tea-things.*]

GOLLGHTLY: As you wish, dear lady – [*He sings.*]

> It is in vain the bold sea-captain
> Steers his ship toward a star
> The world turns round, the star is turning,
> His voyage wanders wide and far.

> He cannot mark the course he's taking
> His eyes are blind with salty scale.
> The storm destroys his very heart root
> As tears the harpoon through the whale.

> The whalefish dies in a bloodred whirlpool
> The sailor dies on the frozen strand.
> Washed up by waves for years that drove him
> Brought him at last to an unknown land.

> The life of man is lost and lonely,
> Whereas the porpoise and the whale
> They both have meaning and conclusion –

[*The song loses coherence.*]

> But he finds no meaning nor conclusion
> He finds no meaning nor –
> Whereas the porpoise and the whale –

I don't believe it! have always said love, Mrs Phineus, I have
always believed it, I must still believe it, you cannot but
credit that I have always certainly held to it, and even if
without true experience, look, I have never really been able
to put it to the proof – oh my dear, dear Mrs Phineus, I have
never killed a whale, I have never *seen* a whale, nor yet
travelled on a ship, except to the Isle of Wight when my
sister lived in Shanklin – but, Love, it must surely be Love,
there is a star that will not turn, I have had faith in this, for
years, years, please, it must be true, *Love* is the meaning, say
it is the conclusion – say it say it – *please!* . . . . Why, you've
finished up all the tea, Mrs Phineus.

The Happy Haven

PHINEUS: Oh no, not all of it. Surely not.

GOLIGHTLY: But then, I suppose, I suppose, why not? Is it not your prerogative? Indeed, dear lady, are you not fully entitled – perhaps there is just a little bit left at the bottom of the pot? Oh dear, oh dear. Well then ... And after all she brought very few sandwiches, and small ones, small ... Perhaps I may have eaten one without actually noticing? I *do* feel quite full, as though I *had* had tea. I am quite absent-minded. Yes.

PHINEUS: Yes.

GOLIGHTLY: Yes?

PHINEUS: I am particularly partial to tomato sandwiches. I am so glad that you are as well.

[*Enter* NURSES *and* MRS LETOUZEL.]

LETOUZEL: Time for your bath, dear. Isn't it, Nurse? Half past five, dear.

PHINEUS: No. Five and twenty to six. I always know the time. I always know the time. I don't think I wish to have my bath tonight. No bath tonight, no bath tonight. No –

LETOUZEL: Oh but you must, dear, you must have your bath –

PHINEUS: No, no, no, no, no bath tonight –

[*Protesting in panic, she is wheeled out by the* NURSES.]

GOLIGHTLY: Give her a bath. Give her a bath. Hot, seething, pitch and brimstone. That's what she deserves. Cruel. Oh: here, here, there's a fish hook, here – [*He touches his throat.*] She's jerking it, tugs at it! Cruel!

LETOUZEL: It's true what I said then?

GOLIGHTLY: I would ask you not to concern yourself, madam, with what is not your concern. Permit me, if you please, to confine my misery to my own private bosom.

[*Exit.* MRS LETOUZEL *then sits down and takes out her collection box and documents. She starts looking over these, making ticks with a pen, etc.*]

LETOUZEL [*as* GOLIGHTLY *leaves*]: Ye-es, well, now that the interference seems to be at least temporarily eliminated,

perhaps we'd better check our current totals, h'm? . . .
'One thousand pounds she thought that she could save . . .'
[*Enter* CRAPE *creeping up behind her. He starts singing, and she jumps to her feet, whipping the documents, etc., out of sight.*]

CRAPE [*sings*]:

> There was an old woman in our town
> In our town did dwell
> And she grafted in a thousand pounds
> But she wanted more as well.

LETOUZEL: Highly diverting, Mr Crape, but it would be more to your credit if –

CRAPE [*laughing fit to split*]:

> Whip she larey tidifoo larey
> Whip she larey oh
> She grafted in a thousand pounds
> But she –

LETOUZEL: I said I had no doubt it is highly diverting, but you don't astonish me, Mr Crape: and particularly I am not astonished to find you creeping about, behind a lady's back, in carpet slippers. It's all of a piece. Go to the devil.

CRAPE: That's a very disagreeable sentiment, Mrs Letouzel. I prefer to ignore it. . . . Heh, ha ha, I see you sent off our little Golightly with a good sharp nip to his backend. Crabs' claws or lobsters', eh? [*He picks up her hand and examines her fingers.*] They look a bit blue, dear. I'd call it lobsters. . . . Let's play the Truth Game. Old Mrs Phineus's thousand pounds isn't as easy to get at as you thought it ought to be? A snippet here, a snippet there, but no real achievement – true?

> Truth or Lie: till the day you die
> Strike you dead if you tell me a lie.

Go on . . . true? All right. *Your* turn. You ask me.

LETOUZEL: I have no intention of being so childish.

CRAPE: As you like then. I'm only playing fair.

LETOUZEL: Wait a minute. Wait: I *will* take a turn.

> Truth or Lie: till the day you die
> Strike you dead if you tell me a lie.

CRAPE: Granted.

LETOUZEL: You have little talks with the Doctor, don't you, two or three times a week?

CRAPE: Eh? Now, now look here, old woman –

LETOUZEL: Truth or lie?

CRAPE: Uh ... true. But don't you go thinking –

LETOUZEL: I know the sort of thing you trot along to tell him, Mr Crape, make no mistake about *that*! But I'm really far more interested in what *he* tells to you.

CRAPE: He doesn't tell me anything – or anyway, if he does, it is under the seal of confidence. I wouldn't dream of infringing it.

LETOUZEL: What about this Bounty?

CRAPE: Bounty? What Bounty?

LETOUZEL: I know because he said so. I went to see him on Friday to make a very justified complaint. I said to him: 'Dr Copperthwaite, the present-day cost of living is very very hard upon we older people who have lived through two world wars.' And he said to me –

CRAPE: 'Bah wah wah wah-wah, Robinson, Smith, clear it up, sweep it away, that's all for this morning!'

LETOUZEL: And I said to him –

CRAPE: 'But for we *older* people, Dr Copperthwaite, who have lived through two world wars, the Old Age Pension is scandalous, the National Assistance gives us nothing –'

LETOUZEL: 'The Socialist Party in 1947 quite deliberately stole my savings.'

CRAPE: 'There are those of us, Dr Copperthwaite, who have lived through two world wars!'

LETOUZEL: And he said to me –

CRAPE: 'Bah wah wah wah-wah, Nurse Brown, Nurse Jones, swabs, basins, towels, liniment, ointment –'

[*They both dissolve into excessive laughter.* CRAPE *emerges from it first.*]

'Mrs Letouzel, you cantankerous old bag, what d'you mean, by complaining about your money! Your board and lodging and medical treatment in this benighted Bridewell is free!

It's paid for by the voluntary contributions of our worshipful Patrons, and also, in part, by the Government. All *you* are asked to provide, God damn your eyes, are those few small comforts which –'

LETOUZEL: Which –?

CRAPE: '*Which* in the fullness of time will be rendered unnecessary by –'

LETOUZEL: 'By the Bounty paid out by the Ministry of Health.'

CRAPE: That's not what I was going to say.

LETOUZEL: No. But it *is* what *he* said. I'm afraid he had lost control. He was most ill-tempered and abusive. But that was what he said.

CRAPE: I've never heard of no Ministerial Bounty.

LETOUZEL: No more had I, Mr Crape. And the Doctor made it perfectly clear that I was not supposed to have done, either. He turned red in the face and went stamping and bumbling away. A slip of the tongue, you see: but what did it signify?

CRAPE: Steady, steady – here comes the Heavy Brigade – 'The Colonel said, die hard my boys. And by God they died hard. . . .'

[HARDRADER *enters. He looks around for his dog, sees it is not with him, then goes back to the door, opens it, calls* 'Hector, Hector'. *The dog (imaginary of course) comes apparently running in and leaps up at Crape. He and* MRS LETOUZEL *react in a panic. The dog barks.*]

HARDRADER: No no, down boy, down – go to heel, Hector, heel, boy, *heel!*

LETOUZEL: Must you bring that dog in here, Mr Hardrader?

CRAPE: Hey, hey, down you devil, down!

HARDRADER: Down, boy, down, leave him alone, he's all right, Crape, don't be frightened, he's as gentle as a goldfish. If you show him you're afraid of him, of course he comes round on you. Now Hector, sit down. Behave yourself. I shan't tell you twice. That's better. There, you see: perfectly disciplined – the word of command. He was only having his

fun. Do you know, we've made a splendid walk this afternoon, Hector and me – eight miles out, eight and a half miles
in again, over the hill past the housing estate, along the
arterial road, railway line, gasworks – out into the fresh air,
beautiful. I composed two verses in praise of nature – then
sharp about turn at the bridge over the motorway, back we
came, eight miles, half a mile detour at the cemetery corner
to visit Mrs Hardrader's grave, flowers on the grave, a few
words, composed a verse in praise of the departed, Hector
gives her a howl too in commemoration – oh he remembers,
don't you, boy? Then home again for tea, fit, tired, splendid.

LETOUZEL: You ought to see he stays in his kennel. It's not
fair on other people. Good boy, then, good boy ... er
Hector, there you are now, Hector – keep him away, man,
keep him away for heaven's sake!

HARDRADER: Hector, I said *sit*!

LETOUZEL: It is quite wrong to bring a dog that size into the
hospital, Mr Hardrader. I'm surprised Dr Copperthwaite –

HARDRADER: Nonsense, Mrs Letouzel. Best friend a man ever
had. Why, he used to live in my own room when I first came
here, but some busybody made a complaint. Do you know
this, Mrs Letouzel: I'm not an unsociable man, but I can
only claim to have had two real friends in the whole of my
life. That's Mrs Hardrader, and Hector. And Hector is the
better of the two. Aha, boy, aha, nearly time for your
biscuits. ... What *you* need, y'know, Crape, is a bit more
physical exercise. Nothing else necessary. A few strong
walks, ride a tricycle, up and down with the dumb-bells! I tell
you what, when the equipment arrives for the Doctor's new
Gymnasium, I'll give you two afternoons a week on the
parallel bars and the climbing ropes. I'll put something like a
framework back inside *you*, man: completely rejuvenate
you in less than a month!

CRAPE: *Parallel bars!* What are you talking about? He's not
going to waste his money getting us parallel bars at *our* age!
Why, I couldn't *possibly* –

HARDRADER: Maybe not now, but I think you'll find you

will. Astonishing what a man can do with a bit of training. The equipment certainly has been ordered, y'know. The storekeeper told me himself. *He* was a bit surprised, as well ... H'm, yes ... Oh it'll do us a power of good! You can give me ten years, I suppose, Crape: but you take a look at me. There's good fresh air in here – [*Thumping his chest.*] What have you got? What have you got there? Smog.

VOICE [*over the loudspeaker*]: Mr Golightly, please. Mr Golightly to report to Sister's Office. Mr Golightly, if you please.

HARDRADER: Ha! Sounds like the silly old pansy's got to have another enema! Hope he enjoys it. Ha ha.

VOICE: Correction to the last announcement. Correction. Mr *Hardrader* to report to Sister's Office, *not* Mr Golightly. Mr Hardrader, if you please.

HARDRADER: Indeed I shall do nothing of the sort! I have no use at all for that sort of treatment. It's merely pandering to one's natural sluggishness. No good. No good. [*He sings, with gestures that alarm Crape and Mrs Letouzel.*]

> I will not stoop, I will not bend,
> I live my life to the uttermost end.
> And when they come to drag me in –
> Ho! Left, right, straight to the chin!
> Bang, crash, ho, ooh, wallop, out –
> Take him away!
> Hardrader, Hardrader,
> Hardrader wins the day.

What do *you* say, Hector?

> Ho! Grab him, get him, sick him, go for his throat –
> Take him away!
> Bold Hector, Bold Hector,
> Bold Hector wins the day –

[*Enter* NURSE BROWN. HARDRADER *nervously tries to escape the other way.*]

Yes, Nurse, right away. Yes ...

[*He tries to drive the dog out the far side.*]

Go away boy, go on, go – you're not wanted, no. Get rid of

    him, Crape. Go on, be off! ... [*The dog is pushed out by* CRAPE *and* LETOUZEL.] Oh, yes, Nurse. Yes. Indeed, yes: Sister's Office, I was just on my way – yes.

    [HARDRADER *goes out with the nurse.*]

LETOUZEL: I shall speak to Dr Copperthwaite. That abominable dog. It's entirely ridiculous.

CRAPE: He says to me rejuvenated? *That* old man – rejuvenated!

LETOUZEL: Rowdiness and rhodomontade, dogs and smells and great muddy boots –

CRAPE: What possible good can any of us get from wanting to be young again? It's only when you're old that you can see how it all sets up – you need experience, you need wisdom – you're not kidding me I'm sorry for my age!

LETOUZEL: Oh? Now you don't believe that, do you, Mr Crape?

CRAPE: Eh?

LETOUZEL: Do you mean to say that there's any sort of value in knowing how to get, when you've no time left you to *spend*? Here we are, look at us, dried up in this Institution, the only things we know how to do are the worst things we ever learned – plotting and planning, avarice and spite. Well, why not? We have no opportunity for anything different.... *We* should stop quarrelling: we ought to be friends.

CRAPE: Ah yes, we ought. ... Oh that stupid Copperbottom, he's wasting his time. What he needs to be working on, if he wants to be worth while, is a *real* rejuvenation! If he could discover a drug that'd make us all young again, yet not destroy our memories – eh? *There* there'd be some value.

LETOUZEL: Who knows? Perhaps he is.

CRAPE: Wait a minute –

LETOUZEL: What d'you mean, wait a minute –

CRAPE: Oh wait a minute ... we're talking flat rubbish. It's too much to hope for ... *He* said: Gymnasium. Why build a Gymnasium? Right?

LETOUZEL: I suppose so –

CRAPE: Wait a minute. *You* said: Ministerial Bounty. Why give us a Bounty? It's not been provided for in any Act of Parliament so far as *I* know. Right?

LETOUZEL: No, you're right, it hasn't . . .

CRAPE: But supposing –

LETOUZEL: Supposing –

CRAPE: Supposing *you* were a mermaid, you'd have a lovely silver tail – right? And you'd need water to swim in!

LETOUZEL: Right!

CRAPE: But supposing, supposing, instead of a mermaid, you was a young woman! You'd need some sort of dowry to start you out in life! And if *I* was a young man – parallel bars! I could *swing* on the parallel bars! Oh my good Lord, I'd be jumping like a monkey!

LETOUZEL: It isn't very likely.

CRAPE: Not? Is it not? [*He pulls out the paper he found in* SCENE ONE.] Now take a look at this. Disregard the mathematics. Look at these names. Optimum ages, estimated reductions, here we are, months, years, you see! He's *doing* it!

LETOUZEL: He must be!

CRAPE: That's what he's doing!

BOTH TOGETHER: He's going to *rejuvenate* us!

[*Startled by a sudden noise, they go rigid, saying:* 'Ssh!']

CRAPE: It's all right: it's nothing. Someone slammed a door. . . .

LETOUZEL: When will it happen?

CRAPE: I was in with him this morning. There was a sort of an accident. Bound to hold things up a little. We've got time to reflect.

LETOUZEL: Ye-es. . . . *How* dare he? *How* dare he? Without one word to us!

CRAPE: Quite right – how dare he. . . . But it stands to reason, after all, he's got to keep it secret till he's worked out his formulas. What *you* want to fix your mind on, y'know, is this question of the Bounty.

The Happy Haven

LETOUZEL: H'm, yes, of course. There is that point of view
... ah, it's bound to be inadequate. Public funds, bureau-
cratic parsimony – and just when I was really reaching my
nose into the true fat meat of *her* savings. . . . I have it! I
shall go into partnership with her.

CRAPE: Partnership in what?

LETOUZEL: In a little Agency, Mr Crape. She'll still have what
I've left her out of her thousand, we'll invest it intelligently
according to my system. All my life, I have been waiting for
this. Scheme after scheme, absolutely foolproof, has been
baulked from the beginning by my never having quite
enough capital to carry it through. In 1945 everything
was set for such a speculation in transport shares that – oh,
that shameful General Election! The black ingratitude
of the British public. . . . Enough of this. I shall set up my
Agency.

CRAPE: What sort of Agency?

LETOUZEL: A general Agency. No staff. Just myself (and of
course, the sleeping partner, dear Mrs P – oh yes, and she
will sleep!). Our clients will write in and I shall conduct
their business for them entirely through correspondence.
The letters come, the transaction is performed, the letters go
out again, and the percentages accrue. Each profit invested,
and investment profitable! Life, Mr Crape: *life*, to be re-
lived once more. I can't wait for the day!

CRAPE: *I'm* going into business, and all. I'm going to open a
warehouse. Export-Import. Y'know, packing-cases, oil-
drums, boxes of porridge-oats – there are going to be *men*
working for *me* – fifteen of 'em, in green aprons and a cap
with a leather peak. 'Three more lorries to be unloaded,
hurry it up, ah, Parkinson, how's the kiddies? And the
missus? Good ... Hardrader! Get them iron girders to the
other end of the shed before lunch-time and when you've
done that you can carry them big bales right up into the
loft.'

LETOUZEL: You're not going to employ *him*!

CRAPE: Ho ho, I am so – you see him young again and out

into the world – he'll be as helpless as a babe! He was put in here in the first place by some of his own family. Too hearty about their house by far, he was. They lived in a semi, y'know, only about a mile away, and he brought all the half-timbering down one night sleep-walking – he strides into a bow window and he carries it straight out into the garden with him! But when he's thirty-five and I'm twenty-six, I'll have that physical phenomenon working for me till the floor-joists rock beneath him! Bow wow, bow wow, down, ye devil, *down*! What about Golightly?

LETOUZEL: What about him?

CRAPE: If he marries Ma Phineus, and he might very well – you won't find much partnership left, will you? A bit of rejuvenation could make a great deal of difference.

LETOUZEL: Then I'd better go and court him myself, I suppose, and you'd better court Hardrader, if you want to make sure of him before he gets his own ideas. But for God's sake keep it secret!

CRAPE: Strike me dead if I utter a word! *We* know, don't we, and nobody else! We're on a stance of power, *we* are – like, hand in hand, aren't we? . . . We ought to get wed! Why, who knows *what* we're going to turn out like? We might be like *Gods*!

LETOUZEL: Ah no, Mr Crape. It's Business is our business, that's all.

CRAPE: Oh, but I used to be handsome – you know, they called me Dandy Jimmy! You wait and see! [*He sings.*]

> To be born into this world again
> As a little child to grow
> Where the young need the old
> For to show them the road –

LETOUZEL [*sings*]: And the old need the young to go.
[*They sing the song through, once more together, and dance out.*]

VOICE [*over the loudspeaker*]: Mr Crape, please. Mr Crape to report to Sister's Office. Mr Crape, if you please.

Act Two

Scene One

DOCTOR [*offstage*]: Robinson! Mr Robinson! Mr Smith! Mr Smith!

[*Enter* DOCTOR, *followed by* ORDERLY ROBINSON *who carries a retort full of liquid.* ORDERLY SMITH *enters by other door and meets them. He carries notebooks.*]

DOCTOR: Notebooks? Have you got the retort? Let's have a look at it . . . Ah, aha, ha. You see, you see – dark blue, dark blue, look at it, and it shades into black down at the bottom. Black sediment: blue: just as I thought. It came in a flash. I never even dreamt – I'll tell you, by God, I think this is it! What a devil of a good chance that damfool patient interrupted us when he did! He doesn't know it, no, but he's speeded up his own chances by a third, by a half, I should think by *threequarters* – you see what he's done? The very fact it coagulated, may be the one clue we need! I must have been blind. This is one of those discoveries in the history of science that –

[*He leafs through his notebooks.*]

Yes, yes – here we are – ha: six point eight-six-nine, seventy-two, four by three by two, *divide*, cross the co-ordinates, bending-moment, bending-moment – quick –

[ORDERLY SMITH *finds a place for him in a log-table and does a quick calculation in the margin with a biro.*]

Good boy, good: right, right – and by the power of three – and there we are! So. Twenty-four hours more: there should be one more change in the colour. I'm certain there will be. Then we'll try it again over the bunsen, add in your accotile and heraclith solution – half-quantities, make a note

– and if it turns green, we've got it! A short cut at last. It's more than a short cut – it's much more than that – I hardly dare say it but it's opening out a whole new field of development. This means, this means that I'm going to be able to put this Elixir straight into full production, straight on the world market! Robinson, I want you to get a draft report made out, as soon as you have time. We must tell the Ministry. It alters our whole timetable. An agonizing – a *wonderfully* agonizing reappraisal of the entire Copperthwaite Project! You know, I'm going to have those five young again by the end of next week. I tell you they're going to skip like mountain bloody goats! All right, Robinson. Take it away. Put it back in the rack. And make sure you check that temperature. Twenty-four hours more. How on earth am I to live through it? Go on, boy, go on . . .

[*Exit* ORDERLY ROBINSON *with retort.*]

Get me the telephone. I want to talk to Charlie Sanderson. You know his number, don't you?

[ORDERLY SMITH *fetches from the recess a telephone on a lead. He rapidly dials a number, then hands receiver to Doctor.*]

Hello – Charlie? . . . Jack. How are you, sport? Ha ha, go on, go on, you don't tell me, he he, watch it, Charlie, watch it, she'll have you at the altar before you've buttoned your breeches. . . . Now seriously, Charlie, look, I'm going to have to scratch from the match on Saturday. . . . No no, of course it isn't because of last week, of course I don't bear a grudge, boy. I was off form and I knew it, you were quite right what you said to me, I'd have told you the same. . . . All right, sport, all right. Forgiven and forgotten. But the fact of the matter is, there's something big coming up at the hospital. . . . Oh the usual line, you know, nothing earth-shaking, bedpans and thermometers – but it may be important and I just daren't commit myself, I'm sorry. . . . Well what about Jimmy Ricketts, then, can't you play him in the second row, make that new type with the big 'tache your hooker – what's his name – Hawkins? – and then swop your scrum-half with – take it easy, Charlie, I know you're the Captain, I know it's short notice. And I may be damn good, boy, but I'm not indispensable – in any case, we're only playing a Teachers' Training College, they'll be outclassed, sport, no question – you'll never even notice I'm not there. . . . Oh, good. Well that's damned accommodating of you, Charlie, I'm bloody grateful, really . . . what? . . . Ho, ho, no! Oh, you look out for *her*, chum – and make sure you know where you've hidden your bedroom key. . . . All right Charlie, I'll remember. I'll put 'em in the post for you. Medical goods, a plain envelope – *I* know the drill. We'll keep you a bachelor yet. . . . Yes, on the Health Service. Tax-payers for ever! So long, sport, so long. And best of luck on Saturday. I'll be round for the beer in the evening. . . . So long. [*He rings off.*] Thank you Mr Smith. Put it away, please.

[ORDERLY SMITH *removes telephone.*]

Oh, while I've got it in my mind – I want you to take a letter – I heard a dog bark in the corridor this afternoon. Before we know where we are, we'll have old Crape along with more of his eternal complaints: so I'm damn well putting a stop to it, *now*.

[ORDERLY SMITH *prepares to take dictation in one of the notebooks.*]

To Mr Hardrader. Dear Mr Hardrader, it has been brought to my notice that in defiance of the permanent regulations of this hospital, you persist in retaining your pet animal on the premises. I would be glad if you would arrange to have the dog removed within thirty-six hours or else I shall have no option but to give instructions to have it destroyed. Yours, etcetera, etcetera, J. Copperthwaite, Superintendent. Sign it p.p. me and see he gets it at once. . . . That ought to make the place a little more hygienic. I don't like dogs anyway. . . . Dogs . . . I may need that dog. Cancel the letter. Write it like this: 'The dog must be delivered to my Office within thirty-six hours or else.' Then get someone who knows about these things to put a value on the beast. I think it's only a mongrel: but I wouldn't want to take it from the old fellow without paying him something.... That'll do for this afternoon. Will you attend to it directly? Thank you.

[*Exeunt severally.*]

Scene Two

[MRS LETOUZEL *enters cautiously. She creeps across the stage to the opposite door, peeps through it, and then flattens herself against the doorpost as* GOLIGHTLY *enters, slowly. He does not see her, nor the mitten which she has taken off and dropped in his path.*]

LETOUZEL: Ha h'm. [*He turns round, sees her, inclines his head, coldly but politely, and continues on his way.*]

LETOUZEL: Mr Golightly! I'm afraid I've dropped my mitten.

GOLIGHTLY: I beg your pardon, Mrs Letouzel. I was in a brown study. Pray forgive me. [*He hands her the mitten and leaves her.*] Good evening ...

[*She gives an exasperated exclamation, and dodges out of the door by which he has entered. He sits down dejectedly. She re-enters by the door of her original entry : or rather, peeps round it to see what he is doing. He gets up and starts towards her, but without realizing she is there. She retreats behind the door, and when he reaches it, pops out at him with a startled little squeak.*]

LETOUZEL: Oh! Mr Golightly, really! ... We seem to be running into each other everywhere! I was just on my way to – well, I didn't expect to meet any gentlemen in *this* corridor, Mr Golightly!

GOLIGHTLY: Good gracious, madam, I really *do* beg your pardon! Excuse me! I will return to my quarters at once.

LETOUZEL [*detaining him*]: Mr Golightly.

GOLIGHTLY: Madam?

LETOUZEL: I am truly sorry for you, Mr Golightly. Please believe me when I tell you that. I know what you came here for, you see.

GOLIGHTLY: You do? Oh ...

LETOUZEL: You hoped to catch some fleeting glimpse, did you not? One last appeal to her implacable divinity, as she is swept from room to room – but it wouldn't be any use. She will never change, never. . . . Dear friend, I beg you: put her out of your mind!

GOLIGHTLY: No. . . . No. . . . I cannot. . . . And you are as bad, you know! Oh yes you are! You gloat and look on. I know what they think – namby-pamby little Golightly, tripping about, ogling, smirking, ha ha, yes, the lady-killer: but all that he's fit for is the queen-bee's dirty work! But I can tell you: when I was a young man I was most certainly admired! It was not considered disgraceful, in those days, to appear spruce and to behave with chivalry. If I could be young – for just one evening, Mrs Letouzel, *I'd* show up the crudities, the brutalities of this age! There are young women who would be *astonished*! And that is no fable!

LETOUZEL: Suppose – why not suppose – suppose that you *were* young. Suppose *she* was too. You'd still allow it to go on, just as it goes on now.

GOLIGHTLY: Oh no I would not.

LETOUZEL: Ah, you would not? You'd tear her right out of you, leap away like a rattlesnake, and ravage alone through the hips and the hearts of innumerable others! Oh you promiscuous, you uncontrolled, you terrible danger!

GOLIGHTLY: I don't mean that either. All I intended to say was that I should be able for once to pay my court where my inclinations have dictated, without prejudice from my old age and my concomitant ridiculous appearance.

LETOUZEL: But I told you: she will eat you up.

GOLIGHTLY: Only because of my age.

LETOUZEL: No! If you were no more than eighteen years old tomorrow, and she no more than – you stupid little man, do you not understand that that's all you are going to be! And she, she, she, will already be more than *thirty*! Mr Golightly, what you need is a *friend*: a loving, loyal, and vigilant friend. [*To the audience.*] I have said too much. [*To Golightly.*] I should not have told you. [*To audience.*] I should not have

228

told him. Business is business. Business isn't passion. Passion and rage: to me, that *must* be business. I have let myself go. I think I am an idiot. But let's look for advantage. [*To Golightly.*] I'll accept it: I've told you. I'd better tell you more. Tell you the lot. Come on.

[*Exeunt.*]

Scene Three

[*Enter* HARDRADER *with a piece of paper, pursuing two nurses.* CRAPE *follows him.*]

HARDRADER [*trapping the Nurses in a corner*]: Excuse me, excuse me, Nurses, I won't keep you a moment. Don't be in such hurry to get away – I may be an old man, but I'm not an old ghost, y'know. I can assure you, if you listen, you'll find yourself edified. There now, sit down, sit down, Nurse Brown –

[*The* NURSES *reluctantly do so.*]

Ha ha, Brown, down, what do we make out of that?

> I watch Nurse Brown
> As she sits down
> On the seat beside Nurse Jones.
> Two diamond stones
> Upon one golden ring.
> To view them both,
> Sets my old heart to sing.
> Hey ding-a-ding, ding.

Only an improvisation, of course. Rough, rough, I know. But what about this? This one's *considered*, this is what I want you to hear: [*He reads.*] To Hector – that's my dog.

> Old fellow. You and I through life
> Have wandered without hurt or strife
> Between us, man and dog. How few
> Of humankind can say so too!
> How few can say, that with a wife
> The years have passed so freely, as with you!
> Alas, how few!

Well, there you are? There's the Sentiment: is it the Truth? Oh, come on, young ladies, don't be bashful. A poem must be true or else it's no good – so tell me, be honest. . . .

LOUDSPEAKER: Nurse Jones, Nurse Brown, to report at once to Sterilization Room. Nurse Jones, Nurse Brown, please. Sterilization.

[*Exeunt* NURSES.]

HARDRADER: Oh. Thoroughly disheartening. Every time I try to teach these young women something, there's something else calls them away. Always the same. They never seem to allow them any free time.

CRAPE: They're supposed to be on duty. Stands to reason they're going to be called for.

HARDRADER: But if they were *off* duty, d'you imagine they'd stay and listen to me for more than two minutes? All they want to do is to jig around with yellow-faced young doctors at these, at these I think they call them 'boogie-woogie' parties, far too late at night. It's not as if they even took any sensible interest in a few out-of-door activities. Look at Dr Copperthwaite, certainly he plays a very respectable game of Rugger every Saturday: but who bothers to support him? No one from this hospital. Except me. No one at all.

[*Enter* ORDERLY SMITH *with letter*.]

Ah Mr Smith? A letter? For me? For me! What's the matter? Er, wait a moment – Mr Smith, I say, I say, please –

[*Exit* ORDERLY SMITH.]

What d'you imagine this is?

CRAPE: I should expect it's from the Superintendent.

HARDRADER: I hope nothing's wrong.

CRAPE: It's just the usual routine bureaucracy – you've been here long enough to know about *that*.

HARDRADER: Dr Copperthwaite only sends notes if there's something wrong. D'you imagine there could be a – a serious discovery, I mean, for instance, my last X-ray? Cancer? TB?

CRAPE: At your age?

HARDRADER: Why not?

CRAPE: Well at your age, why worry? We're all waiting for it, aren't we?

HARDRADER: I have always prided myself on my continued robust condition. I have always been happy to think that when I go, I shall go – straight: suddenly: upright to the end. I have never a cold, never a cough – which is more than can be said for you –

CRAPE [*with a snuffle*]: Colds and coughs are nothing –

HARDRADER: Yes they are, they're symptoms. If there is one thing I have dreaded, it is that something might come – say, cancer, without warning, without *any* symptoms. Every time the Doctor examines us, I say to myself – 'Not this time, oh my God, not this time.'

CRAPE: Why don't you open it?

HARDRADER: Open it. . . . Goddamit, who's afraid? Who cares a brassknuckle for any blasted young sawbones! Ha – [*He tears the letter open and reads it to himself.*] Good heavens. . . . Oh good heavens. . . . Oh . . . Crape: are you a man?

CRAPE: What sort of a man?

HARDRADER: Breathing. Feeling. Living. That sort. Well, are you?

CRAPE: What's the matter?

HARDRADER: Read it. The man who wrote this letter was not a man. Even if this letter is a joke, if it is mistimed pleasantry in a juvenile bad taste, it was written by no man. Because it is an inhuman letter: and I can tell you Crape, it has made me wish to die.

CRAPE [*having read the letter*]: Oh dear dear dear, Mr Hardrader, summon our spirits, man, come on, old chap, cheer up cheer up, rally round the flag, boys. You've still got the dog, I take it?

HARDRADER: I suppose so. I keep him in a potting-shed to the north of the tennis courts. I feed him every day under cover of going to examine the hardcore and the greensward. They all know I like to inspect the sports grounds regularly, and I thought I had been taken for granted down there. Some of the nurses are in the secret, of course. But I said to them: please turn a blind eye. And they are good girls, loyal. They did so. But now – Crape, Crape, what on earth am I going to do?

CRAPE: Give me the dog.

HARDRADER: Give you the –

CRAPE: Get him out of that shed. Let me take him. And don't ask me where. When they come to tell you to hand him over: why, you deny all knowledge. Tell 'em he's run away. What could be easier?

HARDRADER: But what will happen then? Hector can't live without me, why, he –

CRAPE: Of course you'll get him back, old chap, old chap. When the hunt's died down. But don't put him in the potting-shed again. No. Now see: what about the old greenhouse among the rhododendrons west of the cricket pavilion? You go up there to inspect the state of the wicket, don't you? get it . . . eh?

HARDRADER: I would never have trusted Hector to anyone, before, ever. And then, there's another thing. How can I repay you? I am not a man to stand in debt to anyone, ever. You see, I don't even know that I can manage to survive this business. I have not admitted this very often, but I *am* old, Crape, an old man, older than you. And the shock of the separation may –

CRAPE: Temporary separation.

HARDRADER: It is still a separation, and an unendurable one.

CRAPE: It's true you haven't very long to live –

HARDRADER: No. I haven't, now. Under no circumstances, now. Today I know this: I am altogether too old for all those things that I have lived for. Energy. Vigour. Strength of the body. Comradeship. Hector. What does it matter if Hector is destroyed. I am a dead man too. I was a big, strong man. Yes, Crape, I was. But it is finished, you see. This letter –

CRAPE: Oh no, old chap.

HARDRADER: What do you mean?

CRAPE: I wasn't going to tell you – [*To audience.*] I wasn't going to tell him. [*To Hardrader.*] But you're so down in the

dumps, it looks as if I'll have to. [*To audience.*] I don't give a
damn for *her*: do I? And do you? No, you don't because I'm
the quicker of the two of us: you know it – and whatever
she plans, I'll be the paymaster at the end of it all. [*To
Hardrader.*] Old chap, we're going to save Hector. And you're
going to understand how very very much it is going to be
worth it. You talk of repayment? Aha, you'll have your
chance. Come on, and I'll tell you. And then we'll find the
dog. Come on, come on. Old chap. Old chap.

[*Exeunt.*]

Scene Four

[*The telephone rings in the recess.* ORDERLY SMITH *hurries
in, brings out the apparatus, at the same time answering it.
Before he has time to speak, the* DOCTOR *enters and takes it
from him.*]

DOCTOR: All right, Mr Smith, all right – I hear him, I'll take
it. Hello, Superintendent here . . . Eh? What? I didn't catch
it. Hello! . . . Damn nuisance, they've disappeared. You pick
up the phone, there's some silly chicken on the other end,
she says 'burble burble' will you hang on for one moment
please, I'll put you right through! – and I'm damned if I
know who she's putting me through to. Buckingham Palace
for all I'm informed. Hello, yes, your Majesty, how simply
super of you to call! Yes, of course, Your Majesty, five
o'clock would be splendid – shall we wear court dress or is it
going to be formal? Eh, hello, yes? . . . Yes, yes, of *course*
I'm Copperthwaite. . . . What? (Oh my God, it *is* the
Queen – or next best anyway.) Good morning, Sir Frederick
– I'm really sorry, I didn't quite recognize . . . Eh, dear dear
dear, no no no no, Sir Frederick, *any* time of the day is a
convenient time except when I'm . . . Oh. Sunday. I see. . . .
Of course, I can't very well say no. But it *would* be a bit
happier for me if you could see your way, sir, to deferring it
a week. You see, I have to . . . why, if you put it like that,
Sir Frederick, of course. Yes. . . . Sunday. Very well sir. . . .

No question, no. No no no. *Quite* all right, Sir Frederick. Very happy. Very proud to see you here. Yes.... And good-bye to *you*, sir. [*He rings off.*] And good-bye to you, sir. And sir to you, sir. And good-bye, good-bye, good-bye. I'm talking to my peace of mind, that's all. To my careless existence. Good-bye!... There, Smith, it's gone! Look at it disappearing. Flight of a swallow. D'you want to know the reason? Sir Frederick, no less. The Lord Mayor and the Bishop. The Mayoress and Mrs Bishop. The Town Clerk and Mrs Clerk, I dare say. Half the bloody Ministry straight down from Whitehall. They're coming, on Sunday. A ceremonial visit. We'd better buy a flag. Get a carpet. Scarlet. Buns, tea, cream in the buns. But I'm not giving 'em drinks. This is a hospital, not a country club. No drinks, no cinema shows, no dancing, no billiards.... This is Robinson's report, y'know – too damn keen by far, that chap – I *told* him not to make it so melodramatic. They want to see the Elixir, and they want to see it at work. I'm not ready for an audience! Who do they think I am? They'll be asking for a sputnik or a descent in a bathyscaphe before we know where we are.... Well: let's have it organized. Shoulder to the wheel, boy, your back to the wall. They're coming on Sunday. Dial me 36786 will you. And then go away. I want this one private.

[ORDERLY SMITH *dials the number, hands back the phone to doctor and exits.*]

Hello, is that you, mother? Jack here.... Yes, I'm very well indeed, mother – now, look – ... Just a minute, mother, I'm trying to tell you – ... I'm *telling* you, mother, I can't come on Sunday. Well of course I hadn't let you know: I'm letting you know now. Look, I can't come on Sunday because there's a man from the Ministry of Health and a whole lot more of the nobs and they're coming down to look at the hospital and I have to be here.... No, mother, you *can't* meet them. It's not social, it's official, and ... now, look, love, I'm sorry: I like to come home as much as you like me to come ... oh, *was* she? Did I ask her ...? For God's sake let me invite my own girls to tea. . . . I *know* Joyce is a nice girl, I'm sure she's a lovely girl, she'll make a positively splendid wife for some stupid . . . All right, mother. I'm sorry. The tongue is sharper than the sword, or the thought is slower than the knife, or whatever they say. I didn't mean to be rude. Make my excuses, tell Joyce I'm sorry. If you must have her to tea, she can come the weekend after –

[*Barking heard.* DOCTOR *becomes aware of dog on stage.*]

What's that! Get out of it! Get down there! Down! Smith – I say Smith.

[*Enter* ORDERLY SMITH.]

Get this damned dog out! Who let it in? There's a dog in the room, I shall have to ring off. . . . No mother, no, there's a bloody great dog. . . . I'm sorry, mother . . . NO! You can ring me next week! [*He rings off and thrusts telephone at Orderly Smith.*] Where's it gone? Here! No, no, stop it! Here!

[*They pursue the dog round the stage in a flurry.*]

Lord help us, use your sense man, get it to the door – go on, now, go on, don't be afraid of it, it isn't going to bite you –

[ORDERLY SMITH, *bitten, screams.*]

Get it out of the door!

[*The dog is got out of the door and they slam the door behind it, and take breath in relief. The barking starts again at the other side of the stage.* CRAPE *enters, struggling with the dog at that side.*]

CRAPE: Down, boy, down – go to heel, good boy, good dog, Hector, Hector – no . . . Doctor, I'm sorry, it's nothing to do with me – he seemed to run away, I was trying to catch him –

DOCTOR: Robinson – Where's Robinson?

[*Enter* ORDERLY ROBINSON *above.*]

Who let this dog in?

[ORDERLY ROBINSON *shrugs and shakes his head helplessly.*]

Well, we've got to get it out. Entice it, entice it. Get some food for it – *quickly* – How should I know what food – meat, eggs, fish, hurry!

[*Exit* ORDERLY ROBINSON *right.*]

CRAPE: Watch him, Doctor, he's beginning to snarl. I think you've got him vexed.

DOCTOR: Keep still. Just keep still. Smith, I said *still*! Robinson, where are you?

[ORDERLY ROBINSON *enters on main stage with a plate of food.*]

What have you got there? Stew? All right, I dare say it eats stew, now attract him, attract him; lead him along with it – gently, gently – look dog, there's a plate of stew, look at the bloody stew, will you – good dog, good dog – rattle the eating irons, Robinson, make some effort to attract him, man – dinner, dinner, dinner – what do they call him?

CRAPE: Hector.

DOCTOR: Hector, boy, Hector, dinner for Hector, that's right, boy, that's right, come to the Doctor – give me the dinner – [*He takes the plate of stew.*] Doctor's got dinner, dinner for Hector, Doctor for Hector, Hector for Doctor, Doctor, Doctor, Hector, Doctor, dinner, dinner, dinner – [*He has worked his way backwards to the recess and quickly lays the plate down inside, clapping the screen closed behind him as he comes out. The barking is heard muffled.*] Three brass balls and be damned for his dinner. Where did he come from? Hardrader? Is it?

CRAPE: Now, doctor, all I was doing was –

DOCTOR: Poking your nose in, that's all you always do – red nose, Mr Crape, thick nose, carbuncles. Too much blood, Mr Crape. Too much. A nose like that needs a good blistering poultice. I shall bear it in mind. Get out of my sight.

[*Exit* CRAPE.]

Now then, the dog: go in after him – *carefully* – put him in a basket, strap down the basket, come out again, *carefully* – lock the door behind you. Look sharp.

[*Exit* ORDERLY ROBINSON *into recess.*]

So we're all set for Sunday. There's nothing now I need worry about. The Elixir is fermenting all according to plan, Sir Frederick and his friends are all fermenting according to plan, the dog's in a box according to plan – my God, the patients. I hadn't given them a thought. They might none of them be fit – snap check-up, all five, lay it on. X-rays, all the rest of the business. Robinson!

[*Enter* ORDERLY ROBINSON *from recess, carrying empty plate.* MRS LETOUZEL *enters.*]

All fixed? Then get ready. Snap check-up. All five X-rays, all the rest of the business. Smith, do you hear me . . .

LETOUZEL: Dr Copperthwaite, if you please, I maintain that it will not do. This sort of rudeness, simply snatched from my hands, I shall report it to the governors –

DOCTOR: Nurse, Nurse, Nurse Brown, Nurse Jones – All five, snap check-up, get ready, lay it on –

[DOCTOR *and* ORDERLIES *exeunt severally.* NURSES *cross the stage busily.*]

LETOUZEL: They may have given me the wrong diet, I wouldn't know, I wasn't told, but to serve me a dinner, and then to come immediately, simply to snatch it away –

[DOCTOR *crosses the stage, meeting* ORDERLIES *who cross in opposite direction.*]

DOCTOR [*en passant*]: Report cards, temperature charts, blood pressures, quick quick quick; Nurse Brown, Nurse Jones, where have you gone to?

LETOUZEL: I didn't even have time to see what was on the plate. I thought steak and kidney. But what was there with it? Pie crust – suet crust, steamed gravy, potatoes, why, I don't know – I'm not at all fond of steamed suet pudding. . . . But I should have liked to have known . . .

[*Enter* NURSE JONES.]

I tell you, I should like to have known . . .

[*Exit* MRS LETOUZEL *with the* NURSE.]

Scene Five

LOUDSPEAKER: Attention, please. Attention, please. This is important. This is urgent. This is extra, unusual, a breach in routine. Mr Crape, Mr Hardrader, Mr Golightly, Mrs

Phineus, Mrs Letouzel, will you all report, please, at once, to the X-ray department for immediate examination. The Superintendent's instructions. Will Orderlies and Nurses please ensure, at once, that Mrs Letouzel, Mrs Phineus, Mr Golightly, Mr Hardrader, Mr Crape, all report, at once, for immediate examination. Important. Urgent. Attention. Attention. Nurses and Orderlies, please, attention, attention . . .

[OLD PEOPLE (*except* MRS PHINEUS) *run across the upper stage, accompanied by* NURSES. *Then they enter on main stage and cross it going out at opposite side.* ORDERLIES *cross the main stage in the other direction, passing them in the middle. Then the four* OLD PEOPLE *and* NURSE BROWN *re-appear on upper stage and sit down in a row. The* ORDERLIES *re-enter on lower stage, as does the* DOCTOR.]

DOCTOR: Is everybody there? One, two, three, four –

[MRS PHINEUS *is wheeled on to main stage by* NURSE JONES.]

– *And* Mrs Phineus. Right. Nurse Brown, I want to make a complete examination of each patient with as few delays as possible – time's as short as patience, remember that, so have everybody undressed and ready to come in, in turn, the minute I give the word. Right? Mr Robinson, Mr Smith, attend to the X-ray equipment inside and let's have the negatives on the dot, in my hand, the minute I give the word. Nurse Jones, you stay down here in the consulting room, please. Right. Speed it up. I'll start with Mrs Phineus in precisely one minute.

[*The* ORDERLIES *go into the recess.* MRS PHINEUS *is taken out of her wheel chair by* NURSE JONES *and led out of one door. The* DOCTOR *goes out of the other.*]

CRAPE [*sings*]:

There were five green bottles
A-hanging on the wall
Five green bottles a-hanging on the wall
But one green bottle has obeyed the Doctor's call
So there's four green bottles a-hanging on the wall,

Why we're here a-hanging
We haven't yet been told
There's an extra-urgent reason that shortly will unfold
But one green bottle has suddenly gone cold –
At a possible explanation on which his mind takes hold –
As he sits here imagining all sorts of explanations and
emergencies and urgencies and all manner of unforeseen
contingencies, disorders, alarms, provoked or otherwise
called into being by the dark hand or instrumentality of
chance –

[*He sneezes, coughs, and splutters.*]

– Doctor Copperthwaite's examining our health – how is
our health? Mrs Letouzel?

LETOUZEL: Good.

CRAPE: Mr Golightly?

GOLIGHTLY: Good. Except for pains about my heart.

CRAPE: Mr Hardrader? Mr Hardrader? Oh tell me an answer
– you can tell *me* an answer – [*In a whisper.*] I've got him
away, bow-wow, bow-wow, away, away, O.K. *away* –

[HARDRADER *brightens up.*]

Now, how's your health?

HARDRADER: Oh by jove, by *jove* –

LETOUZEL: Mr Crape, how's yours?

CRAPE: Do you know, I think I've caught a cold – I don't
believe it's serious, but you never know, do you, and at this
time of year –

LETOUZEL: Don't be alarmed. I'm not alarmed. I'm relaxed:
and I'm *silent*.

HARDRADER: Crape, you don't imagine –

GOLIGHTLY: Dear lady, you don't imagine –

HARDRADER *and* GOLIGHTLY: That today is the Day!

LETOUZEL: I said relaxed, and I said I was *silent*.

GOLIGHTLY: Ah, yes, the word. Ssh ssh, quite right.

[*He puts his finger to his lips, and looks significantly at her.*
CRAPE *puts his finger to his lips and looks at* HARDRADER,
who puts his finger to his lips and looks at Crape. On the main

stage, MRS PHINEUS, *wearing a sort of white nightshirt, is brought in by* NURSE JONES. *The* DOCTOR *enters from opposite door.*]

DOCTOR: Ah, Mrs Phineus. And how are we today? In good shape, are we? Are the X-rays taken, Mr Robinson?

[ORDERLY ROBINSON *looks out of recess and nods.*]

Now there's no need to worry, Mrs Phineus, about all this bustling about and medical business. I just want a small routine check-up, nothing to it, nothing to it specially, my dear, as you might say, a brief once-over – say Ah.

PHINEUS: Ah.

DOCTOR: Ninety-nine.

PHINEUS: Doctor, if you please – what is the meaning of all this commotion –?

DOCTOR: Ninety-nine.

PHINEUS: But, Doctor, we are not dangerously ill. No, I am in excellent health, Doctor, why do you wish to – ninety-nine.

DOCTOR [*at her knees with his little hammer*]: One, two, three, *hup*.

[*Calls to upper stage.*] Will you get Mrs Letouzel ready please.

[NURSE BROWN *leads* MRS LETOUZEL *off upper stage.*]

PHINEUS: Please what is the meaning –

DOCTOR: One, two, three, *hup*. Good. Good. Waterworks all right?

PHINEUS: I beg your pardon, Doctor? Oh yes, yes, I suppose, I think –

DOCTOR: Yes. I think they are, me dear. Thank you. That'll do. . . . Now then, generally speaking, would you say you're in good shape, Mrs Phineus? I'd say you were, I'd say you were never better, I'd say I was very pleased with you – I'd say many more years, we can give you many more years. All right, me dear, off you go. Nurse.

[NURSE JONES *takes* MRS PHINEUS *out.*]

X-rays ready, Robinson?

[ORDERLY ROBINSON *enters from recess and hands X-rays to Doctor.*]

DOCTOR: Good. Good. Nothing wrong here that the odd dab of iodine won't cure. She'll do. A positive report on Mrs Phineus. Write it down.

[ORDERLY ROBINSON *writes it down.*]

Now for the next, Mrs Letouzel. X-rays taken, Smith?

[ORDERLY SMITH *puts his head out of recess and shakes it.*]

Hurry up about it then and send her in when it is.

[ORDERLY ROBINSON *goes back into recess.* NURSE BROWN *reappears on upper stage.*]

CRAPE [*sings*]:
There was four green bottles
A-waiting in a row
The next green bottle was fetched to go below
So there's three green bottles a-sweating at every pore
Three poor soldiers conscripted for the war
For death or glory or to hear the cannons roar –
I was at Passchendaele, I was, oh what a terrible mess, terrible, four years in the Service Corps issuing new socks to men with trench feet, I can tell you it was a terrible bloody mess, oh God I was fair terrified.

[*He coughs, snuffles, and sneezes.* NURSE JONES *brings* MRS LETOUZEL, *in her white robe, to see the doctor.*]

LETOUZEL: Dr Copperthwaite, this is not the usual routine of the hospital. Now I would like to know, Doctor, because it is only fair to us older people who have been through two world wars –

DOCTOR: Now there's no need to worry, Mrs Letouzel, just medical business, a small routine check-up, me dear – say Ah.

LETOUZEL: Ah.

DOCTOR: Ninety-nine.

LETOUZEL: But, Doctor.

DOCTOR: Ninety-nine.

LETOUZEL: Ninety-nine.

DOCTOR: That sounds all right.

LETOUZEL: It does?

DOCTOR: Oh yes ... One, two, three, *hup*.

LETOUZEL: Hup.

DOCTOR: One, two, three – hello?

LETOUZEL: Doctor, what's the matter?

DOCTOR: Again. One, two, three, *hup*. *Hup*. I dare say it's only local. Clear up by Sunday. Now don't you be worried, me dear, no need to worry. [*Calls to upper stage.*] Mr Hardrader, get him ready, please.

    [NURSE BROWN *leads* HARDRADER *off upper stage.*]

How are you generally, I mean, walking, talking, reading the papers? Waterworks?

LETOUZEL: Oh I'm sure, sure, why quite sure, not a particle of doubt –

DOCTOR: Good, good, you're sure? Waterworks?

LETOUZEL: Oh, yes, I am quite sure, Doctor, really, I am perfectly –

DOCTOR: Let's have the X-rays.

    [*Enter* ORDERLY ROBINSON *with them.*]

Ye-es ... well ... I think so. This is only routine, me dear – but, yes, many more years for you. Splendid form, splendid. Off you go.

    [NURSE JONES *takes her out.*]

She'll do. Positive. Make a note, not too heavy a dose. I don't think we'd better have her going any farther back than, say, thirty-five, thirty. I doubt if she's ever been that far back ever. I doubt if she could do it now. Mr Hardrader, when he's ready – I've no worries about him, nor yet for Mr Golightly. But Crape? We'll, we'll see ...

    [ORDERLY ROBINSON *goes back into recess.*]

CRAPE: Two green bottles a-hanging on the wall. Two green bottles. A-hanging on –

GOLIGHTLY: Don't be nervous.

CRAPE: I'm not nervous.

GOLIGHTLY: I'm never nervous. Why should we be nervous?

CRAPE: I think I've got a cold. Why should that matter?

GOLIGHTLY: Not to me, no.

CRAPE: Nor to me neither. Anyone can have colds.

GOLIGHTLY: Seasonable. Rain. Snow. Sleet. Draughts from the windows.

CRAPE: Anyone can have a cold! [*He coughs.*] Or a cough?

> [NURSE BROWN *re-enters on upper stage.* HARDRADER *in his robe is brought in to the Doctor by* NURSE JONES.]

DOCTOR: Aha, Mr Hardrader. [*Calls to upper stage.*] Mr Golightly, please!

> [NURSE BROWN *leads* GOLIGHTLY *off upper stage.*]

Had your X-rays taken? Good. Now don't you bother your head about all this medical business. A routine check-up, nothing to it – say Ah . . . Ninety-nine . . . One, two, three, *hup* . . . Next one, one, two, three, *hup* . . . waterworks, waterworks, ye-es . . . walking, talking, reading the papers? Good, good.

HARDRADER: Doctor, about Hector. You wrote me a letter –

DOCTOR: Don't you be worrying about that, old boy, all the best and the best of all possible worlds.

HARDRADER: You see, I was looking for him and he seems to be lost. Lost, Doctor, yes, I was trying to find him, I was doing my best –

DOCTOR: We mustn't delay the progress of science, I'm quite sure you understand, that these little sentiments, of no avail really, when looked at in proportion, as we say, the greatest good for the greatest possible number – waterworks all right?

HARDRADER: Why, yes, they're all right . . .

DOCTOR: Mr Golightly ready yet?

> [NURSE JONES *brings* GOLIGHTLY *in, in his robe.* NURSE BROWN *re-appears on upper stage.*]

Now don't you get flustered, Mr Golightly, old chap, about all this medical business, just a brief once-over, routine, routine. Had your X-rays taken? Hurry up with those– Robinson, X-rays, bring both lots in. Ah. Ninety-nine. One, two, three, *hup* – next one, one, two, three, *hup* good, good, waterworks, read the papers do you, good –

HARDRADER: Doctor, I suppose –

DOCTOR: Least said, soonest mended, that's the way, stiff upper lip – where are those X-rays?

[ORDERLY ROBINSON *enters with two sets of X-rays.*]

Let's have a look. [*Calls to upper stage.*] Mr Crape, please!

[NURSE BROWN *leads* CRAPE *off upper stage.*]

Both sets, are they? Good. Nothing wrong here we can't set up with a couple of stitches. Right you are then, positive, positive – many happy years for the pair of you, eh? Don't you worry at all. That'll do, Nurse, take 'em away.

[NURSE JONES *takes* GOLIGHTLY *and* HARDRADER *out as* NURSE BROWN *brings in* CRAPE *at the same door, in his robe.* NURSE JONES *re-enters.*]

X-rays taken, Mr Crape? Now this is just the usual medical business, no need to get flustered. Waterworks all right?

[ORDERLY ROBINSON *goes back into recess.*]

CRAPE: Oh yes, Doctor. Never any trouble. Clockwork. One green bottle a-hanging on the wall.

DOCTOR: Eh, what? Say Ah.

CRAPE: Ah.

DOCTOR: Say it again.

CRAPE: Ah.

DOCTOR: H'm . . . Go on, again.

CRAPE: Ah. Ah . . . Ah . . .

DOCTOR: Hoarse . . . a bit hoarse, aren't we? Ninety-nine.

CRAPE: Ninety-nine.

DOCTOR: Say ninety-nine.

CRAPE: I said it.

DOCTOR: I didn't hear you. Say it again.

CRAPE: Ninety-nine.

DOCTOR: Louder. Like this: ninety-nine.

CRAPE: Ninety-nine.

DOCTOR: What's the matter with you?

CRAPE: Nothing! Nothing's the matter, Doctor, I'm splendid, I'm on the top of the form –

DOCTOR: Bad throat, haven't you? Bronchial.

CRAPE: No –

DOCTOR: Oh yes you are. X-rays ready on Mr Crape yet?

Come on, slap it about! I'm a bit worried about you. You're
not all you ought to be.

CRAPE: Oh, Doctor, don't say that. No, Doctor, please don't.
If it's anything at all it could be a little piece of a chronic
condition I got, back in 1917, y'know. The wet trenches
you see, it gave the boys trench feet and they'd bring in their
socks to my stores to be changed, and it was the constant
humidity in there, all hanging round the walls – but it
hasn't troubled me serious, not for thirty years, Doctor, no
Doctor, please Doctor, really it hasn't –

[*The* ORDERLIES *come in with his X-rays.*]

DOCTOR: Ah ... good, aha ... H'm, h'm, ye-es ... say
ninety-nine.

CRAPE: Oh, Doctor, please – if it's because of the business with
the dog, I assure you –

DOCTOR: Mr Crape: ninety-nine!

CRAPE: Ninety-nine.

DOCTOR: No. It won't do. Put him down provisionally
negative and mark it with a query – maybe six months'
time ... but not now, no. We can't have you prejudice
yourself with a suppurated larynx, can we?

CRAPE: Negative –

DOCTOR: But don't you worry, old fellow, it's only routine.
Usual medical once-over, checkups, nothing at all to be
flustered about. All right, that'll do. Come.

[*Exeunt* DOCTOR *with* NURSES *and* ORDERLIES. *Exit*
CRAPE, *separately.*]

Act Three

Scene One

[*Enter* HARDRADER *and* CRAPE, *severally.*]

HARDRADER: I'm passed. He's passed me. He told me I was positive. He's even passed Golightly. Though goodness knows I've no particular wish to meet *him* thirty years ago ... Hoorah! I say hoorah! – oh, what you told me, bow wow, you know? It *was* true, wasn't it – you *did* do it – got him away?

CRAPE: Eh? Oh that, the dog? Oh, yes, he's away, yes, quite away, don't worry ...

HARDRADER: When do you think we are going to be given it? Will it be a jab, or a pill, or something in a glass? God knows, I don't know, I'd never have dreamt it possible – you know, I asked Copperthwaite, you know I asked him straight out –

CRAPE: You asked him *what*?

HARDRADER: About the dog. I told him, I said: Hector seems to be lost. I said: well, Doctor, what about it? But it didn't seem to register.

CRAPE: I don't suppose it would.

HARDRADER: What's the matter?

CRAPE: I've got a cold.

HARDRADER: Oh dear. Take my handkerchief. Clean.

CRAPE: Damn your bloody handkerchief.

HARDRADER: Steady, Crape, steady. Be a man. Stand up to your new life. It's bound to be a shock, of course, but –
    [*Enter* GOLIGHTLY.]

GOLIGHTLY: He passed me, he told me I was positive, absolutely passed! Hoorah! I say Hardrader, hoorah!

HARDRADER: You're very cheerful. Why? Have you heard something?

GOLIGHTLY: Me? Heard? Oh no, no. It's just that I'm – I'm passed, I'm passed, my physical condition –
[*He sings.*]
> O I am a man and a very healthy man
> I'm a racehorse in my prime
> Ten thousand fields of the brilliant green
> For my pleasuring they all are mine.

But you are cheerful too, yes I can see that – there's somebody knows something – do they? Don't they?

HARDRADER: Oh no, no no, no significance, no. But health and strength and life, man –
[*He sings.*]
> O I am a man and a very healthy man
> A porpoise upon the storm
> I leap and leap ten thousand miles
> From Australia to Cape Horn.

[*Enter* MRS LETOUZEL.]

GOLIGHTLY: Passed? Are you passed? Yes, of course, you are passed, dear lady, oh your features without doubt declare it, bright eyes, glowing cheeks, aha, aha, I shall give you a kiss –
[*He does so, spontaneously.*]

HARDRADER: You too, you too, we all know, don't we, Mrs Letouzel, no question of secrecy now: we've all found out, somehow – we're all passed fit for life –

HARDRADER *and* GOLIGHTLY [*sing*]:
> Boys and girls come out to play
> The moon doth shine as bright as day –

LETOUZEL [*while* HARDRADER *and* GOLIGHTLY *dance round and round*]: Who's been talking? Crape?

CRAPE: Leave me alone.

LETOUZEL [*hissing at him*]: You swore you'd keep it secret.

CRAPE: And so did you, you old scragged rabbit, but *Golightly's* been told –

LETOUZEL: Not by me –

CRAPE: Oh yes he has.

LETOUZEL: And what does it matter? The question is this: everything's moving too fast. The Doctor said to me something about Sunday. Now that can only mean –

CRAPE: It means I'm left out.

LETOUZEL: Out?

CRAPE: I have a cold. I have a cold. Hoarse in my throat. It only began this morning. He said I wasn't positive. But my waterworks are perfect. Ears, eyesight, lungs, bowels, there's nothing wrong at all. Cruelty, damnable, why me? You, you're nothing but a galvanized tin money box on two jerking legs with the slit choked up – [To Hardrader.] You're a lost dog looking for a lost dog, all you can do is howl in the gutter – [To Golightly.] You, you stale doughnut oozing mouldy jam, if they put the drug into you, there's only one part of you they'll ever rejuvenate and then the police will run you in for a permanent obscenity. Who wants to be young again? What'll you find to do when you are? All the things you want to do – why, you'll bloody well have to set to and *do* them! So how will you like *that*?

HARDRADER: I shall like it very much indeed, and I'd remind you, Crape, that you are in mixed company.

GOLIGHTLY: Your own disappointment is no excuse for abusing others, Mr Crape, I think you are very rude.

LETOUZEL: Go on, get lost.

CRAPE: Why don't all of you leave me alone?

[*He goes to a far corner of the stage and sits down to sulk, with his back to the others.* NURSE BROWN *leads in* MRS PHINEUS *and puts her in her wheel-chair.*]

PHINEUS: Thank you, Nurse, thank you. Yes, I'll be easy. Yes.
[*Exit* NURSE BROWN.]
I asked the Nurse to bring me to you, because I wanted to know about what has been happening. All this excitement in the hospital, commotion, disturbances, they're all so abrupt: I don't like it! No! There's no more routine. Mr Golightly, I'm frightened, whatever is the matter? What? What?

GOLIGHTLY: I don't know quite how to express it to you, dear Mrs Phineus, but –

PHINEUS [*jumping out of her chair*]: Tell me. Tell me. Mr
 Hardrader: are we all going to be killed?

HARDRADER: Killed – good heavens, no –

PHINEUS: I think we are. Yes. They are tired of us, they don't
 want to feed us any more. Mrs Letouzel: he's decided to get
 rid of us, that is the truth and you are hiding it from me!

LETOUZEL: No. Oh, no –

PHINEUS: Yes it is, yes it is. Yes. Mr Crape – *he* knows, look
 at him! There he sits, yes, and with no doubts at all. *He* turns
 his back and he cries.

CRAPE [*turning round*]: What do you want to know, old lady –
 hey?

LETOUZEL: Oh leave her alone, she's no idea what she's
 talking about. She's not right in the head.

CRAPE: Be quiet. Now the lot of you, shut up!

HARDRADER: Crape, nobody is talking except yourself.

CRAPE: I'm going to play a jolly game with old Mrs Phineus:
 she'll excuse me – won't you, me old love – if I step for a
 pair of minutes into Mr Golightly's slippery shoes –
 Truth or lie till the day you die
 Strike you dead if you tell us a lie.

PHINEUS: No. No. I won't have you doing it, you must not
 make me frightened, Dr Copperthwaite says –

CRAPE: Truth or lie till the day you die
 Strike you dead if you tell us a lie.

PHINEUS: Why should I play your games? I don't like you, I
 don't want to play with you – Mr Golightly, tell him I don't
 want to –
 [*She falls back into her wheel-chair.*]

GOLIGHTLY: Mr Crape, please, this old lady doesn't want to –

CRAPE: Oh yes, she does. When she plays with *me* she plays
 my game, don't you, you dear old thing, you sweet old
 sweetheart you –

HARDRADER: I say there, steady, Crape, really –

LETOUZEL: Let him be. Just for a little. See how far he goes.
 [*To audience.*] I may use this, you know. I couldn't conquer
 her, but if he can, and I can conquer *him* – more use than

Golightly, wouldn't you say? Watch him, watch him, he's beating her down –

CRAPE: After we've played, I'll get you your tea, how would you like that? I'll feed you your tea, everything you want, scones, and crumpets and tarts and Eccles-cakes galore, oh delicious, delicious – come on, come on, me lovely –

> Truth or lie till the day you die
> Strike you dead if you tell us a lie –

PHINEUS: Truth or lie –

CRAPE: Yes?

PHINEUS: Truth or lie till the day I –

CRAPE: Till the day you –?

PHINEUS: No. No.

CRAPE: Come on, come on, yes! Splendid, you're doing it beautifully – come on –

PHINEUS: Truth or lie till the day I die
> Strike me dead if I tell you a lie . . .

CRAPE: That's right, you've got it! Now we're really playing. Aren't we? I shall give you a kiss. [*He does so.*] There. That's for being a jolly sporting girl! I'll start. Supposing I told you the Doctor *was* going to have us all killed –

PHINEUS: Oh . . . Oh . . .

CRAPE: Supposing he was. What would you think of it? What would you truly think?

PHINEUS: I don't want to have to die.

CRAPE: Why not?

PHINEUS: I don't want to.

CRAPE: Margaret, *why not*?

PHINEUS:

> I'm an old old lady
> And I don't have long to live.
> I am only strong enough to take
> Not to give. No time left to give.
> I want to drink, I want to eat,
> I want my shoes taken off my feet.
> I want to talk but not to walk
> Because if I walk, I have to know

Where it is I want to go.
I want to sleep but not to dream
I want to play and win every game
To live with love but not to love
The world to move but me not move
I want I want for ever and ever.
The world to work, the world to be clever.
Leave me be, but don't leave me alone.
That's that I want. I'm a big round stone
Sitting in the middle of a thunderstorm.
There you are: that's true.
That's me. Now: you.

CRAPE: No, no. Not yet. My turn soon. I'm playing to different rules. I play the *second* time, you see. Yes . . . Now answer me this one. Supposing you died. Today. Here. Now. Just supposing. And then you were born again. Young. Strong. Not beautiful. You never were beautiful until you were old – I've seen your wedding photograph, so I know what you were like, apple-duff and custard, that was you: and your poor little Phineus-man, the pudding-cloth you were wrapped in, he was boiled all to shreds in the water! Suppose you were born again –

PHINEUS: I don't know –

CRAPE: I do. You wouldn't dare to face it. Oh Lord, it would be far too much like hard work . . . Truth or lie? Truth or lie?

PHINEUS: Truth. Truth. But I'd like to be a baby, be born again to be a little baby . . .

CRAPE: Teething, wetting your nappy, teething, struggling to crawl when you've barely learned the strength to move a knee or an elbow, teething, safety-pins stuck into you, squalling, teething, scalded with your bath-water, losing your rattle over the side of the pram –

PHINEUS: No, no.

CRAPE: No! Now you've said it. No. Anyone else say 'yes'?

GOLIGHTLY: I said 'yes'.

CRAPE: Did you? For *her*? Now you've heard what she's just

told you. She was your only reason. Do you still want to do it; for *her*?

GOLIGHTLY: Others – there are plenty of others.

CRAPE: There always were plenty of others. How many of them did you get?

GOLIGHTLY: Never mind, Mr Crape.

CRAPE: I'll tell you what they used to call me. They used to call me Dandy Jim! The only name anybody ever had for you was Little-Wet-Willy-in-a-Half-Pint-Pot. Now isn't that the truth? [*To Hardrader.*] Old chap. Old chap Hardrader. Big strong games and sports, boxing and cricket, badminton and the high-jump, Egyptian P.T. Only two friends and one of them's in her grave – you couldn't make her love you, so you went toughing it on the greensward and bellowing at your dirty dog. If you were to start again, what would *you* find?

HARDRADER: I hope I would find a healthy humane existence.

GOLIGHTLY: No no, excuse me, no: Mr Hardrader. You would be as lonely as ever you were. I know, because *I* would be, too. Isn't it terrifying?

CRAPE: Isn't it?

HARDRADER: I do not understand you, sir. You seem to have changed your mind entirely. But why should you try to change ours?

CRAPE: I'm playing the game of Truth, old fellow. It's three points wilder than a bracing set of hockey –

HARDRADER: Set of tennis.

CRAPE: Hockey, chum, hockey. When *I* call the rules.

LETOUZEL: Crape. Play with me.

> Truth or lie till the day I die
> Strike me dead if I tell a lie.

CRAPE: Truth or lie, ta tum tum-tum, – ah we know the rest of it – you start first!

LETOUZEL: No. You.

PHINEUS: These are the two stout players. Mr Golightly, Mr Hardrader, sit by me and we will watch them play.
[*They do so.*]

CRAPE: You don't want rejuvenation. There's nothing different between you and him, and him and her. All your life you've burrowed for the money: and you haven't got a red ha'penny.

LETOUZEL: Ho ho, have I not?

CRAPE: Mrs Phineus's thousand pounds – you don't have much of that, old woman, and you never really did, 'cos she hasn't got it. It's all in the air, ticker-tape, bog-bumph, Dr Copperbox holds the lot, he gives you pocket money for your China tea and your hair-dyes. All right, she made it over to you, put her scratching old fist on fifty-five miles of stored affidavits – how much of that money have you actually seen? Cash? Coin of the realm? Paid on the Bristol nail?

LETOUZEL: You don't understand the principles of finance. You uneducated old man, what should you know of the poetry and dreams of organized paper? Kleenex to wipe your nose with, that's about your sum.

CRAPE: I've got a cold. I can't help that. It's my bloody curse. Every damned project gets drowned in catarrh. It's a neurotic disability, it's not my fault. Don't you dare mock me with it! But you've told me the truth. You don't want the money: all you want's the notion of it. Here, in here, at your age – that's your luxury. But outside – in the world, between the bus-stops and the supermarkets and the no-parking areas, you've got to have hands on the real jingling metal: or the only place you'll find yourself is back in the Happy Haven, in seventy years' time. What happened to Mister Letouzel?

LETOUZEL: Eh? Keep to the point. What's that to do with it?

CRAPE: We're playing the game. You have to tell me. All right, I'll tell *you*. He didn't exist. You lived all your life a spinster in a little bit of a railway share, and when those rats nationalized, you found you'd no alternative but to give yourself to Copperthwaite.

GOLIGHTLY: Just the same as us.

CRAPE: Poor dears. Poor old dears. Your only safe investment disappeared in the night and if you had any bolder gambles –

LETOUZEL: They were not successful. That was my misfortune. It wasn't my fault. Don't you dare to mock me with it.

GOLIGHTLY: I'm sure if she wishes to call herself Mrs Letouzel she has a perfect right. If she thinks it suits her. It is what we term a courtesy title. You wouldn't be expected to understand that, Mr Crape.

CRAPE: Oh skip it, skip it . . . I think I've made my point. Is there one person here has any single motive for wanting to be young again?

LETOUZEL: Truth or lie. What about you?

CRAPE: I thought that was obvious. I've been rejected.

LETOUZEL: Why, so you have. And don't you enjoy it too, you abominable coffin-carrier. You turn us against our own selves and you disgust us to the very gorge of our throat with what we've all been for the whole of our lives. It's quite made your day, hasn't it? You've never been so happy since the time you were weaned. Ah my goodness gracious me, Mr Crape, at last you've found yourself in power!

CRAPE: Truth or lie, I have.

LETOUZEL: No. Truth or lie, you have not! Now you think, because you snarl and grin and run around between our ankles, that we've all changed our minds and that we'll all stay with you at your term of years and we'll all die together a-keeping you company? Maybe we will. But for a different reason . . . We heard everything you said – good, good, it worked. Yes, we're humiliated. You've made us afraid, you see. Here we are, worms. Old ones. We don't want to die, but we none of us dare state that we want any more life. Let's look around us! Now then, who cares?

CRAPE: I don't know what you're talking about, but I'd say nobody cares.

LETOUZEL: And you would be right. Nobody, not even the Doctor. Not even him, call him our Lord, Priest, and Superintendent, great Guardian of the Mysteries– [*She sings.*]

Take off your hats, bow down:
The High King wears the crown,

He lays out his land with a long directing hand
And the measurements all written down.

The measure of you and of me
In numbers so clearly told –
Say you are a field and I am a tree
And you are a house or a road.

If he wants to root out or rebuild,
Raise up or lay level or burn,
He draws his new line, we obey in his good time:
We suffer, we praise him, we learn.

We learn how to love and submit,
To lie down like a frightened new wife.
Each day and each hour we have given to his power
To the end and beyond of our life –

That's immortality: he grants it to us and then we hand it back. He's the undisputed custodian of everything that's good for us. Security. Reliability. Though some people have said he failed to save the score the other Saturday at football–

HARDRADER: Why – yes –

LETOUZEL: They relied on him to stop the goals; when he came back from the match he was swearing, frustrated – I know because I heard him. He'd let them all through, he had to apologize, I tell you I heard him –

HARDRADER: Quite right, so did I!

LETOUZEL: Apologized – Copperthwaite – in his humility, to the Captain of the Team ... but despite that, you silly children, we are all his worms. And he says 'Turn, worms, turn,' and he thinks we have got no choice!

GOLIGHTLY: I am not a worm. I am not a worm. My name is Henry Golightly and I walk upon legs.

HARDRADER: Two legs. Ten toes. Two arms. Ten fingers. Ribs. Shoulders. Backbone. Backbone. If my backbone *does* bend, it still belongs to *me*.

PHINEUS: Mr Crape.

CRAPE: I read my Bible. God said, he said it to the snake, I remember, he said: 'Because thou hast done this,' he said –

PHINEUS: Mr Crape.

CRAPE: 'Thou art cursed above all cattle, and above every beast of the field. Upon thy belly shalt thou go, and dust shalt thou eat all the –'

PHINEUS: Mr Crape.

CRAPE: 'All the days of thy life. Because thou has done this.' There, that's your true fortunes. Don't talk to me about bones.

PHINEUS: Mr Crape. Please. Please. What is the Doctor going to do? You haven't told us yet.

CRAPE: 'Because thou hast done this,' he said. Done what? Grown old. That's what we've done ... And the doctor – oh, the doctor? He's going to give us medicine, dear, to make us all young again. It's not of importance. You wouldn't like it. Don't bother ...

PHINEUS: But he never told me.

LETOUZEL: Why should he? He's a professional man, dear, he works to the rules.

PHINEUS: I call it very unfair. Very, very unfair. Yes.

HARDRADER: I don't want his Elixir now. You've confused me so much with all of your reasons. But if my backbone bends, it's mine.

CRAPE: Old chap. Old chap. You're the Doctor's patient. You have to do what he says.

HARDRADER: I shall ask to leave the Haven.

GOLIGHTLY: But where would you go?

HARDRADER: Find another Nursing Home.

LETOUZEL: And another Copperthwaite.

HARDRADER: Not necessarily.

GOLIGHTLY: But are you willing to take the risk?

HARDRADER: I don't know ... We can refuse to accept the Elixir. Obviously we can. Free country. Citizens. Voters.

LETOUZEL: He's worked on this for years. Weighed us and dieted us and taken our temperatures.

GOLIGHTLY: Humiliating forms of treatment, with, with rubber pipes and so forth: when I haven't even been ill.

LETOUZEL: He's not likely to let us ruin the masterpiece of his life, is he?

HARDRADER: But what can he do?

LETOUZEL: Turn us out, that's what.

CRAPE [to Hardrader]: Or worse, worse. Supposing he told you you'd got cancer in your lungs. Would you believe him?

HARDRADER: Oh my God, I don't know.

CRAPE: But he could, and it might be a lie – how would you know? He'd terrify you to death. Look what he wanted to do to your dog!

HARDRADER: You mean – vivisection?

CRAPE: What else?

HARDRADER: For a man who'd do that to a poor dumb animal – no punishment could be sufficiently severe.

LETOUZEL: Then why don't we punish him?

HARDRADER: By God, I wish I could ... Oh I would do ... this, and I'd do – that, and I'd do – oh, this, this, that, that –

PHINEUS: I once said to Mr Phineus. 'Why don't we have a little baby, I would so love a little baby to hold and to enclose and to have.' Some women say, oh the trouble and the worry and the noisiness and the naughtiness and the mess – but I said, 'I don't care about that. Mr Phineus shall pay for a good sensible old-fashioned girl to be his Nanny, and later he can go to boarding-school. All I want to do is to hold him and to have him and to enclose him.' I said it to Mr Phineus. And he tried. Yes. He tried to pleasure me and he tried to give me my baby, so many times, oh so often and so many times to no purpose. He was no good. No. No courage in him at all. So he died and there was no succession. I had expected a baby. I had bought all his little clothes and his toys and everything right up to when he would go to the boarding-school, where I suppose they would want him to wear uniform, so I couldn't get that for him in advance. But I bought all the rest and I kept them and I have them all here in my room, locked in my big box. I would so like to have a little baby.

[*Pause.*]

CRAPE: Somebody said he was talking about Sunday. There's something going to happen on Sunday. He hasn't got his drug ready yet, or I'm sure we'd have heard about it. But we have to find out the moment he *does* get it. To find out before Sunday. We must spy on his Laboratory.

GOLIGHTLY: How can we do that?

LETOUZEL: Oh we'll find a way. Use your little brains, you silly little fellow, or else shut your mouth while the rest of us use ours.

[*The* DOCTOR *enters on the upper stage.*]

DOCTOR: Off to bed, now, boys and girls, you're half an hour late as it is – burning the candle at both ends, you know, have to go easy, don't we? That's the way, off to bed, now – Nurse!

[NURSE BROWN *enters on main stage.*]

Good night. Good night, boys and girls.

OLD PEOPLE: Good night, Doctor.

DOCTOR: Good night.

[*Exeunt –* NURSE *wheels Mrs Phineus out. The* DOCTOR *remains above.*]

Scene Two

[*The* DOCTOR *is on the upper stage.*]

DOCTOR: Ladies and gentlemen. Twenty-four hours; and now I'm going to see if it works! In my Laboratory, as you know, the retort with the solution in it – is it or is it not going to turn green? Bear with me a few moments. I'll just make the arrangements, and hey presto, open sesame, abracadabra – I'll tell you confidentially, it is going to turn green. *This* time, I'm right. Mr Smith, Mr Robinson, Lab ready if you please!

[*He leaves the upper stage.* GOLIGHTLY *enters cautiously on the main stage, in pyjamas.*]

GOLIGHTLY: Why me, why me, why should I have to do it? Why not somebody else?

[MRS LETOUZEL *enters cautiously after him in nightgown and hair net.*]

LETOUZEL: Because you're the smallest, that's why. We've told you that ten times –

GOLIGHTLY: But, personally speaking, I have nothing against Dr Copperthwaite – Mr Hardrader has been the worst done by, surely *he* should –

[HARDRADER *enters cautiously at the opposite door in pyjamas.*]

HARDRADER: Golightly, pull yourself together, man. If you've any chivalry at all, remember Mrs Phineus. The man who would deny a woman the child she has craved for is an unmitigated scoundrel.

GOLIGHTLY: Quite right, Mr Hardrader. You have put me to shame, sir, I will do what I am asked. [*He goes into the recess, and we hear him blundering about in there, out of sight.*] The door is locked!

[*Enter* CRAPE *cautiously, in pyjamas, holding a burglar's jemmy.*]

CRAPE: Of course it's locked, you dithering old nightingale – I told you you'd not get in till you'd waited for me! Let me have a look at it.

DOCTOR [*off stage*]: Smith!

HARDRADER: Cave!

[ORDERLY SMITH *enters from the opposite side to the Doctor's shout, carrying a tray of test tubes, etc.*]

CRAPE: Freeze where you are!

[*They all crouch down like hares.* ORDERLY SMITH *crosses the stage and goes out without seeing them.*]

That's the way to do it. You stand stark still and they think you're a bush – I learnt that in France! Now, where's this locked door?

[*He goes into the recess.* GOLIGHTLY *comes out of it.*]

Aha . . . Ha . . . clickety-clock, clock-clock!

[*He reappears.*]

> Dandy Jimmy and his jemmy
> Save us all a pretty penny!

Mr Golightly, in you go lightly! [*He pushes Golightly in again.*] Ha ha, he's in.

DOCTOR [*offstage*]: Robinson!

HARDRADER: Cave!

CRAPE: Freeze.

[ORDERLY ROBINSON *crosses the stage with tray, same business as before.*]

Safe again. I told you. Come on.

[*Exeunt.* COPPERTHWAITE *and* ORDERLIES *enter.*]

DOCTOR: Let's have it, let's have it.

[ORDERLIES *open the recess and bring out the Lab bench.* GOLIGHTLY *is crouched underneath it, and is pulled out unobserved.*]

Bunsen Burner. Right. Now let's see the retort . . . H'm ha. H'm . . . Looks promising, ladies and gentlemen. Sediment developed *just* as I forecast, and the whole thing is approximately the consistency of – of water. Good. Boil it.

[*It is held over the flame.*]

Accotile and heraclith solution? Good. You see what I'm doing? Watch for the change of colour . . . That hot enough yet? Come on, come on, come on –

> Put another nickel in
> In the nickelodeon
> All I want is loving you
> And boil it boil it boil it –

Right! She's boiled. Give it to me. *I'll* pour. [*He pours in the contents of a second retort. It turns green.*] Beautiful. Oh my beautiful. Oh my lovely girl. Green as the leaves on the weeping willow tree, where my true love lies sleeping. I've done it. I've done it. Gentlemen, you may smoke. One of mine? One of mine?

[*They stand side by side. The* ORDERLIES *remove their masks and all three take a few formal puffs at cigarettes. Then they drop their butts, grind them into the floor, and turn back to the work.* ORDERLIES *replace masks.*]

Stage Two. A Practical Test. Go and fetch the dog.

[ORDERLY ROBINSON *goes into the recess. The dog is heard barking.*]

Taking a common-sense point of view, ladies and gentlemen, scientific detachment – I know that this green liquid is the Elixir of Youth, but I can't go administering it to my patients without some further evidence, can I? Besides, how would I know how much I ought to give them, unless we'd some sort of a preliminary run-through, eh?

[ORDERLY ROBINSON *re-enters with a large basket, fastened up.*]

Is the dog all right in there?

[*Dog barks.*]

Seems to be. Put two ounces of the Elixir into a saucer.

[ORDERLY ROBINSON *does so.*]

If anybody in the audience is a little worried at my giving this admittedly unproven drug to an unfortunate dumb animal: there's a lot of silly nonsense talked by so-called humanitarians – would any one of those ladies like to step up here to me and take the place of the dog?.... NO? I didn't think that you would. You look altogether too sensible. Open the box, please.

[ORDERLY ROBINSON *does so. Dog barks.*]

Take him out – *gently.*

[ORDERLY ROBINSON *takes the dog out in his arms – cradling quite a large-sized beast. Dog continues to bark.*]

Saucer on the floor. Dog by the saucer. Let him drink.

[*The dog is set down. More barking. The men watch closely.*]

Doesn't seem very thirsty. You haven't given him anything to drink already, have you? Robinson? Smith? H'm. Come on, come on, doggie, good boy, good boy, drinky, drinky, drinky. Lap lap lap. Oh for Godsake . . . Go on, *drink*! I'm sorry, but it looks like a long wait. We might as well sit down . . .

[*They sit.*]

    Put another nickel in, in the nickleodeon –

Where's he going? He can't leave the room, can he? You've

shut all the doors? . . . Oi, oi . . . Keep still, Smith. You can clean that up later, don't distract him, he's looking for the saucer . . . steady, steady, quiet everybody, absolute quiet – he's drinking, he's drinking – he's *drunk* it! Good dog, good dog, good, good –

[*Dog barks.*]

Now then we shouldn't have to wait long, any minute now, we're going to see – yes – yes –

[*The barks become shriller.*]

Yes! It's worked! It *really* has worked! Oh my God, I'm a famous man.

[*The bark is now a high-pitched squeal.*]

Don't let the dog get out – catch him, catch him, Robinson quick! Oh, the sweet little fellow –

[ORDERLY ROBINSON *is now holding a very small bundle.*] Oh, the dear little puppy, oh, the little chick, there, there, there, did the horrid Doctor givums nasty green water forums dinners, didums didums? Put him inside and give him something to chew – he seems to be teething. That's right.

[ORDERLY ROBINSON *takes the dog out.*]

Now we'll take in my notebooks and the Elixir, please, for safety : and we'll make a proper coordinated report upon the whole business, without any flights of poetic fancy. And let's not get so excited either that we forget the formalities – oh, but this is epoch-making, this is scarcely believable unless you'd been told, this is the greatest experience of your lives and I hope you'll not forget it . . . Come on.

[*Exeunt,* ORDERLY SMITH *carrying the retort and the note-books.* GOLIGHTLY *emerges from under the bench.*]

GOLIGHTLY: Poor Mr Hardrader. However can I break it to him? Still, a little puppy, very tender, very winsome, perhaps he won't be altogether so completely cast-down? There seems to be quite a lot left – now then, a test-tube – quickness of the hand deceives the eye, oh dear, I've spilt a bit, now then – there we are, and there's enough left in the saucer to –

[*He has poured some of the contents of the saucer into a test-tube.*]

DOCTOR [*offstage*]: You've forgotten the saucer!

GOLIGHTLY: Only just in time! My goodness, aren't I brave?

[*He nips off, as* ORDERLIES *come on again from opposite sides. They clear away the bench into recess and go out, taking the saucer with them.*]

Scene Three

[*The sound of church bells. Enter* COPPERTHWAITE *in a hurry.*]

DOCTOR: Excuse me, it's Sunday morning already, listen! I'm in a tearing hurry, the whole place is upside down, nothing prepared, and they'll be here in ten minutes. Who will? I can just spare sixty seconds to tell you. First of all: Sir Frederick Hapgood, makes cars, makes money, and a good deal of the money he makes he puts into this hospital – no question, I've got to impress him. Then, second: a lady from the Ministry of Health – there's a lot of government money put into this, and all – to be quite frank, they pay my salary – so I've got to impress *her*. Then thirdly and fourthly: our own local Mayor, and his good wife the Mayoress. They sit on the committee of this hospital, carry a deal of influence in this district – socially speaking, they *are* this district – county society, very conservative, very well worth keeping in with. And to keep in with them: impress them. There was to have been a bishop, but he's not coming now, thank goodness. I think he's had to go off somewhere to kick a High-church Vicar out of some parish or other … But there's enough of 'em, I say, there's enough. And, by God, I can tell you, they're going to be impressed. Because what they're going to see is my Elixir at work. The World Premiere, that's what. After they've all had coffee, I shall try it on Mrs Phineus.

[*Sound of arrival of motor-cars, horns blow, doors slam, etc.*]

The Happy Haven

And here comes the Establishment. Dead on time. I'd better go and meet them. Do I look sufficiently impressive? Ah well, we're all as God made us, so to speak. The Institution is greater than the Man.

[*Exit. Enter* MRS LETOUZEL *and* GOLIGHTLY, *coffee pots, cups, etc.* (*In this scene the* OLD PEOPLE *are all in their best clothes.*)]

LETOUZEL: Aren't there supposed to be biscuits?

GOLIGHTLY: Mr Hardrader is bringing the biscuits.

LETOUZEL: Good. Everything else all right? Coffee, cream-jug, sugar-bowl, cups, one, two, three, four, and one for the Doctor, spoons, one, two, three, four, and one for the Doctor.

GOLIGHTLY [*producing his test-tube*]: Shall I put it in now?

LETOUZEL: Put it in where?

GOLIGHTLY: I thought we were going to pour out the – [*He waves at the coffee-pot.*]

LETOUZEL: Not till they come in! Now take it easy, Henry, don't be in a hurry, all the time in the world.

GOLIGHTLY: I don't like having to put it in when they're all in the room – one of them might notice –

LETOUZEL: The quickness of the hand deceives the eye.

GOLIGHTLY: Yes, but I wish it didn't have to be *my* hand – Mrs Letouzel, I think I've done sufficient, cannot somebody else –

[*Enter* HARDRADER *with a plate of biscuits.*]

HARDRADER: Here are the biscuits. You have it on you?

[GOLIGHTLY *shows him the test-tube.*]

I'd be obliged if you'd give it to me.

LETOUZEL: Why?

HARDRADER: Dear lady, if you please. *I* should be the one to put it in. Hector would have wished it so. Would he not, Golightly?

GOLIGHTLY: Oh, I'm sure that he would, sir. Here you are. [*He hands him the tube.*]

HARDRADER: Thank you.

GOLIGHTLY: But you know, Hector isn't dead.

HARDRADER: To me he is dead. My Hector is dead. Whatever is alive, it's – it's some other dog. Where the devil is Crape?

LETOUZEL: He's gone to make sure we shan't be disturbed. No nurses, nor orderlies, nobody here except for ourselves, and our visitors, and our leader and teacher.

Take off your hats, bow down.

The High King wears the Crown.

HARDRADER: Cave: Here they come.

[*The* DOCTOR *enters with the four* VISITORS. *He leads them round the stage as though showing them round the hospital.*]

DOCTOR: The Convalescent Wing, as you see, to our left, facing the sun, big balconies, very airy, very spacious. To the right, my Operating Theatre, and ancillary departments, as you might say, perfection of function is in itself beautiful – but of course, Sir Frederick, *you* know all this already – Mr Mayor and ladies, we see over there the Sir Frederick Hapgood Ward, opened last year by Sir Frederick himself, there's a large bronze plaque in the foyer commemorating the occasion, and of course, the Annigoni portrait of the late Lady Hapgood, which we account one of the Happy Haven's most treasured possessions. And now, perhaps, if you'll come *this* way – ah, I see coffee – a cup of coffee awaits us – made and served specially by one or two of our patients – from the Special Research Ward, they are of course to be the subjects in the special experiment I have been explaining to you – I wanted you specially to meet them, before – ah, before we begin – [*Aside to Mrs Letouzel.*] Where's Mrs Phineus?

LETOUZEL: She's having a little rest, Doctor. She seemed rather tired –

DOCTOR: Would you mind fetching her, Mrs Letouzel? [*In a furious whisper.*] When I said all of you, I meant *all*. She ought to be here. Why can't people listen when I give a few instructions? Hurry up and get her.

[*Exit* MRS LETOUZEL.]

Let me introduce – Mr Golightly, Mr Hardrader –

[*The coffee, etc., is handed to the Visitors. When the* OLD PEOPLE *make conversation with them, the* VISITORS *reply in wordless goggling noises which sound both patronizing and genial.*]

HARDRADER: Some five or six years now. And I wouldn't exchange it for home, goodness gracious, no . . .

GOLIGHTLY: A charming place, a very charming place, dear lady, indeed to retire to . . .

HARDRADER: The countryside, the open air, contemplation, peaceful surroundings, nature . . .

DOCTOR [*who has not taken coffee*]: And of course, the beautiful scenery and fresh air in themselves as we say a continual therapy . . .

GOLIGHTLY: Oh dear me no, Sir Frederick, it is often only too stimulating here, when you reach *my* age, a peaceful and secluded existence is really the only one that charms – [*Aside to Hardrader.*] Is it in?

HARDRADER [*aside*]: Not yet. How much?

GOLIGHTLY [*aside*]: About half. We don't want to overdo it.

HARDRADER [*aside*]: All right. Half. [*With his back turned to the company; he carefully empties half the contents of the tube into a cup of coffee, and the offers it to the Doctor.*] Doctor, would you like a cup of coffee?

DOCTOR: No, thank you, Mr Hardrader. I don't normally take coffee. Have some yourself. [*To the Visitors.*] And another point, of course, the freedom from continual contact and only too often conflict with relatives, in itself acts as a –

HARDRADER: Doctor, if you don't care for coffee, perhaps we could get you a cup of tea?

DOCTOR: What? No. No thank you.

HARDRADER: Oh. Very well . . .

[*Enter* CRAPE. HARDRADER *takes him anxiously apart.*]
He won't take the coffee.

CRAPE: Give him some tea.

HARDRADER: He won't take that either.

CRAPE: You've already put it in?

HARDRADER: Half of it.

GOLIGHTLY: And I often say, we were gay then, yes and very happy. Though I wouldn't really have those days again – but there *is* a nostalgia, ah Vienna, Vienna, and the Emperor's mounted band riding round the Ringstrasse, and that wonderful, wonderful Strauss music . . .

CRAPE [*aside to Hardrader*]: Give me the other half.

HARDRADER [*aside*]: Why?

CRAPE [*aside*]: I'll tell you later. Quick.

[HARDRADER *gives him the test-tube.* MRS LETOUZEL *wheels in* MRS PHINEUS.]

DOCTOR: Aha, Mrs Phineus! Sir Frederick, Mr Mayor, ladies, let me present you to our oldest, and perhaps I'd better not say it, but she is, nevertheless, our best-loved and best-privileged inhabitant – ah – Mrs Phineus –

CRAPE [*aside to Mrs Letouzel*]: He won't take any coffee.

LETOUZEL: Then offer him some tea.

HARDRADER [*aside*]: It's no good. He won't.

LETOUZEL: Leave it to me.

[*She goes and whispers to Mrs Phineus.*]

CRAPE [*aside*]: Let him just drink the coffee and we are in the clear. I've locked the communicating doors. Orderlies and nurses can't get in unless they break through the windows. We've got all the time in the world –

PHINEUS: May I have a cup of coffee?

CRAPE [*to Hardrader*]: Give it her. Quick.

[HARDRADER *does so.*]

PHINEUS: Thank you, Mr Hardrader . . . It seems to be rather hot. Perhaps Doctor Copperthwaite, you wouldn't mind taking a sip to test it for me, would you? I'm so afraid of burning my mouth, you see.

DOCTOR: Of course, it's a pleasure, Mrs Phineus – [*He sips.*] Oh I think you'll find it quite cool enough. In fact, it's rather cold. Been poured out a long time, I expect, it –

PHINEUS: Oh dear, it is cold? I don't think, if it's cold, I ought to take it at all. No. You yourself have warned me, Doctor, of the possible danger to the kidneys, have you not? Perhaps you would drink it for me?

DOCTOR: Eh? Oh, well, I suppose I might as well, as I've got it in my hand ... It's not very sweet. Has anyone any sugar?

[MRS LETOUZEL *hands him the sugar.*]

Ah, thank you, Mrs Letouzel ... Well, I put a lot of sugar in, but it's still pretty bitter –

[*To Visitors.*]

Is *your* coffee all right? Sure? Do say if it's not, because –

[*He finishes the cupful, dubiously. Then, aside to Mrs Letouzel.*]

Here, who made this stuff? I feel quite – [*He hurries off the stage.*]

[*The next three speeches are delivered simultaneously, in great excitement.*]

GOLIGHTLY: And always for ever the beautiful climate, the snow on the Dolomites, the sparkle of the wine, the roses and the music, dear lady, the sun in our blood, crying love, love, love, ah the enchantment of the South –

HARDRADER: The one thing I regret here is the absence of the river, a good strong scull up against the tide on a Sunday morning as far as Hobson's Lock, refreshing pint in the Barge and Anchor, then home again with the current and the wind with you, and every artery tingling like quicksilver – wonderful, wonderful –

LETOUZEL: Mrs Phineus is rather deaf, and perhaps a little overexcited, but she wishes to say that she is very happy indeed to meet you, Sir Frederick, and how much, how very much she has always admired you and of course dear Lady Hapgood and the wonderful things you have done for us all!

[*Meanwhile,* CRAPE, *with his back to the others has taken the empty coffee-cup, poured out some more coffee, and is preparing to pour the rest of the Elixir into it.* MRS LETOUZEL *suddenly sees what he is up to. She comes sharply across to him and seizes his wrist.*]

PHINEUS: Yes, yes, Sir Frederick, ah Lady Hapgood, dear good Lady Hapgood, I was so sorry when I heard – was it not so very sudden? But we have the portrait here. That, we shall always treasure.

[MRS LETOUZEL *has been having a silent but strong struggle with* CRAPE.]

LETOUZEL [*aside to him*]: What do you think you're doing?

CRAPE [*aside*]: Please let me do it, let me, let me – just because I had a cold, *he* was trying to stop me but I thought that *you*, you wouldn't be so cruel as to –

LETOUZEL [*aside*]: NO! You don't want it! It's all of us or none of us! There's no more time for tricks – besides, you and me, we need one another: if we're alone, we're lost!

[*She succeeds in getting the test-tube from him. In the final effort, the coffee-cup is thrown on the floor. The* DOCTOR *re-enters.*]

DOCTOR: All well, all well, enjoying your coffee, Sir Frederick? Mr Mayor, Mrs Mayor, er Miss, er – the biscuits all right, are they? You're quite sure, Sir Frederick? Good . . . [*He comes down to Mrs Letouzel. Aside to her.*] I'd have you know, Mrs Letouzel, I've just been extremely sick. What's the matter with the coffee? Who made it? . . .

[*He turns back to the Visitors.*]

Ah, Sir Frederick, if you've finished your refreshment, perhaps we can get on to the next item in our little programme – Er, h'm, patient! Boys and girls, if you wouldn't mind clearing away the coffee things and, er, back to your rooms, and Mrs Letouzel, perhaps you could leave Mrs Phineus here with us, I believe Sir Frederick wishes to –

[*He breaks off uncertainly as he sees that the* OLD PEOPLE *all have their backs turned and are whispering together.*]

CRAPE: It hasn't worked.

HARDRADER: What do we do?

GOLIGHTLY: We'll have to do something.

CRAPE: The coffee, the coffee must have killed it!

LETOUZEL: We've still got the other half – no thanks to *you* –

PHINEUS [*suddenly*]: Here: all to me!

[*They all crouch round her wheel-chair in a tight huddle like a*

[*football scrum. The* DOCTOR *and* VISITORS *watch in bewilderment.*]

DOCTOR: Well, now, I'm not sure what – we must appreciate, of course that these old people have their periodic eccentricities, it's maybe that they feel their little half-hour of recreation with us has been cut short too abruptly – we always find it best to humour them, you know, Sir Frederick –

LETOUZEL: Right. Now. Begin. Mr Crape. Mr Golightly. The bench. Quickly.

[CRAPE *and* GOLIGHTLY *pick up a bench by its end and run against the Visitors with it, pinning them across their bellies against the edge of the stage.*]

DOCTOR: Hey, wait a minute –

LETOUZEL: Mr Hardrader. Neck. Arms. Quickly.

[HARDRADER *grabs the Doctor's arm and twists it behind his back, at the same time bearing down with his other hand on the back of his neck. The* DOCTOR *is forced to bow right over.*]

Right. Now then. Needle.

[MRS PHINEUS *takes from her reticule an enormous hypodermic needle which she opens.* MRS LETOUZEL *swiftly pours in the contents of the test-tube.*]

DOCTOR: Oh, oh, stoppit, leggo, ow, ouch, yarroo –

[*The* VISITORS *gobble.*]

PHINEUS: For a long time I have kept this locked up in my big box. It was lucky I thought to bring it along today. Yes. I said to myself: 'One day, it will be needed.'

LETOUZEL: Needle filled. Screwed up. Ready? [*She hauls up the Doctor's coat and hauls down his trousers.*] NOW!

[MRS PHINEUS *sticks the needle into the Doctor, who gives an appalling yell. The needle is withdrawn.*]

LETOUZEL: Come on. Take him in.

[*She and* HARDRADER *rush the Doctor, still stooping, off the stage.*]

PHINEUS: You can let them go now.

[CRAPE *and* GOLIGHTLY *release the Visitors who still stand where they have been forced, in stunned amazement.*]

This must be a most astonishing moment for you, Sir
Frederick, must it not ...

[*They open their mouths and gasp.*]

Please don't call out.

CRAPE: There's nobody to hear you. I've locked 'em all away.
We're all in this together.

GOLIGHTLY: United we stand. Divided we – you know. I am
not a worm. My name is Henry Golightly and I walk upon
legs.

PHINEUS: But it should also be a beautiful moment because
you will see how much, how very very much, we owe to
you and to poor Lady Hapgood and to the kind ladies and
gentlemen in the Government and in this beautiful countryside around us who take so much delight and interest in our
welfare, and who always look after us like fathers and like
mothers, to watch our every step and stumble, at a time in
our lives when we are, as you know, no more than little
children to wander and to cry and to need nothing more in
life than to be continually looked after by kind fathers and
mothers, who will watch our every step and stumble at a
time in our lives when how few of us know what we want
to do or where we want to go, or what possible good we
are at all, being, as you see, like little children wandering and
crying and in search once again of our fathers and our
mothers –

[MRS LETOUZEL *and* HARDRADER *re-enter, leading the*
DOCTOR *between them. He is now wearing a little boy's suit,
with short pants, and wears a mask that entirely covers his face.
It resembles the actor's own features closely, but is round,
chubby, and childish.* MRS LETOUZEL *puts a lollipop into his
hand and he sucks at it in a formal fashion.*]

Ah, here he is. My baby. Come little baby, come to your
mama, sit him on my knee, dear Mrs Letouzel, I'd like to
sing him a song –

[*They sit him on her knee.*]

Yes, baby, yes, baby, yes ...

PHINEUS [*sings*]:

Now mother holds her little boy
And holds him to her heart
Fall asleep, all you children, fall asleep.
The rising up of sun or moon
Shall never make us part.
Fall asleep and dream the world is all safe and sound.

ALL OLD PEOPLE [*formally*]: Everybody, listen! Take warning from us. Be cheerful in your old age. Find some useful hobby. Fretwork. Rugmaking. Basketry. Make yourselves *needed*. Remember: a busy pair of hands are worth ten thousand times the Crown of a Queen. Go home, and remember: your lives too, will have their termination.

VISITORS: Help. Help. Help. Let us out. Let us out.

PHINEUS: Let them out.

[CRAPE *opens the door and they all run out.*]

VISITORS [*cries disappearing offstage*]: Help! Help! Help! . . .

OLD PEOPLE [*bowing to the audience*]: Good night. Good night. Good night.

[*They all leave the stage. They carry with them the remains of the coffee and refreshments.* MRS PHINEUS *and* MRS LETOUZEL *carefully put the Doctor in the wheel chair, and* MRS PHINEUS *wheels him out.*]

CURTAIN